WHAT STAYS IN VEGAS

WHAT
STAYS IN
VEGAS

THE WORLD OF PERSONAL DATA—
LIFEBLOOD OF BIG BUSINESS—
AND THE END OF PRIVACY
AS WE KNOW IT

ADAM TANNER

PublicAffairs
New York

PublicAffairs books are available at special discounts for bulk purchases in the US
by corporations, institutions, and other organizations. For more information, please
contact the Special Markets Department at the Perseus Books Group, 2300 Chestnut
Street, Suite 200, Philadelphia, PA 19103, call (800) 810-4145, ext. 5000, or e-mail
special.markets@perseusbooks.com.

Cover design by Pete Garceau
Book design by Cynthia Young

Library of Congress Cataloging-in-Publication Data
Tanner, Adam.
    What stays in Vegas : the world of personal data—lifeblood of big
    business—and the end of privacy as we know it / Adam Tanner.—
    First edition.
        pages cm
    Includes bibliographical references and index.
    ISBN 978-1-61039-418-5 (hardback)—ISBN 978-1-61039-419-2 (e-book)
    1. Ceasars Entertainment—Case studies.   2. Casinos—
Nevada—Las Vegas—Customer services—Case studies.   3. Consumer
profiling—United States.   4. Business intelligence—United States.   5. Privacy,
Right of—United States.   I. Title.
HV6711.T36 2014
338.7'617950973—dc23
2014019481

First Edition

10 9 8 7 6 5 4 3 2 1

To Celia, Clarissa, and Adrian

CONTENTS

INTRODUCTION

Spies

The Bad Ol' Days

In 1988, I involuntarily became the subject of old-fashioned data gathering. Spies followed me around Communist East Germany and recorded my every move. That year I was visiting Dresden, the great Baroque art capital that had suffered widespread destruction from the massive Allied firebombing in World War II. Even decades after the war, some of the city's ornate buildings, including the Royal Palace, still lay in rubble. East Germany's government prided itself on operating an especially efficient Ministry of State Security, the Stasi, to monitor suspicious activities and guard against potential enemies. The Stasi mobilized their forces for my arrival, and agents made a concerted effort to learn everything they could about me.

I was researching the Frommer's travel guide *Eastern Europe and Yugoslavia on $25 a Day*, and I spent my days visiting hotels, restaurants, and museums, as well as puzzling out how to do things such as buy train tickets when lines snaked out the station door. Communism was crumbling during these years, yet the secret police continued their dedicated vigilance. Future Russian President Vladimir Putin served in Dresden during that time as a junior KGB spy.

On August 2, a mild day with temperatures mostly in the sixties, I strolled around the Semper Opera, a nineteenth-century structure gutted in the bombing and reopened forty years later, in 1985. The local authorities kept a close watch. Stasi Major Hartmann oversaw a team of ten counterespionage "comrade observers." They monitored my movements. Agents kept a minute-by-minute log, supplementing their efforts with surreptitious photographs. I was code-named "Kiefer" (Pine Tree), perhaps because I am tall. If they were hoping to catch me sneaking off to the homes of dissidents or photographing military installations, they were disappointed; I stuck closely to my guidebook checklist.

"Here, Tanner, Adam, is interested in the exterior of the Semper Opera," a caption for one of the photographs reads, noting the time as 10:35 a.m. "During his stop on Theaterplatz, he did not take any photographs, although he did have photographic equipment (tripod, camera bag). He made only written notes in a notebook."

As I planned my next stop, I studied a city map for a few minutes, then asked for directions. From afar, an agent snapped a photo as that

LAGEFILM B/343/88 " Kiefer "	
Uhrzeit Melder	Sachverhalt
	02.08.88 Ref. 5 08.00 Uhr Beobachtung begonnen 08.53 Uhr ab Hotel mit PKW Lada ICB 9–41 mit 2/1/0 08.55 Uhr Semperoper betreten 10.50 Uhr abgefahren zur Kesselsdorferstr. Antiquitäten Löwe 11.10 Uhr ab 11.40 Uhr Höhe Btz. Str. / Lutherstr. Objekt Pkw entstiegen, Pkw weit Anschließend zu Fuß durch Innere Neustadt u. a. Hotel Rothe burger Hof aufgesucht und sich Hotel und Zimmer zeigen lass u. a. wurde gehört .... er will ein Buch schreiben 12.25 Uhr Str. der Befreiung Geschäftsbummel (Buchladen, Antiquität 13.40 Uhr Hotel Bellevue wieder betreten 13.45 Uhr ab mit Pkw mit 2/1/0 14.00 Uhr Albertinum mit Fototechnik betreten, unterbrochen 18.48 Uhr Hotel verlassen und mit Pkw zur Leipzigerstr. 8 – Agrar La maschinen 19.30 Uhr Hotel wieder betreten

Secret Stasi overview of the day's monitoring of "Kiefer" in Dresden on August 2, 1988. Source: Germany's Federal Commissioner for the Stasi Archives.

random citizen, his finger upon his chin in contemplation, answered the question. The Stasi agents pondered what to do about the man amid suspicions that anyone I encountered could possibly be a covert collaborator. In the end, they did nothing. "The man went off in the direction of the service building of the Semper Opera," the file recorded. "He was not followed."

Eventually I found my destination, the former Schlachthof Fünf, where American writer Kurt Vonnegut survived the February 1945 firebombing described in his novel *Slaughterhouse-Five*. I stopped by the entrance of what had become a state agricultural institute and asked the guard about the building's past. Was this the former slaughterhouse? Reading about the unscheduled inquiry some weeks later, a Stasi official grew alarmed. Likely he was not aware of the site's literary significance.

"We request gathering of information on the reason for such a visit," wrote Lieutenant-Colonel Wenzel. "Did he have state permission to visit? . . . What knowledge of German language did he show, were agreements for further contacts reached?" The Stasi dispatched an agent to find out by interviewing the duty guard and researching the building. "The USA citizen spoke broken but intelligible German," the follow-up report found, citing the guard.

Secret police also ordered a follow-up analysis to unravel the mystery as to why I had stopped at a local budget hotel, spoken to the clerk, popped into a room, and then quickly left. That visit struck my covert minders as highly irregular. East Germany and the Soviet Union required Western tourists to prebook hotels through the state tourism agency. Since the agency vouched for the quality of the establishment, why would anyone need to review a hotel room? Who would doubt the good word of the German Democratic Republic? The Stasi dispatched an agent to question receptionist Karin Zickmantel. She gave my German-language speaking ability a better grade ("good") and explained that I had visited Room 19 on the first floor. The Stasi decided we had not hatched a conspiracy.

The following year, the Berlin Wall fell. After allowing citizens free access to the West and its myriad of choices, East Germany and

Covert Stasi photo of the author taking notes in front of a hotel. Source: Germany's Federal Commissioner for the Stasi Archives.

its vast secret police apparatus quickly collapsed. Reunified Germany opened the Stasi files to those who had come under surveillance. More than a decade after my visit to Dresden I obtained my fifty-page dossier and learned the details of the Stasi's efforts to track me across the city.

Truth be told, for all their diligence, the Stasi did not really learn much. In the Internet era, thanks to meticulous data gathering from both public documents and commercial records, companies today know far more about typical consumers than the feared East German secret police recorded about me. Through public records, private firms know where you live and have lived, which neighbors live near you, your relatives, what property you own, what crimes you have committed. They know your age and telephone numbers. They can research your shopping habits and hobbies, and determine favorite Internet sites. Sometimes they know your ailments, even, perhaps, if you take Viagra. They might know where you are at any time through smart

A line in front of an East Berlin bakery in 1988, a year before the collapse of the Berlin Wall and the end of Stasi monitoring. Source: Author photo.

phone apps and GPS locators. The aggregation of data makes finding out previously obscure information easy. All these years later, an Internet search quickly finds the home address and phone of the very same German hotel clerk who had to explain my visit to Stasi agents in 1988.

Like East German agents quietly trailing their targets, many of today's data collectors remain unseen. Consumers may have a vague notion that companies gather their personal data, yet few have a clear idea about who collects it and how they use it. This book attempts to shine a light on some of the most interesting data gatherers, showing just how pervasive data gathering has become in everyone's daily life. Some firms let customers know they gather information about them and offer significant benefits in return. Others hide their names and whereabouts as they gobble up whatever facts they can.

Revelations about the US National Security Agency and its ability to gather information from our electronic communications illustrate the government's vast capabilities to amass information about us all. But experts believe that the US government does not keep detailed dossiers on every citizen with in-depth personal information accessible at the click of a mouse. Certainly, if the government has reason to gather the information, it has the ability to vacuum up a lot of data about us.

This book is not about those capabilities. It is about how data emerged to become the lifeblood of private industry, the elixir that fuels marketing efforts to compete and expand their businesses. The NSA and the FBI are not interested in the great majority of citizens. Nor do they profit from data. And, however imperfectly, they are subject to governmental, congressional, and judicial oversight. They can be called to account.

By contrast, private companies regularly assemble detailed individual profiles on millions upon millions of people with only minimal restrictions. Data collection has become widespread and extensive in recent years. Companies have fine-tuned efficient methods of gathering information about the lives of others that would make the Stasi green with envy. The land of the free, fueled by the spirit of free enterprise, has become the greatest data collector of all. If you live outside the United States, this trend is making its way to your door any day now, if it is not already in full bloom.[1]

And data collected by the private sector does end up in government hands through sophisticated snooping, the 2013–14 revelations about the NSA show. The NSA and law enforcement agencies—and presumably their foreign equivalents—tap into Google, Facebook, Yahoo, Internet providers, and others to scoop up vast troves of information about us, sometimes without the consent of the companies.

When I visited East Germany all those years ago, I was not producing a continuous stream of electronic data about my activities. If the Stasi wanted to know more, they had to follow people and monitor conversations the old-fashioned way, perhaps by having agents sitting for long hours around cafes and restaurants, or tapping into phones.

In the Internet era, why send ten agents out to trail someone when electronic footprints stored by private firms provide a far richer portrait of that person's activities?

Something as innocuous as playing the game Angry Birds can help the government gather more information on users through their smart phone apps, 2014 revelations from Edward Snowden's documents show.[2] The mobile app for that and other games acquires user data such as contact lists from Facebook, LinkedIn, and other sites as well as location data. US and British officials tapped into such information to learn more about potential terrorism or other suspects. Rovio, the maker of Angry Birds, issued a public statement in response suggesting the US and British governments also tap into Internet advertising networks, which monitor who visits what websites to help companies decide where to place their ad messages.

"The alleged surveillance may be conducted through third-party advertising networks used by millions of commercial websites and mobile applications across all industries. If advertising networks are indeed targeted, it would appear that no Internet-enabled device that visits ad-enabled websites or uses ad-enabled applications is immune to such surveillance," Rovio said.[3]

Governments also turn to data brokers and other companies to supplement their own files because the private-sector data collection is so extensive. Sometimes government agencies such as law enforcement pay for such data. In other cases, according to the NSA documents made public by Snowden, they just take it covertly. Clues to relationships, ailments, sexual orientation, religious and political affiliation, and other intimate details are easier than ever to discern, both for the private sector and for government.

Who are these people in the private sector gathering our data? This book will tell some of their stories. Overwhelmingly, they use our data for legitimate business purposes, essentially to market their products. Some consumers like the personalization that all this data allows, because it provides items or services of interest to them. Others bemoan their diminishing privacy even as they embrace the rich cornucopia of the Internet.

At the same time, there is a darker side. Some firms make money off the misery of others, and this book will tell some of these stories as well. Shaming has never been more profitable or easy. Sites promoting revenge porn, slanderous reviews or gossip, or arrest photos that shoot to the top of Internet searches strike many people as just plain wrong. The ever greater ability to assemble such information is something to be concerned about.

"You can reconstruct, like, my whole day—not just *my* whole day, but for everyone you can reconstruct at a very fine level of detail what they have been up to, what they are doing, and so on," says Vitaly Shmatikov, a University of Texas computer scientist. "Of course, at the moment it requires aggregation of multiple databases and nobody is doing it—I hope. But the technical capability is there. So you've got to wonder what could come out of there."

This book does not directly profile some of the biggest data hunters, such as Facebook, Google, Amazon, and other Internet giants. One reason is that their ever-evolving practices are widely and minutely chronicled on many websites, in the media, and in other books. Another is that their data gathering is often more obvious. If you share details about your life on Facebook or other social media, they will know lots about you. Google and Amazon are such major Internet presences that they have great insights into people's behaviors.

Yet these companies, especially Facebook and Google, return again and again in this book because they cast such a long shadow across the business of personal data. Chapter 9 looks at some less obvious features of Facebook, such as how clues from your friends and "likes" can reveal intimate details about you. Facebook returns in Chapter 11, which discusses casino surveillance. Google searches and advertising play a vital role in the success of the people-search websites in Chapters 6 and the mug-shot websites detailed in Chapter 12.

The Freedom of Old Las Vegas

After researching three editions of the Eastern Europe guidebook in the second half of the 1980s, I spent five years in Russia in the 1990s as a correspondent. I arrived shortly after the collapse of the Soviet Union, symbolized by the moment when protesters toppled the statue of the secret police founder in front of KGB headquarters. But despite the high hopes of many, the clumsy first steps toward democracy led to an economic depression, and many people lived in grim poverty in those early post-Soviet years. Life in the frigid Russian capital at the time often appeared gray and dreary.

One winter during those years I left the deep frost of Moscow and visited Las Vegas for the first time. The glow of the winter sun, the glare of the neon signs along the Strip, the energy of nonstop entertainment, the frenetic spending of money—the whole atmosphere dazzled me. In particular, I remember the opulence of Caesars Palace—its vast casino, endless shops and restaurants, its colorful history with legendary performers such as Frank Sinatra, the skimpy white togas of the waitresses.

In those years, I felt such freedom in returning to America. Communist and early post-Communist countries seemed a world apart. It was fascinating to spend time in that part of the world, but it always felt a bit strange to be a person of interest, someone whose activities attracted attention from others both seen and unseen. One breathed freely and easily on holiday back in the United States, a place where few cared or noted what you did.

In Las Vegas at that time casinos did not ask for my name or any other information about me. I did not sign up for a loyalty program, so the casino had no idea who I was. You put money on the table and they gladly accepted your business, no questions asked. Practiced dealers kept a keen eye on players and manually calculated which high-spending guests might deserve a free meal or room. Lower-end players came and went without garnering much attention. What happened in Vegas stayed in Vegas.

A lot has changed since then.

1

What Happens Here, Stays Here?

The Myth of Sin City

The September 2001 attacks on the World Trade Center and Pentagon thousands of miles away delivered a tough blow to Las Vegas too. After such a tragedy, vacationing in Las Vegas felt frivolous, even disreputable. Many feared Sin City, as a symbol of capitalist excess, could itself become a terrorist target.

Like a champion boxer hit by a stunning blow, Vegas stumbled before it came back roaring with its "What Happens Here, Stays Here" advertising campaign. One TV spot that captured the public imagination showed an attractive young woman flirting with a series of men; to each one she introduced herself by a different name. Another showed a group of women riding in a limo, giggling wildly about some adventure they had just enjoyed. Yet another advertisement opened with a church wedding as a pastor asked, "If anyone present has reason to believe these two should not be wed, let them speak now or forever hold their peace." The camera panned slowly across the worried faces of bridesmaids and groomsmen. An awkward pause filled the church as friends and family looked around uneasily, until the pastor relieved the tension: "No one? Okay, moving on." At the end of each advertisement appeared the slogan "What Happens Here, Stays Here."

It became a national catchphrase, often altered to "What Happens in Vegas, Stays in Vegas." Oscar Goodman, elected mayor in the boom times two years earlier, said the campaign was born of necessity as casinos started laying off thousands of workers right after the 9/11

1

Visitors on Las Vegas Boulevard. Source: Author photo.

attacks. "We started to think in terms of what could attract people to Las Vegas: an adult playland. That's when that change from the family destination came," he said. "And that slogan was a slogan basically of freedom, that people should leave their cares and woes wherever they came from, they could come to Las Vegas and have a good time without any guilty conscience and then return to the aggravation of their own town."

* * *

Throughout its history, Las Vegas has encouraged outrageous behavior. The city promises guiltless eating and drinking, sex, and gambling. And discretion. Casinos do not ask where anyone's money comes from, and dealers might not even utter a client's full name for many years.[1] Casinos whisk their VIP gamblers into private rooms beyond public view.

In the early years of the "What Happens Here, Stays Here" campaign, Facebook and Twitter did not exist. Internet data brokers selling profiles and criminal records about all Americans had barely started to appear. Smart phones and tablet computers ready to snap compromising photos were not ubiquitous. Of course, the limitless freedom to behave badly without consequence never really existed. But back then, it was easier to believe that it might.

During the early years of the ad campaign, I worked as the Reuters bureau chief in San Francisco and frequently visited Las Vegas. In early 2008 I followed then-Senator Barack Obama as he toured the employee areas below the MGM Grand Hotel on the Strip, hoping to win votes from unionized employees in the Democratic presidential caucus. Sensing a bad photo op that could offend voters who did not approve of gambling, he, Hillary Clinton, and other candidates avoided the casino floors. I was intrigued to peer into the vast lower complex hidden from hotel casino guests. Here thousands of workers dine in their own cafeterias, pick up uniforms from massive dry-cleaning operations, prepare meals for guests, and do all the tasks it takes to keep a hotel with thousands of rooms running smoothly.

On another visit to Las Vegas I met Vera Rhodes, who was attending a swingers' convention. A woman in her fifties who said she was a virgin until her marriage at age thirty, Rhodes said she was making up for lost time during the convention's late-night parties. I asked if I could quote her by name in an article. Then, personal data was not as widespread on the Internet. She said fine. Now, years later, Internet searches for her name still turn up her enthusiastic description of her nocturnal exploits. In 2014, I decided to see if I could find her again, even though I had no contact details or clues about her whereabouts eight years later. An Internet search found data brokers offering to sell her address, phone number, and other details for a few dollars—a relatively new development described in Chapter 6.

In the Internet era, it is getting ever harder to keep personal information—what happens in Vegas—to stay in Vegas.

The Inner Sanctum

What changed over the years since I first visited Las Vegas is that businesses everywhere started collecting as much information on their customers as possible. With a lot of money at stake, casinos played an important role in expanding the corporate use of customer data. Starting in the late 1990s, a self-described math nerd became the driving force behind Caesars, making them a widely admired engine of data collection. Boosted by vast banks of computers, Caesars today know the names of the vast majority of their clients, exactly how much they spend, where they like to spend it, how often they come, and many other characteristics. They even know exactly where many of their customers are at any given moment—whether they are sitting at a specific *Wheel of Fortune* slot machine or playing blackjack in the wee hours of the morning. They gather all these details with the consent of those who choose to participate in their loyalty program.

Gathering so much data about customers has proved enormously lucrative. Caesars Palace evolved into the headquarters of the world's largest casino company, called, naturally enough, Caesars Entertainment. Executives from many industries looked to the company and its CEO, Gary Loveman, to understand how gathering information about customers could boost the bottom line.

In 2012, I returned to Las Vegas to ask Loveman's permission to peer into the secretive world of data gathering at Caesars Palace, located at the fifty-yard line of Las Vegas Boulevard, the famous Strip. After navigating through a maze of slot machines, restaurants, cafes, and lobbies, I found the correct bank of elevators for the executive offices. I had expected to find the bigwigs occupying the penthouse level overlooking their empire. But I was told to make my way to the mezzanine level. A lone receptionist to one side greeted visitors after they passed

View of Las Vegas Boulevard, the Strip. Source: Author photo.

through a set of glass doors. She buzzed me into a separate, spacious antechamber. I watched as a waiter in tails trundled by pushing a food cart, a shiny silver dome covering the CEO's meal.

Las Vegas had become a vast data collection machine. Because of the huge amount of money at stake, casinos have used customer information to innovate in a wide array of activities, including direct marketing, loyalty programs, surveillance, and photo recognition technology. Sin City is also a major source of public records because more couples marry here than anywhere else in the United States. If things do not work out, Nevada has long made it easy to split up, and divorce records provide even more information that ends up in public dossiers. Powered by fast computing and cheap storage, businesses from corner stores to international conglomerates gather information about clients from many different sources. All told, private firms, whether in Las Vegas or elsewhere, know more about us, including our intimate secrets, than ever before.

After a few minutes I followed Loveman's assistant along the same path of the waiter. A tall wooden door doubling as a wall in the antechamber slid to the side, and we proceeded to a windowless conference room with wood-paneled walls. Loveman arrived and took a seat in front of his lunch. The CEO had a bit of a baby face although he was in his fifties. Broad-shouldered and oversized enough to require an extra-wide jacket, Loveman was a commanding presence. With a deep sonorous voice, he apologized for dining solo. But, he explained, he did not have time for a proper lunch on that busy day.

He gave the impression of not suffering fools gladly, so after some small talk, I got to the point: I asked if I could follow Caesars from time to time over the course of a year to study how they collected data on their clients. Initially, he expressed some caution.

He had good reason. He had navigated several difficult years. Many casinos had suffered a losing streak following the 2008 financial crisis, but Caesars had taken an especially heavy blow. Revenue had fallen from a peak of nearly $11 billion in 2007 to $9.1 billion the next year and, as things turned out later, would end up stuck in the range of $8.5 billion in 2012 and 2013.

The drop alone was bigger than the annual GDP of entire small nations. For all the company's cleverness in mining customer data, it remained many billions of dollars in debt. Some people wondered if mighty Caesars would ultimately have to declare bankruptcy. A more conventional CEO might have shooed away a writer at such a time. But Loveman decided to gamble. He agreed to allow me to see what happened in his corner of Vegas.

2

A Harvard Professor Comes to Vegas

A Business Professor Rolls the Dice

No one would have ever wagered that someone like Gary Loveman would end up fitting into the casino boss shoes once filled by the likes of Benjamin "Bugsy" Siegel and Frank "Lefty" Rosenthal. Loveman did not grow up in the shadows of the casino world or dream of palling around with the Rat Pack. In fact, through his thirties, he had only once even set foot in a casino, in Monte Carlo, the setting for the first James Bond novel, *Casino Royale*. His encounter with the European version of gaming did not convert Loveman into a regular gambler. He lived in the Boston area; the world of gambling was remote. In any case, wagering invokes the uncertainty of chance. Loveman preferred the exactitude of math and data.

Loveman had grown up in Indianapolis, where his father worked as a supervisor at a telephone manufacturing plant. In college, when classmates were busy chugging beers and chasing girls, Loveman would frequently stay in, pulling out pencil and paper to calculate stock returns and price-earnings ratios manually, just to see how quickly he could do it. After graduating from Wesleyan University in 1982, he spent two years at the Federal Reserve Bank of Boston. He kept on calculating through graduate school, eventually earning a doctorate in economics in 1989 from the Massachusetts Institute of Technology. His thesis examined differing rates of unemployment in the United States, Britain, France, and Germany. That same year in Las Vegas Steve Wynn opened the Mirage, the first new hotel there in sixteen years. The exploding volcano outside the hotel and tropical scenery signaled the start of a new construction boom that changed the face of the city. Yet the bright neon and glitter of Vegas remained a world away from Loveman, who, with his PhD in hand, landed a job teaching at Harvard Business School.

Even within Harvard's rarefied atmosphere, the business school stands apart. Many students and faculty members consider themselves a cut above the rest of the elite campus. Situated on the other side of the Charles River, south of Harvard Square and the historic core of campus, the business school is just far enough away to deter the busloads of tourists who regularly spill into Harvard Yard. With wood floors, stately desks, plush armchairs and couches, and a series of chandeliers hanging above, the main student building resembles the lobby of a luxury hotel. Whereas the rest of campus freely opens its doors to all students, Harvard Business School limits some of its facilities to its own. Future tycoons work out in a deluxe gym closed to others. They compete on their own tennis courts. Dedicated chefs roll fresh sushi in the cafeteria. At another counter, Chinese cooks fry up wok creations on demand. When HBS students mail packages, they need not trouble themselves by stepping into the often harsh Boston winter. The US Postal Service runs a post office in the basement of the central administration building. Customers rarely encounter lines there.

In class, students sit in amphitheater-shaped classrooms. They cannot slink to the back of the room if they're exhausted after a late night studying financial charts. Everyone takes the same seat for every class, behind a prominent laminated name card visible to all. Professors keep large seating maps posted on their office walls, which help them memorize the names of their students. If a student invites a friend to visit a class, he or she must introduce the newcomer at the start. The rest of the class politely applauds. Parents, who often help pay for the astronomical tuition, get a standing ovation, as do spouses.

Loveman arrived when he was twenty-nine, just a few years older than his students. Like a conductor before an orchestra of virtuosos, he faced a daunting task. He had to know more than extremely bright students. Moreover, he had to engage classes of gifted—and demanding—future business leaders. The students had every right to expect a lot. They pay an extraordinary amount of money to rub shoulders with those they expect will become fellow captains of industry, and also forgo six-figure salaries during the two-year program.[1] Loveman mastered this strange new world. Even among an impressive faculty of leading business minds, he quickly established himself as a popular teacher.

Len Schlesinger was one of the HBS professors who worked closely with Loveman on topics related to the service economy. "He was a first-rate, enormously talented young faculty member who was distinguishing himself in a collection of faculty, all of whom were reputed to be great teachers," Schlesinger recalled. "From day one, really, he established himself as having a great presence in the classroom and a real ability to master the art of engaging with students in a case discussion."

At HBS, teachers wield great power. Using the Socratic method, the instructor typically kicks off a discussion by calling on a student, who must outline the day's case study for five to fifteen minutes. This is known as a "cold call." At HBS, those who impress know they are doing well when the instructor writes down a summary of their insights on the white board. Anyone cold-called who fails to give a good spontaneous presentation risks humiliation.

Scott Howe was one student inspired by Loveman's teachings. A Milwaukee native, he came to Harvard after studying economics at Princeton, where he graduated magna cum laude. From Loveman he learned to focus relentlessly on customers. Many years later he still remembered an assignment in which students had to write two letters to two companies, one with criticisms and one with compliments, both suggesting improvements. "He was by far my favorite professor," Howe says. "He definitely made an impact on my thinking." Years later, the student would become CEO of Acxiom, a leading data broker with considerable influence in the universe of personal data.

Loveman enjoyed setting out business problems in case studies. What are the key problems facing a business, what do the data show, what are the possible solutions? Loveman wrote case studies on topics such as American Airlines, Euro Disney, Southwest Airlines, the

Warsaw Marriott, Habitat for Humanity, a hospital company in India, and a Mexican cell phone company.[2] He first gained public attention by arguing that computers added little or no boost to workplace productivity in the late 1970s and early 1980s. His 1990 academic paper on the subject, filled with mathematical equations and data tables, concluded that firms would have been better off putting extra money into things other than information technology.[3] Over time, others began doubting what he called the "Productivity Paradox," and the debate faded as computing power advanced.[4]

In 1994, Loveman coauthored a celebrated article that would become the foundation of much of his work in the years ahead.[5] It proposed the radical notion that the lifetime value of any one customer is significantly impacted by his or her overall satisfaction. Take a pizza restaurant: at a dollar or two a slice, it may not seem that important to pay much attention to any one customer, since pizza eaters tend to hop around. But over a lifetime, a customer who professed high satisfaction with a restaurant was worth $8,000. The lifetime value of a loyal Cadillac owner rose to $332,000. And for a corporate purchaser of commercial aircraft, the value jumped into the billions of dollars. Loveman and his coauthors had set out the logic that would propel companies in subsequent years to gather ever more personal data about customers. "The lifetime value of a loyal customer can be astronomical," the article concluded.

Loveman's transition from academia to casinos happened by chance. Harvard Business School allows faculty to consult for companies one day a week. Loveman started training executives from Harrah's, a company that opened its doors in 1937 as a bingo parlor in Reno, Nevada, and had continued to expand over the years. The sideline proved interesting and far more lucrative than Loveman's $120,000 academic salary.

Casinos provided Loveman with an interesting intellectual puzzle. He was surprised that customers typically showed little loyalty to any one casino company, but instead flitted from place to place. He became convinced that the industry could do better by replacing the gut instinct that often propelled corporate decisions with data analytics. "As

I came to learn more and more about the industry, it struck me that this was a very sophisticated business run by somewhat unsophisticated people," he concluded in his characteristically blunt style.

In 1995, just after Harrah's lost millions of dollars trying and failing to establish successful operations in New Orleans, Loveman wrote an unsolicited letter of advice to CEO Phil Satre in which he suggested ways to use the customer data that Harrah's was already collecting to build and enhance guest loyalty. In 1998 Satre, a lawyer by training, offered Loveman a full-time position as Harrah's chief operating officer. You can try it out for a year while on academic leave, he told Loveman. If you don't like it, you can always go back.

Many HBS colleagues scoffed at Loveman's decision to accept the offer. Not only did the associate professor leave shortly before he would have gained tenure—a job guarantee for life at the nation's most prestigious business school. Making matters worse, he left to join hands not with a venerable Wall Street firm or prestigious firm on the Fortune 100 list but with an outfit that catered to tastes on the other side of the tracks: gambling.

Because he would oversee marketing, Loveman had a simple mandate: use personal data to understand clients better than the competition. By gathering information on millions of customers, he believed the company could lure repeat business, catering offers and promotions to the different tastes of each person.

Loveman joined the corporate world, an academic without any management experience entering a sector famously wary of outsiders. The northerner had to win over employees at Harrah's headquarters at a mansion on a large estate in Memphis, Tennessee. Many thought he would not last long.

Some found him intimidating. Peppering his conversation with words such as "stochastic," "vitiate," and "encumbrance," or talking about "elasticities of demand," did not win over the traditional casino crowd. Even Satre, his greatest supporter, joked that he needed a dictionary to understand Loveman's presentations. One executive, John Boushy, felt confident enough to prod him from time to time: "Gary, I know you know what that word means, but could you tell the rest of us?" To this day Loveman crams so many $20 words into a sentence that he may pause, realize that his listener may need some help, and add, "Let me decode that a little bit."

Loveman found it hard to abandon the university lectern in the style of his presentations. One member of the Harrah's board of directors was Walter Salmon. A former HBS student who had earned a master's degree and a PhD, Salmon had joined the faculty there in 1956. In a long career, he had served on many corporate boards as an expert on consumer marketing. Even years later, he remembered Loveman's premiere performance before the board. The chief operating officer treated the group—his ultimate bosses—as though commanding a class at his beck and call. "If you asked him a question, you got an academic response," Salmon says, implying "that the board member was one step above an idiot, or one step below an idiot."[6]

Several board members approached Satre after Loveman's debut meeting to demand that Satre have a stern talk with his protégé. "He almost got fired," says Satre.[7] "The reaction was that Gary was being too professor-like with the board and lecturing them in his first presentation, and it outraged a couple of board members." The board members were not the first to grumble about Loveman's arrival. At the Harrah's annual meeting, one shareholder complained about the business school outsider. Some employees wrote the CEO privately, asking why he had turned to someone without any casino experience.

Loveman realized he had a lot to learn. In the corporate world, he had to not only possess insights but implement them. Early on he did not always appreciate how much work it took to turn a plan into reality: "I had never managed anything. I really had not had any managerial duties. Oh, there was all sorts of stumbling. I was good at certain things and challenged in others."

Loveman pushed his managers hard. He welcomed differences of opinion, but his wrath came down on those who did not embrace his data-focused approach. David Norton, a former senior vice president who was one of Harrah's top data officials, remembers Loveman growing irritated if property managers were losing money and not focusing sufficiently on data to solve the problem. "He'd pound his fist on the

Gary Loveman at Caesars Palace in Las Vegas.
Source: Caesars Entertainment.

table and say, 'What the hell is going on here!'" Norton recalled. "If we couldn't get the bottom-up compliance, his force of personality would really make people feel badly for not coming through."

Some years after Harrah's bought the Las Vegas Rio Hotel and Casino for $518 million in 1998, Loveman grew displeased with the property's financial results.[8] He met with the hotel's general manager and some top aides, who gave presentations on their operations.

"Don't we need to be thinking about this business differently?" Loveman asked.

An hour into the meeting, he had had enough. "Guys, look, I haven't heard anything that makes any sense here. The problem is ill defined, the analytics is completely absent, and all you guys are talking about is sort of magical, you know, fairy dust stuff."

The hotel casino's manager was quite proud of the style and flair of the property, which had been designed by a legendary Strip architect. He felt his hotel was something special. He puffed up his chest a bit and set his eyes on his new boss: "Gary, you just don't understand: we're the Rio, you know, and all we've got to do is get the panache back in the Rio."

A look of stunned disbelief seized Loveman's face. Within a few weeks the Rio's longtime general manager was gone.[9]

Loveman learned from his off-pitch initial board presentation and changed his tone. The former academic diffused tensions with biting humor, including self-deprecating jokes, and slowly won over members of the team. He communicated effectively and clearly, and he wowed people with his knowledge. But he never became an easygoing, backslapping kind of executive. He was not the type to ask random visitors about the wife and kids or wander through hotel lobbies to greet guests. "I don't think there are very many customers who ever said, 'Gee, I really love Gary Loveman,'" says Satre.

In his heart, Loveman remained simply a numbers guy, a math nerd. He had traded the classroom for the corporate boardroom and was earning money beyond the wildest dreams of most academics. Yet he still thought like a professor. Following the logic of his famous 1994 article, he focused on building long-term customer loyalty. Nothing spelled success better than customers coming through Harrah's doors again and again.

The Elevator Pitch

At every turn, Loveman sought to use data, whether about an individual client or a large group of clients, to gain an edge. One day in the early 2000s, inside a wood-paneled elevator at Harrah's Hotel and Casino on Las Vegas's fabled Strip, an older couple were grumbling to each other. They liked playing slot machines, but their luck had apparently run out.

"I hate Las Vegas," the man said to the woman.

Loveman, who happened to be in the elevator with them, grew curious and decided to strike up a conversation. He learned that the couple were avid gamblers from Philadelphia who usually played at Harrah's in Atlantic City. When he asked them why they hated Las Vegas, the man answered, "The slot machines here are so goddamn tight! We never win any money!"

As Loveman replayed the Philadelphia couple's conversation in his mind, he experienced a "eureka" moment. When it came to slot machine odds, the couple had no idea what they were talking about. In

Exterior of Harrah's Las Vegas Hotel and Casino in Las Vegas. Source: Author photo.

fact, no gambler could tell if a slot machine was loose or tight—with especially good or poor odds—and data could prove his point.

Loveman knew Harrah's slot machines in Las Vegas were looser than those at its property in Atlantic City, returning $95 of every $100 plunked into them. In Atlantic City the company had the machines return just $93, giving them what the industry calls a slot hold percentage of 7. The wheels of his business mind began to spin. Slot machines make more money than anything else in casinos and do not require the extensive costs of table games to operate. Nothing was more important to the bottom line.[10] From the Philadelphia couple's experience, Loveman concluded that a customer has very little capacity to tell the difference in holds from one machine to another. Increasing the hold, even by a tiny amount, might send profits through the roof.

Soon after the exchange with the couple in the elevator, Loveman brought the idea to Harrah's executives. Some on the team resisted. At the time, conventional wisdom held that especially generous slot machines would lure customers into casinos and earn the company more money. Harrah's had even kicked around the idea of launching an ad campaign highlighting the generosity of its slot machines. No one wanted to change tack just because of a rookie executive's chance conversation in an elevator. Loveman needed hard evidence. He loved such a challenge. The idea of developing a way to demonstrate conclusively that the public couldn't perceive the worsened odds intrigued him. A puzzle like this reminded him of his previous life as an academic.

Loveman turned to MIT, the university famed for excellence in math, science, and engineering, to solve the puzzle. He asked some math experts there to test how many times a gambler would have to play the slots to detect any difference in hold over a cycle of millions of spins. The experiment confirmed Loveman's supposition: it would take many, many thousands of times to notice any difference. The math was clear. Still, he wanted to see if gamblers had some special sensory ability to find the better-paying machines. The former professor programmed two sets of slot machines side by side on a casino floor. One kept a 5 percent hold, the other a less generous 7 percent. Casino officials monitored how many people played the different machines, watching closely to see if they would swarm the machines with better odds. Gamblers played the same on each set. Nobody noticed any difference.

Since the chance elevator ride, Harrah's, the world's largest casino company—it renamed itself Caesars Entertainment in 2010—has kept a few pennies more on each dollar plunked into its slot machines.[11] It now sets its hold rates at about 8 percent in Las Vegas, 9 percent in Atlantic City, and 10 percent in some regional markets. Some rivals offer better odds.[12] But the change has brought Caesars hundreds of millions of dollars, maybe even billions in extra revenue.[13] Data had disproved instinct. "Every bit of intuition in the old-time casino business was that we couldn't do that," Loveman says. "And it really was driven by the fact that most people didn't ever understand the difference between the mean of a distribution and what people were experiencing across the distribution."[14]

The former business school professor and his company have not only led the way in tightening the odds of slot machines, but they have bet Caesars' future on harvesting personal data rather than developing the fanciest properties. Loveman has watched as Las Vegas rivals continue to outshine Caesars Entertainment by opening ever more glamorous new casino hotels. The company's flagship Las Vegas hotel, Caesars Palace, dates back nearly half a century. Back then, Frank Sinatra and his Rat Pack friends could also visit the Stardust, Aladdin, Sahara, or Sands hotels. Other than Caesars Palace, all those hotels have met the Las Vegas developer's favored solution for old age: dynamite clearing the way for new construction. Many of the Caesars Entertainment Las Vegas hotel casinos are decades old. Singing gondoliers do not navigate canals in front, as they do at the Venetian, nor do fountains explode in a choreographed dance throughout the day and night, as at the Bellagio.

Still, every day many thousands of people pour through the always-open doors of Caesars Palace and the company's other Vegas hotels, such as Harrah's, the Flamingo, Paris, and Bally's, just a few of more than fifty properties worldwide. That's because Caesars have an unrivaled asset that enables them to overcome their other shortcomings: vast amounts of personal data.

Sometimes, details gathered from individual customers apply to far larger groups. The Philadelphia couple led to Loveman's insights that work broadly on millions of slot players. In other cases, management may know which small group of high-spenders in southern Florida gamble enough money to deserve a free flight to Las Vegas during the March Madness college basketball tournament. That's the power of personal data.

To learn so much about its customers, Caesars followed in the footsteps of the airline industry and set up a loyalty program. By assigning you a number, they can track all of your activities in their establishments, much as American, Delta, and United follow your history of flying with them. If you sign up, which the overwhelming majority of clients do, Caesars record how much you typically wager in a day, to the penny if you play electronic games such as slot machines. They know which games you prefer, what food you like to eat, when you like to visit, and whether you would like standup comedy, '80s rock concerts, or shows where transvestites lip-sync while pretending to be Cher, Dolly Parton, or Madonna. Your personal file may note if you have a favorite hostess at Caesars Palace, whether you prefer the six-foot-tall comely blonde or the diminutive hostess who speaks Chinese.

Mastering data analytics, and customer data in particular, has given Caesars an edge in a business where rivals compete fiercely with the same games. Every casino offers the same product: the excitement of gambling, the dream of sudden riches. The roulette ball bounces and the cards snap with the same unpredictability everywhere. Scoffing at the instinctive approach of fellow bosses past and present, Loveman fills his executive suites with math nerds from prestigious colleges. He lays down the law with a simple mantra: "Tell me what you know, not what you think." And personal data—the minutiae of our likes and proclivities, habits and patterns—lies at the heart of the knowing.

For the former business school professor, the gaming business has become the ultimate research experiment into consumer behavior. He uses cutting-edge technologies to gather personal details on millions of customers—with their consent, even if few understand all the intricacies of what happens behind the scenes. All of this takes place to tweak visitors' experiences in such a way as to get them to open their wallets just a little more. Within the walls of their casinos, Caesars record everything they can about tens of millions of people. And in doing so, Loveman, now CEO, has become a modern-day emperor of customer information.

By prospering on the backs of so much personal information, Caesars have inspired companies across the economy. Everyone wants to learn more about customers in hopes of marketing more successfully. Rivals closely watch to see what Loveman and Caesars will come up with next.

Patti Hart has unusually good access to the biggest casinos and their top management. She is the CEO of IGT, a leading slot machine manufacturer, so she talks with everyone. A rare woman in the macho world of casino management, she has a keen sense of industry sentiment. Over the years she has developed great respect for Loveman's leading role. "He sets the pace for everyone else, and he doesn't always appreciate the fact that everyone else watches him and sets their cadence based on what he is doing. And I think that really is a very tough position to be in, one that he respects and one in which he performs amazingly well," she says. "Gary is not afraid to live in a constantly innovative world. He will even innovate his own idea. I think that really sets him apart from lots of leaders that I work with in every business. Gary is a person that never sees an end in sight to the innovation."

Over the years, Loveman's rivals not only started collecting data about what clients do in their casinos. Some have also turned to outside data brokers to buy ever more personal information. Data brokers learn where customers have lived throughout their lives, whom they marry and divorce, and how many children they have. Data dossiers detail hobbies, economic situation, and consumption habits. Companies across the economy regularly buy and sell information about us all, a trade largely hidden from those whose data are contained in the dossiers.

Even if you never set foot in a casino, companies gather data about you at every turn. If you buy a fishing pole online, the details may be recorded to market to you in the future. Depending on its privacy policies, your gym could let others know you are interested in fitness. Magazine subscribers will often receive offers in the mail and email from companies to whom the publisher has sold their names. Whether you are a gambler or not, the proliferation of personal data affects your life at every turn. Some consumers complain that companies invade their privacy by collecting so much about them. Others like advertising and offers targeted to their interests. In any case, personal data often work in targeting products to the right people, whether by conventional ads or via the Internet. So the trade in such information has increased dramatically in recent years.

Caesars had always shunned outside personal data. The company had focused only on information that its customers gave voluntarily by joining the Total Rewards loyalty program. But continuing economic woes lasting many years after the financial crisis of 2008, and billions of dollars of debt, changed the landscape in Las Vegas. Some of the Caesars data whiz executives wondered if they should do things differently and embrace some of this outside torrent of information about clients. Many businesses were wondering the same thing for their own enterprises.

3

Loyalty

Slot Machine Points

Casinos have long tried to make guests feel special so that they keep coming back. An episode of *The Twilight Zone* that aired in 1960 portrays such hospitality. The city was growing in popular imagination. That was the year the Rat Pack—Frank Sinatra, Dean Martin, Sammy Davis Jr., and others—filmed the original *Ocean's Eleven* and entertained at the Sands Hotel. The *Twilight Zone* episode, written by Rod Serling, opens with an elderly couple arriving at a Las Vegas casino after winning an all-expenses-paid weekend. A well-groomed casino official walks over to greet the couple and asks if their room is comfortable and if there is anything he can do.

"You know, you make us feel . . . important," the wife gushes.

"You *are* important, Mrs. Gibbs. It isn't every day that we entertain celebrated contest winners."

A wary photographer brought along to capture the moment for the hometown paper can't help but interject: "No, not every day. Maybe every other day."

Ever since the days of Bugsy Siegel, casinos have pampered high rollers and special guests, rewarding them with free rooms, food, drinks, and other perks. Dealers kept manual records on gamblers. But without computers and precise calculations, many managers embraced a seat-of-the-pants instinctual style.

Benny Binion, the legendary Texan owner of the Horseshoe, a pioneering Vegas casino that opened in 1951, was famous for making the rounds and chatting with guests. He'd ask their names and where they were from. He might gab about anything that popped into his head. If he decided he liked them, or if he was just feeling particularly generous, he'd take out a slip of paper and authorize a free meal. He would scribble out something like "Feed James lunch," and sign an ornate B at the bottom. "He didn't know if you were playing nickels or dollars," says Eddie LaRue, who moved to Las Vegas in 1962 and fondly remembers the Texan.

Binion drew people into his casino with services such as his paycheck wheel, where customers would cash their paychecks and get a free spin on a wheel of fortune, hoping to win a prize that might be something as modest as a glass of beer. Once their pockets were filled with money, some stayed at the bar or placed a few bets before heading home. The casino owner described his philosophy to a fresh-faced newcomer: "Listen, boy. People hate to be fooled. If you lie to them, they will hate you forever. But people love a chance to fool themselves. And I give it to them."[1] In the early days of Las Vegas, standard accounting may have been a less exact science, and some casinos skimmed money from the till to line the managers' pockets. In the 1950s Binion, not able to fool the government, spent years in jail after a conviction on income tax evasion.

If a chance customer encounter in an elevator could yield a multi-million-dollar change in strategy, how many more millions could be gained through better insights into gamblers' behavior? In the early years of Las Vegas, management did not pay much attention to slot players. Starting from the late nineteenth century, slot machines spun three wheels in random combination. In the earliest days, lining up three symbols on the machine's small window earned prizes such as a free drink or cigarettes. Eventually, cash winnings became standard. For many years players preferred table games such as blackjack, craps, or roulette. But eventually, technology-boosted "one-armed bandits," as the machines are called, became the casinos' greatest moneymakers.

In the 1960s, manufacturers livened up slot machines by adding electronics. They were further augmented in the 1970s with microchips. In 1960, only a slot machine in *The Twilight Zone,* that wondrous land whose boundaries are that of imagination, could talk. But slot machines became ever more exciting as electronics and computerization added flashing lights, video, and audio dialogue. One-armed bandits took on personalities of their own, often grafted from television shows and movies. One manufacturer even introduced a *Twilight Zone* theme. Today some of these machines cost as much as a new car. Such innovation has dramatically increased revenue; slots now bring in nearly two-thirds of casino floor revenue in and around Las Vegas.[2]

As the machines have improved, casino operators have paid more attention to them. In Nevada, a state that beckons gamblers not only to Vegas but also to Reno and Lake Tahoe, casinos decided to reward slot players to lure repeat business. Beginning in the 1960s, slot attendants at Harrah's in Lake Tahoe and Reno noted how much a player put into the machine. Based on their observations, clerks wrote out tickets worth a certain number of points. Gamblers could trade a stack of tickets for prizes such as a blender, radio, or TV. By the early 1980s, the decade when slot machines really took off in popularity, casinos had started installing automatic dispensers that issued tickets for standard amounts of play.

A fundamental problem plagued these early loyalty programs. Until someone redeemed tickets, management had no way of identifying who the biggest players were. US retail loyalty programs had faced the same challenge since the late eighteenth century.[3] The best-known pre-computer era program started in 1896, when Sperry & Hutchinson introduced Green Stamps. Stores gave away the stamps based on the spending of customers, who in turn could redeem them for a variety of goods. Stores bought the stamps to boost business, but the program did not gather information about customers, making it of limited value to the retailer. Like the businesses that eventually abandoned Green Stamps, casinos did not want to just give out free prizes. They wanted to learn about their best customers so they could market more effectively.

* * *

US airlines led the way in compiling information about their best customers by introducing the modern-day loyalty program. When American Airlines designed the first frequent flyer program in 1981, it turned to outside consultant Hal Brierley. A Harvard Business School graduate who founded Epsilon Data Management, a leading personal data marketer (see Chapter 7), he had a simple mandate: build a database of people and track their flights to better target news and offers to the right people.

American had to motivate passengers to give not only a name and address but also a number that linked them to their previous purchases. That way the airline could understand the value of each passenger. The lure was the chance to earn a free ticket. "If they could identify their best customers, they thought they could better reallocate their marketing spend to the right customers and hopefully gain a bit of market share," Brierley said. "The goal was not to give away two tickets to Hawaii."

Airlines and other businesses are ready to give away perks to identify their best customers because they represent such a disproportionate percentage of total sales. When Brierley worked on airline loyalty programs in the early 1980s, he says the top 2 percent of passengers generated 25–30 percent of revenue, and even more important, the top 0.2 percent generated 7–8 percent of revenue. Other airlines quickly followed American's lead. Looking back, it seems obvious that someone would develop an airline loyalty program. But at the time, the program represented a game-changing innovation. Car rental agencies, hotels, supermarkets, and many other businesses later embraced similar programs, allowing them to accumulate information about their best customers.

It might appear that airlines should be able to figure out their best clients on their own, since passengers give their names, phone numbers, and credit card information when they buy a ticket. Yet Brierley says the airlines needed a unifying number to identify them correctly. "They had spent a lot of money trying to develop customer databases in a more stealth manner matching names and phone numbers," he says. "But when you have a lot of Bill Smiths and people use different telephone numbers, they had very little luck figuring out who it was that was flying back and forth to London."

As casinos sought to keep better tabs on slot customers, they too looked to the US airline industry's loyalty programs. Over time, casino companies such as Caesars gathered an especially wide array of transactional data about customers.

Tracking Players

When airlines adopted frequent flyer programs, they only had to record a customer's number in the centralized reservation system. Collecting loyalty program numbers from thousands of slot machines proved more challenging. Casinos had to reconfigure the machines to bring together information about who was playing. Setting up card readers proved an especially expensive proposition. John Acres wanted to find a cheaper solution. He found inspiration from an unlikely source.

Like Gary Loveman, Acres cherished mathematics and applied his knowledge to tinkering and inventing for the casino industry. He had already figured out how to build ticket dispensers for slot machines, eliminating the need for clerks to write out tickets to reward frequent slot players. But such retrofitting cost about $400 per machine in the early 1980s (about $1,000 today, adjusted for inflation). Even at that price, the ticket dispensers could not identify players by name.

On Christmas Eve 1983, as Acres was wrapping gifts for his children, he paused to marvel at a game called Speak & Spell. For less than $50, the manufacturer offered a plastic keyboard, electronic display, and electronic voice. He wondered how it could do so much for so little money—at least in terms of what computer parts cost at that time. Santa took out a screwdriver and dissected the toy on his kitchen table. He looked inside and marveled at the low-cost circuitry. He then thought back to a visit he had made a few weeks before to the Sun City Casino in South Africa. There Acres had seen an electronic plastic hotel key for the first time. He felt a flash of inspiration. Within a few weeks he had devised a prototype card reader for slot machines to identify who exactly was playing the game. On that Christmas Eve, however,

*Inserting a Total Rewards loyalty card into a slot machine at Caesars Palace.
Source: Author photo.*

his probing destroyed the toy. It never spoke or spelled again. Santa delivered one less gift to the Acres home that year.

Like a credit card that identifies shoppers from a small slab of plastic, Acres's new card reader allowed casinos to track their slot players accurately by name. Gamblers happily whipped out their cards and gave up data. Harrah's officials crowed about how they helped personalize service, added people to their mailing lists about special events, and counted a player's bonus points precisely.

Gathering data on gamblers expanded from there. In the 1990s, Harrah's CEO Phil Satre wrote personal letters to customers who had visited multiple properties to ask where they planned to visit next. His staff tried to track the responses, but found that system time-consuming and difficult to maintain. Harrah's spent years and millions of dollars installing a common database across all of its properties, and in 1997 the company introduced the first full-scale casino loyalty program.[4]

Harrah's WINet (Winners Information Network) quickly gathered five million names.[5] The executives hoped the new database would allow them to target their direct mail offers with greater precision. But things did not work out as hoped. "To be honest with you, I was disappointed with the early results, which is one of the reasons I hired Gary," says Satre. "I didn't think we were getting enough traction with our customers. We were getting the data, but we were not using the data in a sophisticated way to market back to the customer with offers and rewards that would meaningfully change their behavior."

As the new chief operating officer plotting changes at Harrah's, Loveman started searching for new aces to pilot his customer data operation. He turned first to Rich Mirman, a consultant at Booz Allen Hamilton.[6] Mirman was a math whiz who had dropped out of a PhD program at the University of Chicago. He was a newcomer to the world of casinos, but Loveman saw him as a like-minded data analytics guy. As the new chief marketing officer, Mirman learned the ropes and created many models to fine-tune the company's approach.

One showed a decision tree of customers, divided into those who came a lot and those who did not. The next level down showed those who spent a lot when they came and those who did not. The next level showed customers who had a high predicted budget and those who did not. Along each section of his marketing map Mirman identified what he called "opportunity segments." Such groups might be gamblers who came often but spent little, even though they appeared to have money. Another potential group might be those who came infrequently but could be encouraged to come more often. The company would market differently to each segment.

Mirman also thought about the life cycle of a typical casino customer, one of Loveman's favorite themes. When new customers first arrived, Harrah's could observe only part of their long-term value to the company, because they might be sharing their business with other Vegas casinos. For long-standing customers, the company might already have a good idea of their full potential to spend. So Mirman started spending more money than before marketing to new customers with bigger long-term potential.

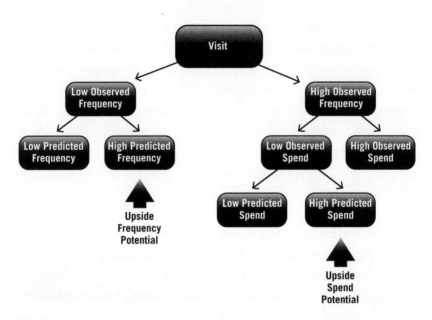

Rich Mirman's chart of opportunity segments that had previously been neglected. Source: Rich Mirman.

In another model, Mirman tried to figure out when customers would be most likely to come back to Las Vegas. He found that gamblers were many times more likely to return exactly twelve months after their previous visit. Marketers would gain an edge if they sent offers around the time gamblers began planning their return visit—usually around nine months after the previous visit. Studying the customer database, Mirman also noticed the greatest business opportunity not from "whales," the biggest spenders, but from those who played $100 to $400 per trip. Such players were far from the most lucrative on any one day, but in a year they might spend $1,500 to $5,000. This group represented 80 percent of the opportunity for growth, he calculated.

"We built our entire strategy around that one insight that surely we could do better and convince a customer to give us a larger share of their wallet," Mirman says. At the time, Harrah's estimated that customers gave 64 percent of their business to other casinos. With little incentive to show unwavering loyalty to any one establishment, clients

Customers at a Total Rewards counter at Caesars Palace. Source: Author photo.

regularly gambled away most of their money elsewhere. "Everything that we did was based on the mantra that we were going to convince them that it was in their best interest to consolidate up their play."

Soon after Loveman hired him in 1998, Mirman toured Harrah's in Las Vegas, a former Holiday Inn located across the Strip from Caesars Palace. As they passed a long line leading to a restaurant buffet, the property's manager kept stopping to greet people.

"Who are those people?" Mirman asked.

"Those are some of our best players," the manager said.

Mirman was taken aback. "Our best players are standing in line waiting for the buffet? Why would we do that?" he thought.[7]

Harrah's eventually replicated the model embraced by US airlines and added different membership levels. The most active customers would get greater perks, including shorter buffet and check-in lines.

Buffet line at Caesars Palace. Source: Author photo.

Mirman and his team toyed with whimsical tiers such as "Lucky Cherries," "Three Sevens," and "Diamond Jubilee." They tested the ideas on customers and found they hated the goofy names; they took their gambling seriously. In 2000, Harrah's settled on Gold, Platinum, and Diamond levels, inspired by conservative names used by credit card companies.[8] The company added a new top level, Seven Stars, four years later.

After Mirman, Loveman hired David Norton. Norton thought a lot about the people traditionally ignored by casino management. He saw great value in the retired grandmother quietly feeding a steady stream of coins (and later paper) into slot machines in the corner of the room. Under the old system, such players did not spend enough on any one day to merit special attention. But they came twenty, thirty, or forty times a year for their Friday or Saturday night entertainment. Norton concluded that the vast majority of the company's most valuable customers followed such a pattern.

"Previously in the industry, people who were good daily value customers got special treatment," says Norton, who ended up as the senior vice president, serving until 2011. "You could spend $500 a day once a year and be a VIP, and you could spend $100 a day and come thirty times a year and you weren't a VIP."[9]

Norton considered how a sixty-year-old woman who lives in New Jersey near Atlantic City would stack up against a twenty-eight-year-old guy from Manhattan. It may be that two visits a year to Atlantic City is all they can expect from the New Yorker, but the nearby retiree might come ten times. Thus the company should give her special deals to show up more often, based on her specific profile. "We are going to talk to her differently and say, 'If you are more loyal to us, you could achieve Platinum or Diamond status,'" says Norton, an MBA with a background in the credit card industry. "Because we think she is going to the market somewhere else and we are only getting a small fraction of her spend."

Norton recommended to Loveman that Harrah's create more benefits for the repeat customer who spends modest amounts on each visit. Loveman agreed. So the company started offering these regulars special perks such as free valet service, faster check-in, and better buffets. The New Jersey regular and other customers like her felt special. They kept coming back.

Harrah's still had its headquarters in Memphis when Norton started. He received a cushy office in what he felt was a country club atmosphere. As he dug into the company's database, he was impressed to find that Harrah's had centralized gambling information on customers from across what was then fifteen different properties. Yet he soon realized local managers did their own marketing, often disregarding the data and following their instincts. They largely ignored headquarters, even though the great value of all the customer data could only be realized with a unified approach.

Norton struggled to get local casinos to embrace the mantra of personal data. One day he visited Harvey's Lake Tahoe, a company property that lured gamblers from San Francisco and other parts of California. He told them he wanted hosts at the casino to spend one day a week calling new clients and encouraging them to return. The message was not welcome. "The daggers I got from those hosts was amazing," he said. "But it completely revolutionized the business."

Some on Loveman's staff ruffled feathers with unbridled arrogance. Norton recalls one Harvard graduate on his team who was as smart as anyone he had ever hired. Yet he fired her after a few months. No one ever wanted to work with her because of her attitude. Sometimes, the old-timers *did* know more than the whiz kids. The math nerds, many of whom had cut their teeth on Wall Street and as well-polished consultants, were often surprised by who spends the most gambling. They expected that lawyers, doctors, bankers, and consultants would be their best clients. Yet often the big gamblers ran small businesses such as dry cleaners, Chinese restaurants, or plumbing companies. "They don't look like the people you expect to have money," said Randy Fine, a former Loveman student who later became head of Harrah's Total Rewards loyalty program. "Most Harvard Business School people struggle in the business and most wash out. And the reason is that people who go to a place like Harvard Business School believe that people who have money look a certain way."

As Harrah's relentless focus on personal data and marketing showed results, old-timers grumbled that the whiz kids had subverted the spirit of old Las Vegas. "Casinos used to be run by individuals," says Eddie LaRue, who still tells stories about Benny Binion from half a century ago. "Now it's a total disaster. You've got people who don't know anything about running a casino."

Former Vegas Mayor Oscar Goodman, who worked as a criminal defense lawyer in that era, remembers going to the now-defunct Thunderbird Hotel with his wife, where he would see singers such as Sarah Vaughan and Frankie Laine. "They didn't charge. They would bring us a free drink and hope that if we had any money in our pocket we would leave it there," he recalls. "Now everything has changed. Now the bottom line, the bean counters have said that every department has to make money."

4

Casino Data Gathering in Action

What the Casino Knows

Gary Loveman and his math nerds do not wander casino floors personally sizing up customers as Benny Binion and old-time Vegas hands once did. Rather, they study data about customers' past visits and project their potential future value. Just watching someone at a gaming table or slot machine for as little as sixty minutes makes it possible to predict how valuable a gambler may be in the future. It all comes down to how much someone typically bets, how many bets in a row he places, and how skilled he is. Such personal data is so valuable that Caesars sometimes reimburse newcomers for up to $100 in losses if they sign up for the rewards program and gamble for an hour.

The data gathering begins soon after a gambler walks into the cavernous casino lobby. A slight haze may linger from smoke (in the United States most casinos are among the last great refuges for those who enjoy cigarettes). A subtle perfume scents the air, pumped in to create a specific memory sensation. The gambler looks for her favorite slot machine and plops down. She reaches into her wallet and pulls out her Caesars Total Rewards loyalty card. She reaches toward a card reader surrounded by dotted orange lights. It turns green after she inserts the plastic card. From that moment, the casino records everything, starting with how much cash and paper ticket value she puts into the machine (coins were phased out more than a decade ago).

Caesars know exactly how many times she pushes the button triggering the electronic wheels to spin in random combination. They know how much she is losing (or, less often, winning) from the moment she starts. The law of averages means that everyone will lose over time. Yet the casinos want her to keep returning, so they will do everything they can short of rigging the machines to mitigate a particularly bad day. If she loses far more than she traditionally wagers and far worse than the game's mathematical odds predict, a host, tipped off by a message to a smart phone, might arrive with a coupon for a free buffet to cheer her up. The logic? A bad day could inspire a gambler to defect to another casino to change her luck.

From time to time a host will greet elite-status slot machine players. At Caesars Palace, that might be Holly Danforth, a striking six-foot-tall blonde in her late twenties who aspires to become an actress or model. She introduces herself and addresses the player by name, which she knows from the data on her cell phone. "Most of the time they are very shocked," she says. "They ask, 'How do you know that?' I tell them it's by their participation in Total Rewards." She then gives out a business card and invites the player to contact her for any future assistance. If the player is a man who makes a pass at her, something she says happens all the time, she tries to gracefully extract herself and continue toward the next VIP.

Taking a break in the action, the gambler heads to one of the casino's many restaurants. The maître d' asks if she is a Total Rewards member. The waiter hands her a menu with two rows of prices, with a few bucks off each item for loyalty members. Or she could sign up for six all-you-can-eat buffets within a twenty-four-hour period at the discounted price of $47.99.[1] Caesars record exactly what she orders and over time chart her favorite foods. Capping off the evening at a show, she hands in the card to buy tickets, giving the management insights into what kind of entertainment she prefers.

In a fast-moving table game like craps, a supervisor notes down bets by visual observation, less precise monitoring than with slot machines. A player can later check credited points on a casino computer. If the gambler feels shortchanged, management can review a videotape of betting.[2] The supervisor also keeps a close eye out for players trying to game the system. Some bet especially heavily when the supervisor comes into view, hoping they will be credited with more loyalty points. Others quietly pocket some of their own chips to exaggerate their losses (casinos are especially keen to lure back losers with generous future offers). The company is considering spending tens of millions of dollars to buy chips embedded with radio-frequency ID transmitters, which would allow the casino to track bets to the exact dollar.

In all, Loveman says, Caesars casinos know: "Did you respond to an offer when you came to the facility? Are you a resident with us at the hotel or not? When do you come? How long do you stay? What game do you play? How intently do you play it? What's the average wager? What sort of success did you have in the game? Were you a big winner, a big loser, an average winner, an average loser? Did you eat when you were with us? Did you go to the show? What kind of dining habits do you have? Do you shop?"

Rod Serling's old *Twilight Zone* episode, titled "The Fever," portrays a slot machine that knows the elderly husband's name, Franklin, and beckons him in an ominous voice. His obsession eventually drives him mad.[3] Today Franklin might receive a direct solicitation for his business by mail, email, or smart phone. A host might also call him up to see how he is doing.

Some critics say all this clever marketing exploits those with a particular weakness for gambling, especially those who suffer from gambling addiction. Loveman responds that while gambling addiction is a real issue, 98 percent of his clients can dispassionately decide whether to take advantage of a marketing promotion. These clients can rationally decide to buy or not in the same way they might review a new offer for books or products from Amazon.com.

"For the 2 percent of the people who are addicted, there is no evidence to suggest being good marketers is really the issue. The addiction has to do with lots of other issues, and there are mental health circumstances," Loveman says. "It's not whether or not the guy who runs the casino is especially capable or incapable of offering them things that they care about."[4]

Catching Whales

By tracking a gambler's last visit, a casino has information that can help lure him back in the future. Such logic motivates many companies far from Las Vegas to collect our personal data. Whether it is a local restaurant, airline, or online retailer, businesses want to know as much about us as possible, hoping to gain an edge in marketing. Some firms are more successful than others in using customer information, and that's why many have studied Caesars for insights.

Caesars give customers a choice to share their data, and patrons like Daniel Kostel do so willingly and enthusiastically. A salesman at an asset management firm in Los Angeles, Kostel visits Las Vegas about once a month. The bachelor loves blackjack and typically wagers $100 a hand. On a good night, he wins a few thousand dollars. If things go less fortuitously, he heads out the door that much poorer. He is not a huge gambler—what the industry dubs a "whale"—but he spends a lot more than a retiree cautiously playing penny slot machines. For years, Kostel alternated between casinos along the Strip, making him what the industry labels "promiscuous." One night he dropped by Caesars Palace at the Strip's fifty-yard line.

People still rave about the glamour of Caesars Palace in its heyday. Former Las Vegas Mayor Oscar Goodman can wax lyrical about the old Caesars Palace: "They had a restaurant called the Bacchanal where you sat in this beautiful ornate room with Filipina waitresses who would give you a back rub and peel grapes and toss them down your gullet. I mean, that was pretty neat."

Hollywood has long portrayed Caesars Palace as a den of excitement and adventure. Robert Redford, dressed in a purple cowboy suit dotted with flashing lights, slowly rides a horse across the casino floor to the bemusement of patrons in *The Electric Horseman,* then proceeds down Las Vegas Boulevard. Dustin Hoffman and Tom Cruise win so much money at blackjack in *Rain Man* that management becomes alarmed. George Clooney and Catherine Zeta-Jones flirt over a meal there in *Intolerable Cruelty.* Mobster Tony Soprano, played by James Gandolfini, stays at Caesars Palace after the death of his nephew

Christopher Moltisanti. In the first and third *Hangover* comedies, the guys drink on the roof, recover from a wild party in their suite, play blackjack, and engage in other high jinks there.[5] And in an example of life imitating art, some of the movies and series filmed at Caesars Palace, such as *The Hangover* and *The Sopranos,* eventually become themes for slot machines.

In terms of history, no Las Vegas casino can outshine Caesars Palace. But in a city changing as rapidly as Las Vegas, the hotel casino is no longer the unrivaled belle of the ball. Trendsetters have migrated to more luxurious rivals. The crowd at some of these newer, more upscale casinos often appears more refined and perhaps a bit younger, more likely to wear designer evening clothes.

Dan Kostel typically favored more elegant hotels such as the Bellagio, but one December weekend he decided to try his luck at Caesars Palace. He had joined Total Rewards about fifteen years before, but only patronized the casino from time to time. When he signed up for the loyalty program, he gave his name, address, date of birth, and other information. He reasoned that such details were already out there in the public realm. The casino would also know how much he had won or lost at the tables, something he did not consider particularly private.

Kostel sat down at the blackjack table and handed in his Total Rewards card. A supervisor swiped the card through a computer reader. The scan showed that Kostel had previously shared financial details with Caesars to get a line of credit. The supervisor returned with a few thousand dollars in chips, which he placed onto the green felt table, and recorded Kostel's initial purchase on a touch-screen computer tilted away from bettors. The screen also included notes on customers on preformatted fields that included sex, race, build, and age. The supervisor, moving around a cluster of tables, kept returning to note how much Kostel was betting and how well he played a game where skill can enhance—or at least mitigate—the luck of the draw. When the thirty-nine-year-old player cashed out twelve hours later, the program calculated his total earnings and time at the table. Kostel proved an excellent client: the house made thousands of dollars off him that night. Management definitely wanted him back.

Dan Kostel at a blackjack table at Caesars Palace. Source: Author photo.

By allowing Caesars to gather a significant amount of data about his casino activities, Kostel hoped to receive benefits much as an airline frequent flyer earns free flights. That is exactly what happened. A few months later, the world's largest casino company mailed a letter to Kostel, offering him a free room and $1,000 in free play during his next trip.

Kostel liked luxury. He liked to feel he was staying someplace special. At Caesars Palace, he had noticed some gamblers with extensive tattoos, and even a few guys wandering through without a shirt, escaping the desert heat. Many of his fellow gamblers were retirees, long into their golden years. He preferred a more refined ambiance. The offer of a free room was nothing special, Kostel thought; other casinos do that for big spenders. But $1,000 in chips to kick off the trip made it worth returning to Caesars Palace. "It's older and the crowd is not as sophisticated and as upmarket as some of the newer hotels, but if I have a choice to stay at one place and they give me a thousand bucks, or stay next door and they won't, I'll stay at a place that won't be as nice and keep that money," he thought.

By signing up for Total Rewards, Kostel agreed to share an intimate view of his activities on the company's properties. Caesars know that he appreciates a visit to the hotel spa and that he likes southwestern food as well as blackjack. They record that he sometimes dines alone. Yet unlike many transactions in the current world of personal data-gathering, this process lets him know who is gathering the data and what they are gathering, and he receives clear benefits in return. Anyone who does not want to share their data can decline to enroll in the program and gamble anonymously. "The complimentaries that you can get can be considerable, and you are not going to get anything if you don't use the card," he says. "A substantial part of what makes gambling somewhat worthwhile in terms of its cost are the complimentary room, food, beverage, etc. that they can give you."

Kostel could afford to stay at any Vegas casino, but the generous $1,000 in free chips lured him back to Caesars Palace. About a month later, Caesars sent another $1,000 in free chips, followed by another grand the month after that. He became a regular, visiting every month. By the time he felt enmeshed in the loyalty program, Caesars lowered their offer to $300. Kostel liked the $1,000 offers better, but he kept coming regardless.

Kostel is just one guy, of course, but Caesars target millions of customers to come again and again. Maybe you think Jerry Seinfeld is hilarious. Caesars may invite you out to Las Vegas for one of the handful of days a year the comedian performs stand-up at Caesars Palace. Or maybe Caesars know that you are a fan of Elton John, or Rod Stewart. If they know a bachelor party might lie in your future, they may serve up a promotion for a *Hangover*-themed package. Many people respond to such offers. Overall, the company says its personally targeted offers have generated billions of dollars over the years.

Even if you have never set foot in a casino, many businesses—credit cards, banks, alarm companies, magazines, divorce lawyers, you name it—are trying to serve up individualized offers based on their interpretations of your personal data. You don't get a pile of free chips from those companies, of course. But you might get a free flight, meal, or other benefit based on your value as a customer.

When gamblers such as Kostel sign up for the loyalty program at Caesars, they know who is collecting the information. The casino does not sell the information to anyone else. Management could, however, buy data about the gambler's activities outside the walls of their hotel casinos to learn even more about their customers and help persuade them to gamble more with Caesars. Who are the person's friends and relatives? Does he or she make a lot of money? Does the person have an arrest record? What else does he or she spend money on?

If you are a business trying to understand customers, it certainly is tempting to look at this kind of information. The company was reluctant. Like a professional baseball slugger shunning steroids even after the drug became widespread, it watched from the sidelines as the use of third-party data grew. It only collected information about its own clients, within its own walls, with their permission. The know-it-all data brokers would call from time to time to try to sell additional information. How about details about customers' income level, job status, or friends, family or work associates? they would ask. The answer was always no. Caesars steadfastly refused.

The company first adopted the "no outside data" policy in the mid-1990s as it ramped up its own data collection. In 2000, it published a public code that pledged to conduct the business "with honesty and integrity, and act in accordance with the highest ethical and legal standards." After Harrah's bought Caesars Entertainment in 2004, the company reconfirmed its "no outside data" policy. To gather outside information from third-party data brokers would violate the trust Harrah's had established with its clients, officials felt. "We were not going to overlay external information that is really potentially intrusive even if a vast majority would not find it intrusive," recalled John Boushy, who worked as an executive at the company from 1979 to 2006.

But not everyone agreed, especially rivals who envied Harrah's lead among casino loyalty programs. Over time, competitors caught on and established alternatives. Eventually some newer Caesars executives began to wonder: was the company voluntarily shackling itself when everyone else was going data hunting?

5

A Celebrity, a Private Eye, and a Hit Man

Finding a Hollywood Star on Holiday

Former US President Gerald Ford died shortly after Christmas in 2006. I was working at the time in San Francisco as a wire service reporter. When news broke, I often had to find people quickly to interview. For a follow-up story the next morning, I wanted to talk to veteran comedy actor and writer Chevy Chase, star of the *National Lampoon's Vacation* and *Fletch* movies. Through his portrayal of Ford during the first season of *Saturday Night Live* in 1975–76, Chase had helped cement the public image of the unelected president as a bumbler.

To reach celebrities, journalists typically must penetrate a barrier of agents, publicists, and lawyers. A formal request for an interview can take days or even weeks. Celebrities often refuse when they have no movie, CD, or book to promote. A data broker website I used did not have a phone number for Chase, but a search for others at his address did produce a number in his wife's name.[1]

Chase's daughter answered the call on what turned out to be her cell phone. She chirpily explained she was skiing with her dad in Colorado. She said he would call back after they glided to the bottom of the hill. Within the hour, the actor was sharing his recollections of how Ford once took Chase and his wife on a tour through Grand Rapids, Michigan, and proved a genial and welcoming host.

Back at the ski lodge that evening, Chase called again, this time angry and upset. He had realized that decades of filtering outside contact had not exempted him and his family from appearing in data broker files. How had someone found his daughter's cell phone, he wondered? "I'm just a guy who made some fun of Gerald Ford in 1976 and I prefer to be left alone, really," he said bitterly.

Old-Style Private Eye

In the era before computers, unlisted phone numbers and public records were hard to come by. People had to travel to the courthouse or the county clerk's office to see important documents, and if one company learned such information, it was hard to share with others. Only insiders could quickly assemble a dossier on any particular person. A scene in *Guess Who's Coming to Dinner*, the 1967 film about interracial marriage, illustrates the way such techniques were deployed half a century ago. Spencer Tracy, playing a wealthy newspaper publisher, calls up his office to learn more about his daughter's fiancé, played by Sidney Poitier.

"Call the library and see if they've got any dope on a John Wade Prentice. Prentice. He's a doctor of medicine. Fellow about thirty-five, thirty-six. Oh, Matt. He's a colored fellow," the publisher tells his assistant. "If they haven't got anything, call up the medical association and see what they've got. Get anything you can, will you, Edie? All right. Hurry and call me back." Edie does call back a few minutes later with Prentice's year of birth, education, and professional details, as well as the year of his first marriage, which ended when an accident killed his wife and son.

Of course, that was just Hollywood's version. In real life, 1967 marked a banner year for Las Vegas public records. Elvis and Priscilla Ann Beaulieu got married at the Aladdin Hotel—but only after driving to the county courthouse to get their marriage license at 3:30 a.m. Billionaire Howard Hughes bought the Desert Inn, bringing a new face to casino ownership in the city. Both events are typical of the kind of activity captured in public records. But in the rough-and-tumble world of old Las Vegas, long before the era of Gary Loveman, personal data was much harder to come by. And sometimes it was a matter of life and death.

Oscar Goodman's clients from his life as a criminal defense attorney included some of the biggest names linked to the mob, including Meyer Lansky, Frank "Lefty" Rosenthal, and Anthony Spilotro (the latter two inspired the Robert De Niro and Joe Pesci characters in the film *Casino,* in which Goodman played himself as their defense lawyer). "In the old days, what you would do is that you would call a private detective," Goodman said. He might ask for an address or phone number. How the detective got the information was not his concern.

Goodman's old go-to guy was Eddie LaRue. Even the name sounded like a relic of a film noir private eye. Many of Goodman's most notorious clients have since passed away, but LaRue was energetic and working on cases in Las Vegas. I contacted him and he agreed to meet. Two days later we had lunch at the Golden Nugget, one of the city's oldest casinos, dating back to 1946. LaRue wore a Bluetooth earpiece for his cell phone and a short-sleeve shirt that hung over his slacks. He appeared a little more weathered than his seventy-one years, perhaps the result of half a century chasing leads in the desert sun. We sat at his favorite table, where he chatted amiably with his favorite waiters and waitresses (who are often great sources for information).

Over lunch LaRue told stories about some of his famous clients: Elvis (always polite, saying "Yes, ma'am" and "No, sir" to everyone); Sinatra (arrogant, had people in his circle deal with people he did not know); Spilotro (didn't talk a lot, didn't make a lot of jokes); Rosenthal (very arrogant, the kind who deserved to be blown up); and Howard Hughes (who, true to form during his reclusive Las Vegas years, never met LaRue even when using his services).

So, back in the day, how did he get personal data? First, LaRue bought the Criss Cross city directory, which surveyed households to learn who lived where, where they worked, how many children they had, their addresses and telephone numbers, and whether the person owned the apartment or home.[2] Then he read *Nevada Legal News,* which published all sorts of public information, including when people had utilities turned on or off. He also looked up public records such as vehicle and voter registrations, although many of the characters he was looking for were not regular voters.

Over the years he developed sources at utility companies who were willing to share information. In the 1960s and '70s, LaRue had a good contact at the local power company. Once a week he would show up bearing a basket of fruit, a couple dozen donuts, or some other gift as well as the list of people he wanted to learn more about. After that contact left the utility, he had to pay someone else $5 or $10 per name.[3] Insiders at the gas and water companies were not as helpful because they did not have as comprehensive coverage as the power utility. He would pay a telephone company employee $25 to $100 for a private number. The proliferation of carriers, cell phones, and then Internet telephony after 2000 made one-stop shopping for numbers impossible.

In LaRue's line of work, the stakes were high. Finding a key person could make the difference between winning a multimillion-dollar lawsuit or getting a client acquitted in a criminal case. There was a darker side to this kind of personal information. In the days of mob influence, details dug up by a private investigator could lead to intimidation, an assault, or even death—if the information landed in Frank Cullotta's hands. From the 1960s until the early 1980s, he worked as an enforcer for the Outfit, as insiders called it, close to Tony Spilotro. If someone was behind in his payments, Cullotta would mete out a beating. If someone was considered a sufficient threat or nuisance, a boss might ask Cullotta to rub the person out. In the movie *Casino*, he was portrayed as the character mediating between the Las Vegas and Chicago mob bosses. Cullotta himself appears briefly near the end of the movie, gunning down people. In researching this book, I found no more serious impact of personal data.

Cullotta, who was born in 1938, had a falling-out with Spilotro, and in 1982 he agreed to provide evidence against some of his former associates. He entered the witness protection program and still lives under an assumed name. I wanted to find him and followed the old-school path. I called his former FBI debriefer and asked if he might pass on my contact details. He questioned me for some minutes, then agreed. A few weeks later, Cullotta called and agreed to discuss how the Outfit had gathered personal information.

The mob went first to a private investigator and asked for details on people. Then it would turn to helpers like Cullotta to do the job at hand. Cullotta did not concern himself with how the investigator turned up his leads. "How he done it, I don't know, nor did I care," Cullotta said, speaking in his no-nonsense Chicago accent.[4] He might also visit a relative or friend of the person the mob was seeking. He had a convincing way about him when gathering details. "Of course, they would disown the person we were looking for, but yet they would know just about where they were, and they would reveal information," Cullotta said.

Private investigators who worked with tough guys made a point of not asking why someone needed personal information. "It was their job—they didn't have to know why. They didn't ask why. They just wanted to get their money. They didn't want to know the reason why you wanted them. If you told them, 'I want to kill the guy,' they are going to run away, that makes them part of a conspiracy," Cullotta said. "You've got to remember something. The private investigator you would get is a little shady anyway. So you are not going to hire somebody who is not shady. You have to find somebody that is hooked up to somebody that is shady. And in the world I lived in, there was always somebody available."

Cullotta recalls receiving information from another private investigator, not LaRue, whom he knew as well. The PI would tell him where the person lived, worked, family circumstances, and more. "You'd get a complete rundown, depending on what they wanted you to do," he said. "If they wanted you to whack him, you'd get this from your direct boss, whoever your direct boss might be at the time. If they wanted you to break his head, then you took that on yourself, how to do it. You'd break a leg or break an arm, you know, to make him pay. Because if you kill him, you don't get your money."

Given what his line of work was back then, Cullotta said things worked just fine without the Internet and easily accessible databases. "Our way of doing it probably was, I think, a little more efficient than all this Internet shit," he said.[5]

But whether the old-timers liked it or not, everything changed with the Internet. Today, anyone ready to pay a few dollars can "get the dope" on anyone. You don't need to hire a private investigator or own a newspaper's archive. Big firms, private investigators, corporate headhunters, lawyers, and others have long had access to background check services, an industry that grew when computers made it possible to store databases of information after the late 1960s. The Internet and digitization of public records brought such services to the masses. Already in the 1990s, some online firms started selling unlisted phone numbers for $69.[6] "This is the information age, and information is power! Controversial? Maybe; but wouldn't you sleep easier knowing a little bit more about a prospective business partner, employee, baby-sitter, neighbor or significant other?" a company called DocuSearch advertised in 1996. "Now any Internet-savvy individual can locate lost friends, track down debtors and deadbeats, or discover the secrets of the people with whom you associate. It's all totally professional, completely legal, and entirely confidential." In the 2000s, more entrepreneurs opened Internet businesses selling personal data built upon public records from thousands of government entities. Companies have created a host of websites that allow anyone to conduct background checks on most of the 318 million people in the United States. They advertise heartwarming reasons for their services, such as reconnecting old friends and lovers, reunifying families, and empowering singles to check potential dates.

US law restricts the trade of some personal information, such as medical and financial data, and how personal data can be used in hiring and financial decisions such as granting loans. But for the most part, the new data entrepreneurs can buy and sell our information to their hearts' content. By the 2000s, when Gary Loveman became the CEO of Harrah's, the new gold rush of personal data was under way, and all types of entrepreneurs were entering the field.

Marketing to Newlyweds

Data brokers gain information about Chevy Chase and the rest of us by collecting the electronic clues we leave behind just by living a normal life in the modern world. Landmark days in our lives generate not just especially happy or sad memories but public records as well. These records not only document our lives for the government but give insights to marketers, including casinos, into who we are.

Consider the couple traveling to Las Vegas to get married. This happens quite a lot. Every month thousands wed there, making Vegas the US marriage capital. Nearly three times more people wed in Clark County, Nevada, than in the Chicago area, a city with more than double the population, and more than four times as many as in Miami, which also has a larger population than Las Vegas.[7] The bride and groom may tie the knot with a Cleopatra wedding package at Caesars Palace or opt for an Elvis theme at a petite wedding chapel. But at some point they must interrupt the fantasy and stop by the Clark County Clerk's office to obtain a marriage license. They pay $60, provide their birth dates and places of birth, address, parents' names (including mothers' maiden names), the parents' places of birth, details about any previous marriages, and Social Security numbers.

Everyone goes through the same process, whether a drunken couple stumbling in for a spur-of-the-moment matrimony or a celebrity pair's well-choreographed pageant. Over the years Elvis Presley, Angelina Jolie, Jane Fonda (with Ted Turner), Frank Sinatra (to Mia Farrow), Paul Newman, and Kirk Douglas have all obtained Las Vegas marriage licenses. After the wedding ceremony, the presiding official has ten days to send the marriage certificate to the Clark County Recorder's office, which scans the document and enters the data. If the couple ends up buying property, the recorder's office logs those details, as well as liens, court judgments, financing, and other relevant documents.

All of the personal information captured in this process is public. Anyone can see it, record it, and pass it on or sell it to others. And that's exactly what a handful of individuals such as Marc Hall do. They spend their days trolling through public computers at the Clark County Recorder's office hunting down information to sell to others such as banks and title companies. Hall, an "abstractor," works freelance for a number of companies. An alarm installation business pays him $35 a day to gather the latest home purchase registrations. He types in up to 200 new registrations a day, recording them as soon as they are posted. Speed is important because a homeowner will buy only one alarm system. After Hall passes on his updated list, the company sends salespeople door to door. Other companies hire abstractors to look up new house registrations for landscaping services and pest control.

Another company pays Hall $40 a case to research a property's history, including liens, judgments, mortgages, and tax information. Companies might use such information to refinance loans, for example. Clark County places summary information from many of its public documents online, but not the actual documents. Hall's value comes from extracting details from the scanned copies of the original documents, which may contain Social Security numbers (in more recent documents these are redacted from public view), dates of birth, and fuller details. Companies doing background searches on potential hires ask him to check court records about people, earning him anywhere from $4 to $10 per person.

He got into the field working for the legal reference service Lexis in Los Angeles. In 1999 he struck out on his own in Las Vegas. He does his job when he wants to and makes anywhere from $80,000 to $150,000 a year. He writes up his reports from home. Just days before I met him he had added a new public record of his own into the system: he had married for the first time at age thirty-eight.

Of course, you don't have to hire an abstractor to find public records. The documents are there for anyone to look up, increasingly via the Internet as well. Want to know what boxer Mike Tyson paid for his home or when he married? The details on him and any other local celebrity can be found in a few clicks.[8] A search for Steve Wynn, one of the most important people in Las Vegas, turns up dozens of public documents.

Until the Internet era, people who wanted to see marriage licenses or other public documents would have to go in person to a government office and apply to see a specific document. After a wait of some minutes, the visitor would peruse the papers in a reception area under the watchful eye of a department employee. Copying pages was expensive at $1 a page.

Casinos looking to generate new business sometimes turn to public records to develop leads. For example, starting in 2011 the deluxe Wynn Las Vegas and Encore Resort asked both the county clerk's office and the recorder's office for an ongoing list of everyone who had married in Las Vegas three months before.[9] The casino already knows the couples who wed at its resort. But it wanted to lure a far broader group of newlyweds to return. So it decided to invite couples to Vegas half a year after their wedding. The clerk's office charged $1,500 to do the initial work to gather the data, and then $150 a month for continuous updates—spare change for a massive casino that might comp a good client that much in a night.

The Wynn marketing campaign was apparently not a big success. Clark County officials say the casino operator stopped asking for the information after about a year and a half.[10] But many companies have solicited new clients from public records, and the practice has grown for many years. Turning to outside data such as marriage records was exactly the kind of information Caesars executives had long declined to collect. But should they?

Shy Data Brokers

For an industry focused on revealing information about others, data brokers are awfully shy. Take Spokeo, one of many data brokers offering services to the public, which long advertised itself as "not your grandma's phone book."[11] Several graduates of Stanford—where Google's founders had also studied—started the site in 2006 and offered especially detailed dossiers. I wrote cofounder Harrison Tang to ask if I could meet him. Eventually the company invited me to visit its headquarters in Pasadena, California, and confirmed a date. I purchased a plane ticket from Boston. Days before the departure, the company abruptly withdrew the invitation without offering a reason for the change of heart.[12]

With a nonrefundable ticket to Los Angeles in hand, I tried instead to meet Jeff Tinsley, who founded MyLife.com in 2002. His assistant said Tinsley's schedule would not permit a visit at that time but said we could talk by phone later. He scheduled and then abruptly canceled interviews four times over a period of weeks. Eventually he stopped responding to emails.[13] Jim Adler, then the chief privacy officer of the data broker Intelius, did not respond to four emails over a period of many weeks, but he subsequently agreed to speak after we met by chance at a congressional briefing.[14]

PeopleFinder.com distinguished itself by including a short description of its management team on its website, something few online data brokers did, especially in the earlier years of the industry. The company's website also showed a photo of three men and two women.[15] The photo looked a little too perfect. A Google image search revealed that PeopleFinders was not, in fact, showing the real people who ran the company but a group of models in a stock photo. Available for just $19 online, the same image appeared on sites such as the Bank of Ireland and the Ontario Real Estate Association. Rob Miller, the Sacramento-based PeopleFinder.com founder and CEO, initially said he would review questions by email but then did not respond.

Then there was PeopleSmart, another site that tried to differentiate itself by respecting privacy even while dealing in personal data. The two brothers running the company grappled with the same issue as Caesars: in gathering and using data, what is effective and what is morally appropriate? The company published real photos of its management and actually revealed how commercial data brokers gather information. The company was even willing to reveal some insider secrets to me.

6

Dossiers on (Virtually) Everyone

Seeking Disruptive Ideas

Three and a half years apart in age, the Monahan brothers—Matthew and Brian—grew up in Murphysboro, Illinois, a town of eight thousand people. Their mother worked as a sixth grade teacher; their dad sold mobile classrooms—a type of mobile home used by schools undergoing renovations or unable to afford more permanent structures. The parents encouraged reading and limited TV watching; the Monahans did not own a computer until 1998, when Matthew was in high school.

While at the University of Southern California, Matthew set up an e-books company, where he wrote about how to get into college, how to do well in the SATs, and similar topics. He built his business by advertising on Google and Yahoo. When people looked up words such as "scholarships" or "scholarship tips," his ads encouraged them to visit his sites scholarshipsecrets.com and collegeshortcuts.com. Those who clicked on the ad found some basic tips and a pitch to buy his $29 book.

The site made him sound a bit like a carnival pitchman. "When I graduated high school I had won over $130,000 in free scholarship money, aced the SAT and ACT, and had admission offers from Harvard, MIT, Penn, Georgetown, USC, Wake Forest, and several other top-notch institutions," he told visitors to collegeshortcuts.com. "Then I went on to attend the college of my choice—for FREE."

Even though he was indeed enjoying a free ride in college, Matthew dropped out after two years, in 2004, to focus on being an entrepreneur. A North Carolina company eventually bought his business, and he moved to the company headquarters. He stayed for two years and, with the economy booming, left in 2006 with $1 million in his pocket and a burning desire to create his own Internet business in Silicon Valley. He just wanted to be part of the exciting 2.0 expansion of the web and create a platform of some kind. To prepare for his new life, he changed his first name, which had been Air'n. He found the name too unwieldy; people couldn't spell it, didn't know how to pronounce it, and could not figure out the gender. He went through the formal legal process and became Matthew.

He searched for ideas, and sought out successful businesspeople for advice. Later that year he went to an Internet conference in San Francisco. After a dinner speech by Niklas Zennström, one of the founders of Skype, Matthew queued behind others in the audience to approach him for a quick word of private insight.

"How do you guys come up with these huge disruptive ideas?"

"Just look for things that have yet to be totally digitized, because as things become digital everything changes."

In May the following year, along with thousands of others, Matthew traveled to Omaha, Nebraska, for the annual meeting of Warren Buffett's company, Berkshire Hathaway. (He did not own the premium A class shares then trading at $93,000, but a few of the company's cheaper class B shares, which were going for about $3,000 each.) He rose at 4 a.m. on the big day anxious to ask a question of the finance guru and his right-hand man, Charlie Munger. On a rainy and windy spring morning, he stopped at a twenty-four-hour Walmart store en route to the convention center to buy an umbrella. As the foul weather tested his patience, he waited in line for hours for the convention center to open. Finally, the doors swung apart and the early birds put down their names to question the Sage of Omaha.

Later that day, with a record crowd of twenty-seven thousand shareholders attending, the predawn maneuvers paid off. Matthew stepped up to the microphone. His voice trembled as the many thousands in the audience focused on his question. An echo bounced off the back of the hall a second or two later as he spoke, throwing off his concentration.

"I'm twenty-three, I have some resources, I sold a small e-book business, and I'm looking to start a new company. If you were in my shoes, what types of fields would you look into or what types of criteria would you use?"

Buffett started by recommending that Matthew read everything that he could: "You need to fill your mind with various competing thoughts and decide which make sense. Then you have to jump in the water—take a small amount of money and do it." Buffett, famous for his folksy manner, continued with a salty analogy that made the crowd laugh: "Investing on paper is like reading a romance novel versus doing something else."[1]

Munger followed up: "Of course, the place to look when you're young is the inefficient markets."

Buffett then finished up the thought: "You should do well in games with few other players."

The wise men had spoken. Matthew set his goal: he needed to build a technology-driven business in a large inefficient market. If he did not know exactly what kind of business that might be, he had already settled on where he wanted to be: Silicon Valley, the center of the tech universe, and close to Facebook. In fact, just a week before making the pilgrimage to Omaha, he had signed a lease for an office on the third floor of 101 University Avenue in Palo Alto, immediately north of Stanford University. He wrote out a security deposit of $20,149.50 and agreed to pay more than $10,000 a month for 2,100 square feet of office space. He did not have contacts in Silicon Valley and hoped proximity would help make magic happen. He set the orbit of his life around that office and rented an apartment just four blocks away.

Matthew eventually set his sights on public records and directories. He realized it had the potential to be big, but saw a highly fragmented and inefficient sector. He thought he could improve on what was out there, but found that he had to do far more than just identify an opportunity. He had to build a business from nothing. "It was tough, it was really tough, because the data industry isn't the easiest to understand as an outsider," he says.

His brother, Brian, still in college, pitched in from afar and traveled to Palo Alto during his breaks. He studied the search results made public by Google and Yahoo and noticed many people looking up telephone numbers. Yet those searches typically did not lead to helpful results. From that insight, the brothers set up reversephonedetective.com.

Having settled on an idea, the brothers needed to get unpublished cell phone numbers. Brian researched companies that aggregated phone numbers and hesitantly called. Surely, he thought, he would have to hop through a lot of hoops to obtain such intimate information. He explained his idea to one company.

"We're building a website where people can do self-service caller ID."

"Oh, yeah, we can do that. You can give us the number and we can provide you with the results."

"Seriously, you can do that?"

Brian was surprised that a college kid could get the information so easily. A new business was born. The brothers set up the site in December 2006. The site listed many reasons to reverse search phone numbers, such as finding the source of prank calls, hunting down suspicious numbers on a boyfriend's or girlfriend's phone, looking up a number on a phone bill, or checking out missed calls. They charged $14.95 for the number's owner and address. "Get INSTANT ACCESS to owner information, address history, carrier, connection status, and location details for any phone number," the site advertised. "Your search is 100% legal and strictly confidential."

By the time Matthew signed the expensive office lease in Palo Alto, the site was bringing in tens of thousands of dollars in sales a month. Yet very little profit resulted because of the high cost of assembling and marketing the phone numbers. Matthew paid the data provider just $2 per number searched.[2] Yet the main cost came from luring customers via Google ads, the promotional copy that appears in small boxes alongside search results when people look up words and phrases. Companies pay only when Internet users click on the ads, which might cost 10 or 20 cents for a person's name. The ads appear not only on Google.com but on other websites with their own search boxes, such as *The LA Times* and *Wired,* which host Google ads in exchange for a share of the revenue.

Through continuous experimentation, Brian figured out how to generate a Google ad for thousands of different numbers by using just a fragment of a ten-digit phone number, such as the area code and first three digits. This insight was important because at the time Google limited the total number of keywords an advertiser could use. Also Brian had to enter the numbers manually. Even with music or a movie playing in the background in his dorm room, such rote data entry proved mind numbing. In the end, fragments of 75,000 to 100,000 numbers generated ads for millions of phone numbers, a technique rare at that time. "Who owns 303 703 1436?" the reversephonedetective.com ad might read. "Find out who owns 303 703 1436 with this Reverse Phone Lookup."

Brian tried different combinations to see what would work best. How about numbers in a row without spaces? What happens if you add dashes in the phone numbers? He experimented with variation after variation. Testing key words that people might enter into Google allowed the company to shave fractions of pennies off the ad costs. Such tiny amounts added up to real money when placing thousands of ads.

The ads lured many people to reversephonedetective.com. Yet almost everyone wanted the information for free. The Monahans typically paid 10 cents per AdWords click, but only one out of a hundred people would actually pay for a lookup, thus adding a cost of $10 per new customer. On top of that, they paid another $1.50 to process the credit card charge and $1 for customer service. By the time they were done, the service left them with about 50 cents' profit for a first-time customer. Repeat visitors would obviously prove much more lucrative.

Valentine's Day Goes Sour

Brian dropped out of Harvard after his sophomore year. Like Facebook founder Mark Zuckerberg, who had left before finishing college three years earlier, Brian felt ready to take on the world. He abandoned a full scholarship, swapping his elite college dorm room for a couch in his older brother's apartment in Palo Alto, California.

Business developed slowly in the early years. The brothers lived off the $1 million Matthew had earned from his first venture. They spent much of their money on rent—principally the centrally located office and their nearby apartment—and software development. For more than three years they did not even own a car. They focused on work. They also created several other sites. One gave information about classmates. It failed. A website that helped consumers gather telephone numbers and file complaints against telemarketers (callercomplaints .com) did not succeed either.

On most days they ventured no further than a triangle between their office across from Stanford University, their apartment four blocks away, and a Whole Foods supermarket. On occasion they made it as far as a few local restaurants. The brothers dedicated all their energy to making the business succeed. They embraced the mantra "Burn the Boats," a reference to Spanish explorer Hernán Cortés, who destroyed his ships upon landing in Mexico in 1519 to ensure that his men could not retreat from conquering the Aztecs.

By early 2008, a year after starting the site and half a year after Brian quit school, they were making $300,000 to $500,000 a month in sales. That amount left roughly $50,000 in profit, which they reinvested. Leaving Harvard looked like a smart decision.

Few things could draw away the brothers' attention from work, but Brian planned a rare break to fly to Boston for Valentine's Day, which fell on a Thursday, because he hoped to continue his relationship with his college sweetheart. His girlfriend had recently returned from a semester in Paris, and Brian wanted to rekindle the romance. On the big day, the couple strolled across Harvard Yard. He felt happy to spend time with her, but that winter's day, with temperatures just above freezing, did not provide an especially romantic setting. Rain fell from gray skies; the tall bare elm and oak trees provided little cover.

A message on his cell phone interrupted their walk. Matthew had bad news. Intelius, a leading competitor, had just slashed its caller ID lookup prices dramatically. Not 10 or 20 percent less, or a few dollars less. A full three times cheaper than reversephonedetective.com. Brian called back at once. "Dude, Intelius just dropped their prices to $5. We are looking at the conversion rate, everything is plummeting," the older brother blurted out, referring to how many of the visitors to their site actually paid to look up a phone number.

Alarm bells sounded in Brian's mind. Just a few weeks ago, Intelius had unveiled plans to take the company public. By cutting prices so dramatically, the firm could put the brothers out of business. Both realized all their sacrifices stood a hair's breadth from miserable failure. Not only had they turned down many thousands of dollars' worth of scholarships, but they also had spent far more trying to build their company, burning through much of Matthew's savings along the way. On the regular job market, they were just two dropouts with enough college credits between them for one diploma.

Brian, overcome with guilt that he had left Silicon Valley in the middle of a workweek, put his date on hold. He rushed in from the rain to Lamont Library to get online. He read everything he could about what had just happened. He plotted with Matthew on what they should do next. The people-search war was under way, a fight that would last for years. Brian's relationship with his girlfriend proceeded on a terminal path.

As the Monahans expanded their business, they faced many competitors, but none more ambitious than Intelius. Founded in January 2003, the company initially played up patriotic themes sweeping the country after the 2001 World Trade Center attacks and the 2003 Iraq War. A photo composite on the company's home page in those early months showed fused images of the Statue of Liberty, the US Capitol, and an American flag. The site quoted founder Naveen Jain as saying, "The next war will not be won based on who has the most powerful weapons, but by those who have integrated intelligent information." The Bellevue, Washington–based company became a dominant on-line vendor of public records. It advertised itself as the "world's largest and most accurate public records source." Revenue soared from $18.1 million in 2004, a year after it started business, to $122.9 million in 2008. Even more remarkable for an Internet startup, it reported a profit throughout that time.[3] To gain market share, the company advertised heavily. Eventually one million people were visiting the site every day.[4] Coming up with the core product—personal data on adult Americans—came relatively cheaply. Gaining attention proved more costly: advertising represented more than half of total expenditures for Intelius between 2004 and 2008.[5]

In January 2008—the same month two private equity firms purchased Caesars in a leveraged buyout—Intelius filed paperwork for an initial public offering. With investors looking over its financial numbers carefully, the company hoped to boost sales and subscribers. In 2007, it had started allowing people to search for private cell phone numbers (the Monahans and others would only allow people to look up numbers received via incoming caller ID, but not names). Outraged citizens and some important voices in Washington complained. Intelius withdrew the service. Weeks after announcing its plans to go public, Intelius lowered the cost of its reverse phone lookups to $4.99—or 99 cents as part of a monthly subscription.

The dramatic price reduction hit the Monahan brothers hard. The original $1 million in the bank had dwindled to $200,000; they started losing money every month. They ran fewer ads and hoped to weather the crisis. They outsourced some of their programming to a small team in Kiev, Ukraine. Five months later they were also hit by the unexpected death of their father, who collapsed at age fifty-seven while exercising on an elliptical training machine. Not long after that Matthew looked at what remained in his bank account. "Where did all the money go?" he wondered.

Still embracing their "Burn the Boats" philosophy, the brothers pressed on. Eventually, Intelius and some of the other data brokers experienced setbacks. The media and government authorities began looking into reports that some firms unfairly roped people into expensive subscription plans without their knowing consent. Some companies also suffered black eyes by exaggerating the quality of their information. The Federal Trade Commission and other authorities stepped up scrutiny. In 2010, Intelius agreed to pay a $1.3 million settlement after the Washington State attorney general alleged the firm had acted un-scrupulously by enrolling one-time users as subscribers without their consent.[6] The company did not admit any wrongdoing as part of the settlement.[7] "The only reason we get these things is that we were the biggest. We are the biggest," said company founder Naveen Jain.[8] "Our customers love us as is evident from our A+ BBB rating," he added, referring to the Better Business Bureau, a nonprofit, nongovernmental group that monitors consumer complaints.[9] In 2009, Jain won vindi-cation in an earlier legal tussle. In May 2003 a federal district court had issued a summary judgment that Jain had purchased stock in his previous company, InfoSpace, within six months of selling the shares, a so-called short swing that was not allowed because he had been an officer of the company.[10] He appealed the ruling, and in 2009 the US Court of Appeals for the Ninth Circuit dismissed the case.[11] But in 2010, a second Intelius cofounder was jailed for perjury related to having sex with strip club dancers.[12]

Other data brokers got into hot water as well. The same year that the Monahans started reversephonedetective.com, several Stanford graduates set up Spokeo. Business picked up considerably after 2010, when the site started adding data from more than ninety social net-working sites.[13] But in 2012 Spokeo agreed to pay an $800,000 FTC fine for advertising its services as a way to check out potential job hires, a violation of the Fair Credit Reporting Act.[14] "We wanted to put this behind us," said Emanuel Pleitez, Spokeo's chief strategy officer. "Any company goes through their own internal calculations of how much legal fees and things they cannot do for X amount of time, where they lose productivity and they lose the ability to create new products, and you make an assessment on whether you settle or not."

Other people-search sites faced lawsuits over their marketing. A 2011 class-action lawsuit charged that MyLife.com, which advertises that it will tell "who's searching for you," was sending out emails suggesting people were looking for users even when nobody had expressed any in-terest. To gain access to the site and learn how many people are looking for them, users provide their name, age, and ZIP code. To test how MyLife.com works, I randomly picked a name, age, and city to see what

would come up. The site said that more than twenty people were searching for my imaginary person—James Parker, a nineteen-year-old with
a New York City ZIP code. More than fifteen of them were female.
Perhaps there is a lucky guy in the city called James Parker with a lot
of lady friends. The lawsuit quoted one web developer who had tested
the site: "I went to the site and put in a fake name like sfsf sdgfsdgf and
a real age and ZIP code, and guess what?! 7 people were searching for
sfsf sdgfsdgf!"[15] The lawsuit also charged that the company hacks into
users' email address books and invites their contacts to join MyLife.com.
That feature is given in the fine print of a user's privacy policy: "Contacts
who are not registered. Members will receive an email invitation from us
on your behalf inviting them to join. We may follow up such invitations
with a limited number of reminder emails to some contacts if they do
not respond." Jeff Tinsley, the company founder and CEO, said the case
was settled out of court in 2012: "There was absolutely no merit to the
case, and the claims are outright false."[16]

Such tactics, even if spelled out in the fine print, rubbed a lot of
people the wrong way.

Many people-search businesses did not always seem on the up-
and-up, and their reputations suffered. Rivals continued to struggle in
the following years. In 2012, a former CEO of LocatePlus Holdings
Corporation, which sells personal data to professional groups such as
law enforcement, pled guilty to conspiracy to commit securities fraud
and was imprisoned through 2017.[17] In a related case, in 2013 a US
district court sentenced another company official who had served as
chief financial officer and chief executive officer to five years in prison
for securities fraud that included an effort to inflate revenues.[18] He is
also set for release in 2017.

As rivals ran into turbulence, the Monahans began to recover.
They had avoided some of the industry's more dubious tactics, such
as subscribing users to the service after one mistaken click. They also
tried to differentiate themselves by offering a money-back guarantee
on searches. Between 15 percent and 20 percent of users took advantage of the offer. Sure, some users complained, but the Monahans escaped high-profile lawsuits and inquiries. "As the site got better and

as our customer base grew larger and as we made more updates and understood the customers better, that's ultimately how we survived the Intelius price drop. We had enough customers that kept using us," Matthew says.

Building on the cell phone ID service, the brothers started gathering more information on people. They wanted to compete against the more comprehensive offerings of rivals but in what they called a privacy-friendly way. They figured out who were the personal data wholesalers and started frequenting the annual conferences big data firms attend, like that of the Direct Marketing Association. Some vendors initially resisted working with the baby-faced brothers, but they gradually warmed as the Monahans established a track record. For their part, the Monahans found some of the personal data aggregators sleazy and some of their rivals a bit unsavory. But they thought transparency would help them win market share over the long term.

"There are a lot of people, they are not bad people, they are just aggressively trying to make money, very aggressively," Brian says. "You're talking to these people who are like, you know, creepy and weird and not someone that I would ever invite to my home and not someone I would want to spend time around, but not evil. They are not trying to hurt people even if their business practices do, and a lot of that is because they're only scraping by too."

Matthew says dealing with such people was not the most fun aspect of the job. "It has also been an industry—direct marketing as well as data providers—that attracts maybe a little bit more of an aggressive or, I don't know, renegade style," he says.

In September 2010, the Monahans launched their first full-fledged name lookup service, PeopleSmart.com, the core of their business today. They raised $30 million in investor funding and christened their parent company Inflection. "By aggregating billions of public records into one easy-to-use interface and managing the information with cutting-edge privacy technology, PeopleSmart makes it fast, easy, and safe for people to find and learn about one another online," it advertised.[19]

In gathering public records from government agencies, the Monahans also discovered a deep well of historical documents. Prodded

Matthew and Brian Monahan at Inflection's corporate headquarters.
Source: Author photo.

by their mother, who became interested in genealogy after their father's death, the brothers set up GenealogyArchives.com in 2009 to help people research their ancestry. Eventually they bought the domain name Archives.com for $170,000, an incredible investment at the time, which ended up paying off big. In 2012, rival genealogy site Ancestry.com bought Archives.com for $100 million. The brothers planned two trips with their share of the windfall: to the Burning Man festival in Nevada, which they attended in 2012, and into space, a journey that still lies in the future.

Inside the Cheez Whiz

So where does the information sold by companies such as PeopleSmart come from? It begins with public records. But rather than contact a myriad of local government agencies such as the Clark County Recorder's office—as Wynn did to find Las Vegas newlyweds—companies buy from data wholesalers that purchase directly from government agencies. These are typically firms you have never heard of such as AccuData, a direct mail marketing company based in Fort Myers, Florida, and CoreLogic, a data company in Irvine, California.

The process of assembling such data has become dramatically easier in recent years. The Clark County Recorder's office says that until 2004, firms obtained bulk data on microfiche. Data broker clerks had to painstakingly re-enter the information into their own systems. In 2004 Clark County started providing computer disks, and in 2007 data wholesalers began acquiring the information directly from FTP file transfers on the Internet. Nowadays, it costs $374 to buy a month's worth of marriage data from the Clark County Recorder's office.[20]

After obtaining public data, people-search sites sprinkle in phone book information, details from marketing lists, commercial records, and other information. Through such documents, data brokers know where you live and have lived, your phone numbers—often including cell phone—your neighbors and relatives, educational history, past lawsuits, bankruptcies, criminal history, and many other details. The data broker websites mix all this information together, much as a food manufacturer pours twenty-five ingredients into a batch that becomes a packaged snack. Think Cheez Whiz. Once the Cheez Whiz glops onto your plate, there's no telling where its ingredients originally came from.

Today Inflection spends between $3 million and $5 million a year to buy and rent the personal data that appear on PeopleSmart.com. Inflection relies on ten to fifteen companies for the bulk of its personal data, with another ten to fifteen adding supplementary information such as educational backgrounds and criminal records. Confidentiality agreements bar Inflection from naming its suppliers, but they are among the big personal-data companies. Top players in the field include Acxiom, Epsilon (see Chapter 7), Experian, TransUnion, and Equifax, the latter three best known to the public for their credit bureau operations.

Wholesale data prices vary greatly, with more reputable aggregators charging more. Some charge 10 cents per address; others charge 50 cents for the same information. Some data wholesalers offer all-you-can-eat

What Makes Up a Listing?

Photos
Social networks & websites.

Web Profiles
Social networks & websites.

Home Information
U.S. Postal Service, state & county property records.

Work Information
Corporate filings + SEC data

Telephones
Phone books, commercial data vendors & aggregators.

Education + Classmate Information
Universities, alumni groups, and high schools.

Emails
Commercial data vendors & aggregators.

Court Records
County, state, and federal court offices.

Professional Licenses
Licensing & accreditation groups.

Genealogy + Family Tree
Historical archives organizations, churches, and cemeteries.

PeopleSmart gathers personal information from many sources. Source: Inflection (reprinted with permission).

plans. Unlike the bargain Las Vegas food buffets, unlimited access to records on most US households costs hundreds of thousands of dollars a year. Government agencies charge anywhere from $60 to $6,000 for access to batches of records, Matthew Monahan confirms.

The data wholesalers do not have a prominent public profile. Few consumers know CoreLogic, but the firm advertises itself as "the premier supplier of U.S. real estate, mortgage, consumer and specialized business data." It employs more than five thousand people to supply a stream of public- and private-sector information into its data files, and reported a $130 million profit on $1.3 billion in sales in 2013.[21] Rick Lombardi, the vice president of data solutions licensing at CoreLogic, says the company does not sell to the general public because such a business is expensive to operate.

Another company little known by the public, LSSiDATA, advertises that it can supply more than one hundred million cell phone contacts[22] and one hundred thirty million landline records, including unpublished numbers and Voice over Internet Protocol (VoIP) numbers.[23] The company obtains the data directly from local exchange carriers and other telecommunications providers. "Contact information is also sourced from cable companies, VoIP providers, CLECs, and wireless carriers across North America to create one of the most robust contact resources available," it says.[24]

The United States Postal Service plays a vital role in the data broker ecosystem. Whenever a person changes an address or forwards mail, he or she signs a form whose fine print authorizes the USPS to share the information with companies "already in possession of your name and old mailing address." Such information allows data brokers and companies to update older lists continuously. For example, the 1999 Gramm-Leach-Bliley Act limited the use of credit header data, the information on top of a person's consumer credit report. Such information contains name, address, telephone number, Social Security number, and date of birth. Some data brokers use the USPS change-of-address records to keep that old credit header data updated.

A New Rival Emerges

After the hugely successful sale of Archives.com, the Monahan brothers kept reinvesting in their people-lookup business, which had become a major player in the field. By 2014 the Monahans oversaw a full-time team of about ninety people in Redwood Shores, in the heart of Silicon Valley, and 170 worldwide. Their offices overlooked a verdant park with ponds and ducks; among their neighbors were Electronic Arts and Oracle.

They embrace the Silicon Valley ethic promoting a healthy work-life balance and encourage employees to work from home on Tuesdays and Thursdays, a welcome perk in a region plagued by traffic jams. As at far wealthier Silicon Valley companies, Inflection caters lunch every day and provides snacks, all free of charge. Workers take a daily recess together. The company organizes yoga and massage classes. Beanbag chairs in the conference rooms invite staffers to relax as they work.

The company continues to advertise with Google, as well as with Bing and Yahoo, on eighteen million individual names (John Smith, John Jones, John Williams, etc.), so that an ad for a searched name often pops up to the side of the search result. Because many people share the same name, that number allows PeopleSmart to advertise most of its records. As in the past, Inflection, as the advertiser, pays 10 to 20 cents every time someone clicks. A dime a time adds up to tens of thousands of dollars a day, or millions of dollars a year.

More than ten million unique US visitors came to PeopleSmart .com monthly in 2012 and 2013. Yet the old math in attracting customers still proves true. About 1 percent who click on search ads become customers, and about a third of those pay $35 to $720 for annual subscriptions, with rates depending on how many services and look-ups customers use. When people do pay, the Internet connects them to an underground server vault in Santa Clara, a Silicon Valley town home to companies such as Intel. If they call customer service, they reach a call center in Omaha, the same town where Warren Buffett had inspired Matthew years earlier. And programmers in Kiev, first contracted during tough economic times, continue to develop the software powering the site.

As Inflection has tried to establish itself as a transparent and more honest leader in the industry, it has lost money in recent years. Despite tens of millions of dollars a year in sales, Inflection still expects to lose a few million dollars over the next few years as it invests in product development and hiring. (Caesars has also lost money in recent years, having acquired massive debt after their leveraged buyout shortly before the 2008 financial crisis.)

PeopleSmart does not list cell phone numbers, it removes celebrities and VIPs from its database, and it enables users to send email to people they're trying to locate but does not give out the addresses. Still, some people object that the Monahans sell any data. "I am also wondering why they then have the RIGHT to make a profit off of my private information that I did not authorize," one person asked about PeopleSmart on an Internet bulletin board. "How are they able to OWN my information when I did NOT sell it to them?"[25]

The brothers understand such sentiment and say they make it easy for people to opt out of their databases. "It's a legitimate vein of sentiment that says, 'Hey, my information is out there and I don't want it to be out,'" Matthew says. "There is no one who said, 'Okay, Inflection, you are blessed to be the government's provider of personal data and you are officially doing a public service here.'"

Both brothers say they can help millions of people reconnect without harming privacy.[26] "I don't think it's evil. You need to be careful, you need to be responsible," Brian says. "If people don't want to be in our database, we don't want them there. We've always made opt-out free and easy and online."

Not every company is as cautious when it comes to personal data. The Monahans learned about a new rival via spam that highlighted a different approach to marketing such information. "Damaging Information Posted: MAY EFFECT HOW OTHERS VIEW YOUR CHARACTER," the headline on one email read. "DONT RISK this information staying online publicly too much longer. It could ruin your life by ending personal relationships or even your current career. The time is now to view it."

Another email read: "RISK ALERT: Very Negative Information Was Added To Your Online File (See what it was). Unfortunate news just came across my desk that I thought you should know about. Negative information was added to your personal online records about 30 minutes ago. There is still time to correct this."

The email did not mention the name of the sender, but when Matthew clicked on a link, it led to the home page of what became his company's latest nemesis, Instant Checkmate.

Be Cautious When Using This Tool

Instant Checkmate embodied the clever and brash kind of company seeking opportunities on the Wild West frontier of personal data. By using aggressive marketing, it attracted a stream of new users. Even within a young industry, it surpassed existing businesses to become a leading site selling personal dossiers to the public, with a focus on criminal records. Its rivals took notice.

"Whereas Intelius was our most irritating nemesis and someone that we focused on differentiating ourselves from in 2008 and 2009, Instant Checkmate is now that company. They have grown to be quite large, and their site gets more traffic now than Intelius," Matthew Monahan acknowledged. "It is arguably our biggest challenge from a competitive perspective."

His brother Brian added, "These guys are incredibly sophisticated at marketing."

The success of the Monahans' early site reversephonedective.com came after they figured out how to place ads for millions of phone numbers. Instant Checkmate also flourished by understanding how to gain attention when the raw data—the criminal or marriage records, for example, or contact details such as addresses and phone numbers— are often the same among competing companies. Marketing savvy is essential, and Instant Checkmate stood out from the moment someone arrived on its site, when an eye-catching pop-up screen appeared.

"This site contains REAL police records (driving citations, speeding tickets, felonies, misdemeanors, sexual offenses, mugshots, etc.), background reports, marriage/divorce history, address information, phone numbers, a history of lawsuits and much more. Please BE CAREFUL when conducting a search and ensure all the information you enter is accurate," it said. "Learning the truth about the history of your family and friends can be shocking, so please be cautious when using this tool."[27]

Coming online a few years after the Monahans entered the business, Instant Checkmate called itself the "most popular background check website on the Internet."[28] It attracted around twenty million unique visitors a month in early 2014, according to the site compete.com. Traffic had tripled from 2012, making the site among the one hundred most visited in the United States, ahead of PeopleSmart and other rivals.[29] A counter on Instant Checkmate's home page advertised that it had conducted more than 180 million searches by the spring of 2014.[30]

The company's marketing brilliance lay in convincing people they needed regularly to conduct background searches. For example, Instant Checkmate suggested that parents should conduct online criminal searches to keep their children safe and secure. "Parents will no longer need to wonder about whether their neighbors, friends, home day care providers, a former spouse's new love interest or preschool providers can be trusted to care for their children responsibly," the company advertised.[31] Children should also do a background search on their parents: "Do you want to liven up the upcoming holiday dinners with family? Background check your folks and see what sort of mischief they got themselves into before you were around."[32]

Check Your Mate

When Californian entrepreneur Kris Kibak started Instant Checkmate in 2010 along with a partner, he was inspired by the growth of online dating and came up with his site's name thinking of "check your mate." "We were astonished to see how much time was spent on dating sites and their increasing popularity in our society," he says. "We then thought about the danger that women (and men) could face when meeting someone they met online in person—what if you were chatting online with a sexual predator or a person with a violent criminal history?"[33]

Since dating sites at the time did not provide background checks, he decided to provide access to personal data, including arrest records. The FBI does allow the public to look up individual names in its sex offender registry for free, but people have to know such a site exists.[34] In addition, that service does not offer a broader background check. "Our primary concerns revolved around sexual predators or other dangerous people using dating sites to find victims," Kibak said.

"We had an idea I liked (protecting vulnerable people from potential dangers) and that I thought was good for society, and I was excited to pursue that idea."[35] He worked from San Diego but set up a call center in Las Vegas, across the highway from the Strip, down a quiet street at the back of a parking lot no tourist would ever stumble across. It shared the Vegas address with the public as its mailing address.[36]

Less than six months younger than Matthew Monahan, Kibak is the son of a professor at California State University, Monterey Bay. He grew up in Santa Cruz, a beach town that embodies the California dream, with a boardwalk and an amusement park along the Pacific Ocean. He has ruggedly handsome looks, with some photos showing him with a few days' beard. Kibak set up his first website at age twelve.[37] Before graduating from the University of California, Santa Cruz, in 2006, he had already established several Internet businesses.

From its early days, Instant Checkmate issued many blogs and press releases. Some detailed the merits of conducting background searches before giving away an unwanted pet,[38] explained why it is a good idea to conduct a search on yourself,[39] and noted how well stocked Instant Checkmate keeps its refrigerator.[40] Even if sometimes trivial, the postings and news releases can help boost search engine ranking. Google and other search sites look for links to a website, among other things, to rank popularity when deciding its results.

At first Instant Checkmate did not feature Kibak's name or image. By 2013 the site for thecontrolgroup.com, which says it developed

Instant Checkmate, began including photos of staff members with more information about the company.[41] The front-page photo of the site shows Kibak and the staff, almost all in shorts, on a beach on a cloudless day above a banner headline that reads, "The Control Group—Developing Good Times." The company also generated positive publicity in the San Diego area by sponsoring a local beach cleanup and other events.

To drive traffic to its site, Instant Checkmate also turned to third-party affiliates. Such marketers have an incentive to grab attention because they are paid only when someone clicks an ad or email and becomes a customer. Some sent out provocative emails, sometimes in stilted English. "I just found out my new babysitter is a thief!" one email said. "Is the report I listened to legitimate? Your friend informed they conducted a criminal check on your aunt and it showed they have a felony. Just click this link to read it and see."

Kibak has distanced himself from such messages, saying they were sent by third-party affiliate marketers who used techniques he does not approve of. "Instant Checkmate would not create or send emails of that nature, and those emails absolutely violate Instant Checkmate's policies," Kibak said. "My best guess is that the emails were created and sent by an unscrupulous third-party affiliate advertiser. To reiterate, we do not condone this in any way."[42]

Real money is at stake for affiliates who win new clients. In March 2014, for example, one affiliate site promised payment ranging from $18 to $29.50 per Instant Checkmate lead that resulted in new customers.[43] Another site referred to a previous rate of $22.75 per lead.[44] The company also offered a special incentive to its top producers—a trip to Dubrovnik, Croatia, for the "publisher who generates the most revenue running Instant Checkmate offers between February 1–June 30, 2014."[45] The contest was aimed at a sporty crowd with the lure "to sail, cliff jump, paddle board and jet ski."[46]

Kibak points out that Internet companies routinely use third-party affiliates, and many well-known businesses such as Netflix and Amazon have used such services to help find new clients. "I believe we do a good job in making sure that third-party affiliates only send approved emails," he said. "When we learn that a third-party affiliate has sent emails that we do not approve, we take swift action to ensure the third-party affiliate no longer works with Instant Checkmate."[47]

One such instance occurred in early 2012 when a Facebook ad briefly ran showing a dark-skinned man with small beady eyes, thick elongated lips, a massive nose, and a pointy head. He wore what appeared to be an orange prison jumpsuit: "You Can Now See Arrest Records of Anyone! Click Here to Search!" "We did not create that ad and were not aware of its existence until we read a blog post about it, at which time we immediately demanded the ad be taken down," Kibak says.[48]

As Instant Checkmate grew, it typically quoted a spokesperson, Kristen Bright, in company statements. All efforts to reach her over many months led to dead ends. No returned calls. No emails. Public record searches for her did not produce an obvious match. Was she an especially shy spokeswoman—whose job was, after all, to talk with the outside world? Or was she a fictitious corporate creation, like Betty Crocker or Aunt Jemima?

Instant Checkmate also gained prominence for its Google ads in a very competitive marketplace.[49] Like the Monahan brothers, Kibak and his team placed Google ads on millions of names, which meant an ad for the company's services would often pop up when someone searched for a particular name. The company invested enough so that its messages would often appear on the screen above those for PeopleSmart and other competitors. At times the ad message would ask if the individual had been arrested, such as "John Doe, Arrested?" Google ads lie at the heart of the search company's business, generating billions of dollars in annual revenue.

Shock Value

In 2012 and 2013, Instant Checkmate's success continued to grow.[50] The upstart surpassed PeopleSmart in web traffic. It expanded its staff and in 2014 moved into new corporate offices in San Diego.[51] Yet data brokers more broadly were going through a turbulent time.

Congressional committees and the Federal Trade Commission stepped up examination of industry practices. Some called for more regulation. Computer programmer Thomas Lowrey IV, who worked at Instant Checkmate, believes the personal data industry is in desperate need of a legal overhaul. He wonders why companies that cannot guarantee the accuracy of their data are allowed to stay in business. "Most of these companies try to market themselves as a tool to assist in discovering more about people you don't trust," he says. "The problem is, how can anyone trust these companies themselves when they practice extremist marketing and exploit people's lack of trust for one another?"[52]

Kibak strongly disagreed with the assessment, calling Instant Checkmate "a due diligence or precautionary tool." "The quote above is like saying that ADT Home Security systems or manufacturers of locks for doors—are 'exploit[ing] people's lack of trust for one another.' Obviously that's not true—those companies, like Instant Checkmate, provide tools that people can use to protect themselves."[53]

Another complaining about Instant Checkmate's approach was Meagan Simmons, a Florida woman whose mug shot appeared in an ad for Instant Checkmate beside text that read: "Sometimes the cute ones aren't so innocent." She filed a lawsuit in 2014.[54]

"The ad contained her arrest booking photo and did not identify her by name," Kibak said. "There is greater freedom under the law with publishing public records, like arrest booking photos, because this is a matter of public interest and the photo is not owned by the person arrested. We also did not suggest that she was endorsing or a spokesperson for Instant Checkmate. In any event, we are defending the lawsuit and are no longer running the ad."[55]

A month after that lawsuit was filed, an even bigger blow hit Instant Checkmate. The FTC charged the company with violating the Fair Credit Reporting Act by advertising its services to users including landlords and employers. The complaint alleged the company did not take reasonable steps to ensure the reports were accurate or that those coming to the site had a permissible reason to receive such reports.[56]

How Instant Checkmate advertised its services, both on its site and on Google, proved key to the case, as outlined in a March 21, 2014, complaint that noted: "The company, through its Google Ad Words ad campaign, ran advertisements that would appear in search results when users sought background checks on 'nannies,' 'babysitters,' 'maids,' and 'housekeepers.'"[57] It also quoted from Instant Checkmate's website: "GOOD REASONS to get instant criminal checks on anyone right now. . . . (2) Check out tenants before they rent."

The company issued a statement referring to "a technical violation" of the Fair Credit Reporting Act. "The FTC recognized that Instant Checkmate is a responsible company and agreed to a settlement where Instant Checkmate did not admit liability," it said. "The few ads that concerned the FTC ran briefly over two years ago and are not representative of Instant Checkmate's advertising."[58]

Instant Checkmate agreed to settle the case and pay a fine of $525,000.

Matthew Monahan says it is a challenge to compete when rivals or marketers working on their behalf attempt to stir up fear when advertising their products. "When you say things like, 'Your neighbor may be a sex offender, find out the shocking truth, click here and see the mug shot photos,' you create their whole entertainment, shock-value kind of approach. It drives a lot of eyeballs, it drives a lot of curiosity," he rued.

Caesars faced a similar dilemma in Las Vegas. Could they ignore outside supplementary personal information from data brokers when their rivals aggressively used such insights for marketing? Unlike the Monahan brothers, who had a cushion of cash for long-term investment, Caesars did not have the luxury of time after the financial crisis. With a massive debt load, the casino chain faced more urgency in boosting revenue. Rivals such as Wynn were using raw public records on Las Vegas weddings to market directly to newlyweds. But a different type of data broker working directly with businesses offered far more sophisticated insights, sometimes thousands of pieces of information about any one person.

7

Direct Marketing

How Would You Like to Earn $10,000 in a Summer?

After enrolling at Wesleyan University in 1993, Joshua Kanter returned home to New Jersey for the first time over Thanksgiving. His mother had gathered his mail into a four-inch stack, most of it junk. One envelope grabbed his attention. "How would you like to earn $10,000 in a summer?" a bold headline from University Painters asked. Working the summer before college had brought in only $1,200, not enough to fulfill Kanter's dream of buying a car.

At that time University Painters sought out college students in certain ZIP codes so it could target key markets. To find the right entrepreneurially minded youth, the company rented lists of students at universities within a few hours of their family homes. Kanter did exactly what the direct marketer intended: he called University Painters to find out more. He learned that the company would grant him a house-painting franchise in exchange for 26 percent of sales. He received choice terrain to test his business acumen: Princeton, New Jersey, a prosperous town with strong business potential.

Kanter started returning home from Connecticut on weekends to knock on doors with the offer of free house-painting estimates. The teenager might have deterred some potential customers with his shoulder-length hair, but he showed energy and sincerity. People sensed he was a good kid and responded positively to his sales pitch. Over summer break, he went into overdrive, making the rounds and organizing his growing enterprise ninety to one hundred hours a week.

Occasionally he pitched in and painted, but he focused on finding new clients and training employees.

University Painters' direct mail pitch far underestimated Kanter's actual earnings. The first year he piled up $45,000. The second year, after getting a conservative haircut and suspending his studies for a year, he really hit the jackpot, earning $105,000. He bought his first car, a maroon 1982 Honda Prelude that had already journeyed 250,000 miles. Kanter had become a convert to the magic of direct marketing. Less than two decades later he would help lead a massive direct-marketing operation at Caesars that sends out 750 million offers a year.

The founder of University Painters, Joshua Jablon, found Kanter's name through a data broker called American Student List. Now part of ASL Marketing, the firm rents lists of students and recent graduates, and allows buyers to specify age, grade point average, hobbies, sports interests, ethnicity, and other categories.[1] Nowadays, ASL Marketing says it has mailing addresses of 4.3 million high school students and email addresses for three million.[2] Jablon appreciated that he could target specific students in key New Jersey ZIP codes such as Princeton and Lawrenceville. "They are affluent neighborhoods, and if you have a college kid that lives there and he goes to school within a few hours away, that was ideal," he says.

Sophisticated segmenting allows direct marketers to rent very specific lists. Among the countless variations on offer are Americans of Iranian, Albanian, or Vietnamese descent or other ethnic origins; contributors to AIDS research; male virility supplement buyers; depression medication users; and cancer victims. Also available: gays who own boats; recently divorced African Americans; tobacco chewers; rich baseball fans; birth control users; readers who buy books about drug and alcohol abuse; women who have bought porn or sex toys; concealed weapon permit holders; online gamblers; and subscribers to *The Dairy Goat Journal* (just 4,025 households at the beginning of 2014).

Las Vegas casinos have used direct mail for decades, typically targeting their own clients. When Caesars send out their 750 million pieces of direct marketing annually by mail and email, people get messages tailored to them.[3] Some get two to three offers a month, others as many as twenty. That's certainly a lot, but the company has found that the more offers it sends, the more responses it gets. Overall, offers to come on a specific date generate half of Caesars' revenue, CEO Gary Loveman says. MGM Resorts, Caesars' main rival in Las Vegas in terms of total properties, whose holdings include the MGM Grand, Bellagio, and ARIA, sends out forty million to forty-five million pieces of direct marketing a month.[4] That's at least two hundred million fewer offers per year than Caesars, but it's still a lot. "We are all guilty of 'Are you ready to buy, are you ready to buy?'" says Adam Bravo, MGM Resorts' director of campaign operations.[5]

Loveman believes customer data can also improve the client experience: "It drives me fucking crazy that in so many settings companies ought to know a lot more about me than they do." He thinks firms such as cell phone providers, cable companies, and others that know a lot about what their customers buy should do more to cater to them—but they still fail to personalize the experience. Loveman scoffs at personal-data-rich firms that don't provide individualized services. He gives the example of his own American Express Black Card. He paid $7,500 just to get the premium card and shells out another $2,500 annually to keep it. "God knows why," he says. "As far as I can tell, there is absolutely no service that has been provided to me based upon what they have learned about me."[6]

Loveman would like to use the data he knows about his clients to target offers more intensively even within micro-neighborhoods. For example, someone in Philadelphia who lives closer to a rival casino may get a more generous offer than someone who lives closer to Harrah's in the same city. "We want to treat every single person differently, based on what we know they care about and what we can afford to give them," he says. This desire guided Caesars as executives crafted their evolving strategy toward collecting customer data.

Origins of Database Mining

Although Loveman has introduced many innovations in marketing during his time at Harrah's and Caesars, he follows a long American tradition of appealing directly to customers at their homes. Companies started gathering home addresses en masse for mail-order sales in the nineteenth century. Mail-order companies such as Montgomery Ward and Sears, Roebuck and Company bypassed the expense of operating stores wherever their clients might be. Other firms took a similar approach in Europe. A century before Amazon.com, mail-order companies dazzled customers with their wide array of goods. They made exotic products available to even the most remote rural areas. Sears, Roebuck's 770-page 1897 catalog offered nerve and brain pills for 60 cents, Dr. Rose's Obesity Powders, a "sure cure for the tobacco habit," "Peruvian wine of coca," "57-cent princess tonic hair restorer," and "bust cream or food unrivalled for enlargement of the bust." Whether you wanted a banjo, a pack of diapers, a feather boa, or an array of farming tools, it was all in there.[7]

Prices were quite high compared to what one could buy in Las Vegas in that era. A state land act made land available for $1.25 an acre, just a bit more than some Sears, Roebuck nerve pills and the tonic hair restorer. But people loved shopping through the mail. With such an exciting array of products, shipping goods directly to the home address became a big deal. By 1939, two years after Bill Harrah opened his first bingo parlor in Reno, Nevada, 434 mail-order businesses were operating in the United States—not including department stores, which also sold by mail.

Directly targeting potential new customers through lists dates back nearly as long. Entrepreneurs mined telephone books to accumulate names as early as 1903—two years before Las Vegas was even established as a city. Back then, just owning a telephone line suggested wealth. A company called Multi-mailing, located across from City Hall in Manhattan, was selling lists of six hundred thousand names and addresses it had copied from phone books in New England, New York, New Jersey, Ohio, Pennsylvania, Maryland, Delaware, and Washington, DC.[8]

***

After learning computing basics at NASA, working briefly for IBM, and getting his MBA from Harvard, Hal Brierley launched a company to automate his fraternity's national list of 150,000 members. It was 1969. Out in Vegas, Caesars Palace was enjoying its heyday.

Using exotic new things called computer printers, Brierley and others replaced conventional labels and tailored messages on an individual basis. Customization made it seem as though the person pitching you something really knew you. The computer stored information about when people had gone to school, where they graduated, and what they had contributed to the fraternity in the past. The technology helped boost fundraising tenfold within a few years. A letter might begin, "Dear Brother Brierley," then mention the year he joined and his member number, thank him for his recent gift, and close with an appeal for a little more this year. "We discovered that using the computer as a fundraising tool for segmentation and personalization significantly raised more money," Brierley says.

Over time, his company, Epsilon Data Management, attracted hundreds of nonprofit clients. Eventually it moved into for-profit work and became a direct-marketing giant. In the decades since Brierley cofounded the company, the explosion of digital records has allowed direct marketers such as Epsilon to gather an unprecedented amount of data on almost every American. Today the Irving, Texas–based company, part of publicly traded Alliance Data, brings in more than a billion dollars a year in revenue.[9]

Epsilon caters to catalog and retail companies that share information about their clients in a data cooperative so they, in turn, can receive information about prospective new clients. From this information Epsilon filters a person's purchases into more than twenty categories, such as home electronics, pet supplies, food and beverage, apparel, cigars and tobacco, and religious merchandise.[10] It has information on 250 million consumers and sends out more than 40 billion emails annually, which it says makes it "one of the world's largest permission-based email marketers."[11] That's a fancy way of saying that it is not spamming people but sending out messages to people who have agreed to receive the emails.

Controversial Practices

The same year Brierley started building what became Epsilon in 1969, an Arkansas businessman founded a direct-mailing company that eventually became one of Brierley's main rivals, Acxiom. Using phone books and a computer, the Arkansas company sent out direct-mail pieces for Democratic Party candidates. The business continued to grow, and today Acxiom enjoys annual revenue of more than $1 billion. Clients include nearly half the Fortune 100 list of America's largest companies, eight of the ten top credit card issuers, seven of the ten top automakers, four of the five top banks, and five of the thirteen largest federal government agencies. The company has widened its political focus too: Republicans buy its data as well.[12]

The largest part of Acxiom's business comes from supplementing information companies have collected on individuals. Getting more data from Acxiom helps boost marketing across sectors including the Internet, mobile, direct mail, call centers, and interactive TV. For example, if a company knows a person's name and address, Acxiom may be able to add a phone number, email address, and demographic information about average wealth in the neighborhood. A smaller chunk of the business comes from selling lists of potential customers.

Acxiom knows a staggering amount about people. It starts with public records, then amalgamates information volunteered on warranty cards and online surveys about hobbies and lifestyle information as well as commercial data from magazine publishers, retailers, and catalog companies. Acxiom also aggregates other identifying data, such as credit header data, the nonfinancial information at the top of your credit report that includes addresses and phone numbers. It may also include sensitive data such as Social Security numbers, which, the company says, are used only for fraud prevention. Acxiom's file does not detail that you once bought a $269 TaylorMade Men's Burner Super-Fast 2.0 TP Driver golf club, but it may indicate that your household has an interest in the sport.

The end product combines thousands of sources on a given person into two main dossiers. One is for marketing purposes and the other is for "risk mitigation," with only the data needed for that purpose. The company provides data from these products to companies, nonprofits, and government agencies that have passed a credentialing process.

Acxiom has data on almost all US consumers. Just reading the list of information it has can prove a little overwhelming. As consumers learn how much a company like Acxiom knows, some grow uneasy and concerned. "It is new and people don't understand what is happening. That feels a little bit creepy, that feels a little bit uncomfortable," said Tim Suther, Acxiom's former chief strategy and marketing officer, who insisted that consumers should not be afraid of the company.[13] He stressed that it does not make this data available to just anyone or for just any purpose. Thus Acxiom data do not determine whether you get credit, or health insurance, or a job. "We use it generally for one thing, and that's to help advertisers be more efficient with their messaging and who they want to talk to," he said. "If that information were used in a way that disadvantages you—'Hey, wait a minute! I've noticed you've gained a little bit of weight here. Do you mind if I share this with your insurance company?'—well, that would be a little freaky."

* * *

A few years after the initial incarnations of Epsilon and Acxiom, an Indian immigrant started his first direct-marketing efforts, which would eventually make him a millionaire invited to spend the night at the White House. Vinod Gupta grew up in a poor village north of the Indian capital, New Delhi, without water or electricity. He studied engineering and came to the United States in 1967 to get a master's degree and then an MBA in Lincoln, Nebraska. After finishing university in 1971, he got a job at the Commodore Corporation, a mobile home manufacturer, as a market research analyst earning $850 a month. (That same year, Harrah's sold shares to the public for the first time.) The following year, seeking to boost sales, Gupta asked the national telephone monopoly AT&T to deliver a copy of every local phone book to him. Because Commodore had a costly toll-free 800 number that made it an important business client, AT&T sent a massive order of about four thousand books, free of charge.[14]

When his boss protested the massive size of the shipment, Gupta had the phone books delivered to his garage. The piles of directories sat there for a few months. Then, over the course of a few days, he compiled a sample list of mobile home vendors in Nebraska, writing them out by hand. Others programmed the data into an IBM System/3 computer, inserting punch cards to store up to ninety-six characters of data, about as much information as a line of text in this book.

He offered to sell a master list of US mobile home vendors to his company for $9,000 to compensate for his extra labor or give it to Commodore for free—provided he could market the list to rival firms as well. Commodore chose the latter option. Within a month Gupta had received $22,000 in new orders and started compiling data from other states, charging 10 cents per listing. It took three months before the list was ready. He started his own list-building business on the side and left Commodore the next year, 1973. Over time he expanded the lists to car dealers, boat dealers, and others. By 1981 he had made close to $1 million in sales.

In the mid-1980s Gupta added lists of people across the United States, layering public and commercial data onto basic phone book listings. Computer storage was becoming far cheaper, and his firm could do a lot more. "Once you know the name and the address, you had the home value, you had the phone number, then you can estimate the income of the household and then you can also overlay other information anytime a person fills out some stupid warranty card," he recalls. "Suppose it's a warranty card and some coupon for an arthritis drug, then you know this guy has got arthritis. So we had a lot of these clearinghouses who basically are selling that information."[15]

Gupta included whatever categories made sense from a commercial standpoint. For example, he says, he would not have had a problem listing that someone suffers from HIV. Yet with fewer than 1.8 million Americans in that category, he says, there is not enough marketing demand, so he does not include such information.[16]

In 1992, Gupta took his company, then called American Business Information, public. His wealth led to greater social prominence. He

donated generously to both Bill and Hillary Clinton's political campaigns and was invited to spend the night in the White House's Lincoln Bedroom, a perk shared with top donors and friends. He appeared
on *60 Minutes II* to explain data broker lists. After Bill Clinton left
office, he hired the former president to consult for his company at a
cost of $3 million over several years.[17] Gupta traveled on a corporate
jet and enjoyed a life of luxury. Eventually he sold his company, which
was later renamed InfoUSA, for $680 million in 2010.[18] By then he
and his family had homes in Omaha; Aspen, Colorado; Washington,
DC; Miami; Yountville and Hillsborough, California; and Maui and
Kauai, Hawaii.[19]

His high living attracted the attention of federal authorities. In
2010 the Securities and Exchange Commission charged him with
milking his former company for $9.5 million in unauthorized perks
between 2003 and 2007, including personal use of jets to Italy, the
Virgin Islands, Cancun, and other places, as well as billing for expenses
related to his yacht, a winery in Napa Valley, twenty cars (including
a Jaguar, two Mercedes, and a Hummer), life insurance, credit cards,
twenty-eight club memberships, and other expenses.[20] "Gupta stole
millions of dollars from Info shareholders by treating the company
like it was his personal ATM," said Robert Khuzami, director of the
SEC's enforcement division.[21] Gupta agreed to pay millions of dollars
to settle the case but did not admit or deny the allegations as part of
the settlement.[22]

After selling his company in 2010, Gupta formed DatabaseUSA,
which continues to compile data. The service lists one hundred million
cell phone numbers.[23]

Despite so many years of work in direct marketing, or perhaps because of it, Gupta is contemptuous of many in his field. He says about
half of today's list brokers are "shysters" cutting corners or lying about
the quality of the personal data they are selling. "They are basically like
traitors," he says. "They never tell the truth, you know. They claim to
be like a multi billion-dollars company and at the home they only got
one employee."

The DMA

Many of the firms arousing Gupta's ire gather every year at a convention hosted by the Direct Marketing Association, the leading industry group, whose roots date back nearly a century. The event, held in 2012 at the Las Vegas Mandalay Bay Hotel, celebrates data gathering and capitalism. Data merchants set up booths in a vast convention center. Even as they try to find new clients for their lists of consumers, they continue gathering data on one another. Some sponsor old-fashioned raffles, encouraging visitors to plop their business cards into a bowl for a chance to win a prize. As I approached one businessman's booth, he asked if he could scan my convention badge. The matrix code contained my name, address, phone number, and email.

Different brokers advertise different specialties. A company called T5 Healthy Living asks people to share intimate details via online surveys on subjects such as constipation, bipolar disorder, depression, cancer, and other conditions. Participants "receive information and exclusive offers with valuable coupons and savings on the latest products available." One question asks if you or a partner have had a sexually transmitted disease. The end of the form asks users to confirm: "I authorize T5 Healthy Living and its trusted third party partners to use my personal and household information to send email, postal, and valuable information to me."

Another broker even sold lists of the deceased. In Nikolai Gogol's satirical novel *Dead Souls,* the protagonist buys identities of those who have passed on to boost his apparent wealth and standing. That was not the goal of Omaha, Nebraska–based CAS Inc. It wants to improve clients' chances of selling to the living by purging the names of others in the household who have died. "Sending direct mail to the recently deceased adds insult to injury for the remaining members of a household," a company brochure said. "Not only is this practice bad manners, but it is also bad for business."

The US Postal Service has a large display stand at the convention, advertising its services to update addresses for direct marketers when people move.

One conference highlight is the DMA head's keynote speech. In 2012, with Congress and the Federal Trade Commission stepping up scrutiny of data brokers, DMA acting CEO Linda Woolley struck a fiery tone as she rallied thousands of gathered marketers in a large ballroom.[24] She said firms spent $168.5 billion on direct marketing in 2012, which generated more than $2 trillion in incremental sales— nearly 9 percent of US gross domestic product.[25] "Our data-driven world is a better world," declared Woolley, a former consultant and lobbyist. "It's not just that we have big data, it's that we are using it to give customers what they want."

Then she portrayed a dark future in which the Federal Trade Commission and "privacy zealots" had gotten their wishes and persuaded Congress to bar the collection of personal consumer data without their permission. The nightmare-scenario law would bar Internet tracking and prohibit the use of public records to gain insights. "Consumers even have the right to say: 'My marketing data is mine, and it's private, and you can't use it or sell it,'" she said. Woolley's vision aimed to rile up the crowd much as talk of a new prohibition might horrify a convention of brewers. "In this picture of the future, marketers didn't fight back hard enough, and the FTC and the privacy zealots got this bill passed," she continued. "Is this the picture of the future that you want? Of course not!"

She closed her remarks by leading the crowd of several thousand in a chant of "We are DMA! We are DMA!"

One developing area of marketing on display at the annual DMA conference is marketing through racial targeting. The field is attracting some interesting entrepreneurs who are making new uses of big data. After immigrating to the United States from India in 1997 at age thirteen, Ajay Gupta became fascinated by the important role minorities played in politics. He ultimately started developing software to identify the ethnic origins of millions of Americans from their names and other clues.

In high school in San Francisco, he taught himself computer coding by helping to develop a website on professional wrestling. He studied financial economics and creative writing in college and graduate school, but saw better career opportunities in big data and formed his company, Stirista, after his 2008 graduation. He bought lists of registered voters across the United States, and cross-referenced names with those on the rolls in eight southern states that also listed ethnicity. Using this and other data he could eventually predict ethnic origins and religions for most names and could discern unusual patterns. For example, of Ann Smiths, he detected that about three-quarters are white and the rest black. But 70–80 percent of Annie Smiths are black.

Gupta learned as well about the need for multiple clues such as combinations of first and last names, ZIP codes, and other details. A surname like Sen could be Bengali or Scandinavian. Das could be Indian or German. "What is the most challenging is when you have a name like Obama. There are only going to be about twenty people in the country with that," he says.

As he built his database, big companies started buying the data and his software. Cable operators including Dish Network, Time Warner, and DirecTV promoted Russian, Hindi, Chinese, and other foreign-language channels. Phone and VoIP telephony providers appealed to emigrants with ties to the old country. For example, Vonage could directly advertise very specific offers such as three thousand minutes a month to the Philippines for one cent a minute.

Ever more detailed personal data allows well-known names in retail, finance, health care, and other fields to tailor messages to different ethnic groups. McDonald's, T-Mobile, Diageo (distiller of brands such as Johnnie Walker whisky and Guinness beer), Wells Fargo, Blue Cross Blue Shield, and Procter and Gamble have all embraced what they call multicultural marketing.

Throwing away notions of a color-blind American society in a giant melting pot, data scientists and entrepreneurs like Gupta have stepped up efforts to use big data to segment customers into ethnic, racial, and religious categories. This ability is one of many areas in which marketers are gaining ever more intimate insights about customers who typically are unaware such information is being gathered.

"There was a sense that people came here and they were expected to take on the American culture, so you marketed to them as that. And now there may be a growing awareness that people maintain their ethnicities," says Donna Lillian, president of the American Name Society, a group of a few hundred experts who specialize in the study of US names.

For Stirista, a San Antonio, Texas–based startup where top executives include Gupta's wife and mother-in-law, this awareness has translated into rapidly growing revenue. It expected to bring in $3 million in 2013, up from $1.4 million in 2012.

Such targeting may be as simple as swapping ad photos to show a different ethnic group. Other times the message varies to reflect cultural sensitivities, a practice the American Heart Association embraces. "In certain cultural groups there is a certain guilt or lack of trust in working with their doctors," says Gerald Johnson II, the group's chief diversity officer and senior vice president. "There are the cultural nuances that say that messaging would be different."

In other cases, marketers will only target certain ethnic groups. "If I send out twenty thousand emails just for a Hispanic grocery store, for example, the response is not necessarily that great," says Lynwood Shackelford, director of sales for the Washington Suburban Press Network, which helps firms with marketing. If they can narrow that original mailing list to just Hispanics with the right messaging, the ad may deliver ten or twenty times better results, he says. In another campaign, he promoted a new Native American museum to people of that heritage.

Direct marketers have gathered information about ethnicity, race, and religion for decades, but advances in computing allow ever greater sophistication in modeling a person's likely origins, as well as details such as whether someone is a first-generation immigrant likely to speak a foreign language. Before the 1990s such marketing was often based on surnames or ZIP codes, with religion assigned based on broad assumptions (for example, designating those with Italian surnames as Catholic).

"There was a lack of trust and common knowledge that compiled lists through inferred information were not accurate," says Peter Brownstein, former chief information officer at Ethnic Technologies, a leading ethnic data broker and processor. Today Ethnic Technologies uses multiple sources of information to predict 95 percent of the names it encounters. "As that marketing method evolved, they started looking at geography, neighborhood analytics," says Karen Sinisi, director of sales.

Today, large data brokers such as Acxiom buy ethnic data and related software from companies such as Stirista and Ethnic Technologies, making the data widely available to marketers. Gupta says his program starts out by seeking matches to the five hundred thousand most common US surnames that make up about 70–80 percent of the nation's total. Another five hundred thousand surnames account for everyone else, he estimates. For less common names, his team studies emigration and government records for clues. First names help determine if people are first- or second-generation immigrants. US-born citizens are likely to have Americanized names, with the exception of Indians, he says. Some marketers also rely on self-reported ethnic data from surveys, but Gupta says people do not always answer truthfully.

On its website, Stirista shows how it can supplement basic information about a customer. Jennifer Pham? A Protestant of Vietnamese ancestry who speaks Vietnamese. John Washington in Palmetto, Florida? A Protestant African American. Marshall Begay? A Catholic Native American Navajo. Sometimes the first name contains the decisive clue.

The software is predictive, which means it is not always right. Both Stirista and Ethnic Technologies said their software would likely wrongly guess that Barack Obama would be a Muslim of Kenyan extraction. Stirista predicted that I would be Western European, "typically English or German." They were a few countries off, and missed the Italian half of my heritage, obscured when my mother, with an Italian surname, married my father. It suspected that American Name Society president Donna Lillian was of Irish ancestry. She does have some Irish, but also English, Scottish, and a dash of Native American heritage.

Political campaigns also increasingly use ethnic data. "In politics it's like marketing on steroids. So you've got a one-day sale where you have to get all the shoppers to the store," says John Phillips, CEO of Aristotle, which uses personal data to help US and foreign candidates.

"Political marketing based on ethnicity or nationality is increasingly important." He cites campaigns in India, Mexico, Tunisia, and elsewhere where nationals living abroad are a vital source of both donations and millions of votes.

Although Gupta is open about his business, many selling and using the data are reluctant to reveal much about racial targeting. Sinisi of Ethnic Technologies spoke at the 2013 DMA convention, but her CEO and other officials have declined to answer subsequent questions. The president of List Service Direct, a rival company, emotionally shooed me away at the DMA convention in Las Vegas in 2012, saying he had been unfairly portrayed as a racist in the past. He did not return later calls and emails.

"When you look at certain ethnic populations and their kind of negative historical experiences with the majority treatment of the minority, there is no surprise that there are some sensitivities," says Andy Bagnall, executive vice president of strategic direction at Prime Access, an advertising agency specializing in multicultural health-care marketing. "Something that we are very aware of as an agency and the industry is aware of as well is the delicate dance that we play when it comes to hyper-targeting, especially based on ethnicity, because we never want to come across as 'Big Brotherish.'"

Daniel Ocner, director of strategic marketing and development at multicultural marketing agency MediaMorphosis, says companies must avoid stereotypes such as using a sumo wrestler to seem more Japanese or a kung fu fighter to sell to Chinese. "These are all very cultural segments that don't apply to everybody. Similar to how we cannot assume that all Americans are cowboys," he says. Targeting too narrowly could backfire, as Ocner's surname shows. Stirista's software took him for "Hispanic (typically Mexican or Brazilian)." In fact, his family is from Argentina and Jewish.

"Any communication that comes across as very stereotypical is not going to get a good reaction from the intended audience," says Bagnall. Here again, big data can establish the boundaries by testing the results of the marketing. "What has really increased exponentially is our ability to measure whether an ethnic campaign is working or not," he says. Because of sophisticated use of personal data, such campaigns often do prove effective.

Yet many marketers are cautious about going too far. In a presentation at the 2012 DMA conference, Acxiom's Suther urged marketers to show restraint even if they could make ever more clever uses of personal data. He told a room full of peers that they would be tempted to go to the dark side and use sensitive data about people.[26] "Please do not do it," he said. "Ask yourself: am I doing something *for* the customer, or am I doing something *to* the customer?"

Acxiom regularly solicits Caesars for business, boasting that over the past few years it has sold information to four of the five largest gaming companies, to good effect.[27] A former executive for Wynn Resorts says the company made extensive use of Acxiom data and estimated that at the peak, before 2008, its marketing with that data contributed at least 15 percent of the hotel's occupancy—a number Wynn's spokesman disputes.[28] Acxiom also sells a "casino gambling propensity score" for millions of people. That score combines interest expressed in surveys as well as data on past activities.[29]

For a long time Gary Loveman and the top Caesars brass were skeptical about the utility of outside data, whether specifying a person's background or estimated propensity to gamble. "We don't need to know the income level in Adam's ZIP code or whether he bought a lawn mower last week or whether his wife had a baby," Loveman said in one of our early meetings. "We don't play in any of that stuff. We're taking a look at whether we are missing something by not doing much of that, but historically we haven't."

But everything started to change when the clouds darkened over perpetually sunny Las Vegas in 2008.

8

Recession

The Economic Crisis Hits

Gary Loveman had made Caesars so attractive by 2006 that two private equity firms, Apollo Global Management and TPG Capital, swooped in to take Harrah's private. Financial markets were soaring, so they paid a staggering $30.7 billion. The firms financed the deal, which was completed in January 2008, by taking out a huge amount of loans. The debt saddled the casino company with big interest payments it would be obligated to pay long into the future. Everything would be fine if business kept growing.

It turned out to be an especially inauspicious time to buy a massive casino company. Vegas was heading into dark days. After continuously building ever more grandiose structures, the industry faced unprecedented debts and liabilities.[1] A glut of new rival casinos under construction as the crisis hit worsened matters. Interest payments on past debt claimed an ever greater percentage of revenue.

Loveman started making cuts and other pre-emptive moves to stabilize the business. The numbers were daunting. In Nevada, casinos lost $15 billion in the four years after 2008 before federal income taxes.[2] In 2008, Harrah's lost $5.2 billion. Those guests who continued to come noticed the cutbacks. In a 2009 company survey, customers said they had the impression that the recession had hurt Harrah's more than it had hit their own pocketbooks. They did not want to come as often, not so much because of their tighter belts but because of the difficulties experienced by the casino chain. "We had cut labor,

Massive Total Rewards sign on the side of Bally's Las Vegas.
Source: Author photo.

they didn't think the property was clean, we had cut marketing offers, maybe some of their favorite employees weren't there," said David Norton, the executive who had worked for years to attract steadily spending regulars who had not traditionally been considered VIPs. With the recession putting his back against the wall, Loveman had to squeeze even more value out of his most valuable asset: the personal data in the Total Rewards program.

The New Personal Data Guru

Loveman wanted to hand over the mantle of Total Rewards to someone with fresh ideas and energy, someone who might be able to help the company emerge from the slump. He spent more than a year searching for the right person. In June 2010, after others had conducted preliminary interviews, Loveman invited Joshua Kanter, then a thirty-six-year-old consultant at McKinsey & Company, to lunch at an Italian restaurant across the street from the Harvard Club in New York City. Kanter, with a round face giving him a choirboy look, projected an image about as different from the rough-hewn casino underlings of yesteryear as possible. He wore half-frame eyeglasses and a Harvard class ring on his right hand. He had come a long way since his University Painters days.

Kanter was born in Phoenixville, Pennsylvania, a town outside Philadelphia where part of the cult 1958 sci-fi movie *The Blob* had been filmed. Growing up, he had devoured math classes; he scored 790 on his math SAT scores, a tad shy of perfect. He had gone to college at Wesleyan, Loveman's alma mater, dropped out to tend to his painting business, and then resumed his undergraduate studies at Harvard. He had graduated the same year Loveman left the business school across the Charles River to join Harrah's.

Kanter had first visited a casino as a college student when he went to Foxwoods Resort Casino in Connecticut with his girlfriend and roommate in the middle of the night. When he arrived, he took $100 out of the ATM and decided he would leave with either a second Benjamin in his pocket or nothing at all. Within minutes he had lost $75 at the roulette wheel. He lasted another hour or so at the blackjack table before losing his last dollar. After college he became a consultant in New York. He distinguished himself by working from seven in the morning to eleven at night and by wearing his long black hair far past his shoulders, all while navigating the button-down world of financial services.

About forty-five minutes into their lunch, Loveman paused, tilted his head a bit, and looked straight at Kanter: "I want you to take this job." The CEO then told him why he should discontinue his twelve-year career as a consultant and join the casino business.

Loveman viewed Kanter as "a very sophisticated, quantitatively literate marketing guy." He saw the consultant as his third hire of the same ilk, a data F-14 pilot following in the footsteps of Rich Mirman and David Norton, both of whom had served as chief marketing officers. By then Mirman had left the company to become a private consultant in Las Vegas, and Norton was soon to go.[3]

Later that day a Harrah's recruiter called Kanter with a job offer and details of a generous package.

The night Kanter accepted the job, he recorded his thoughts in his leather-bound diary. He would not move to Las Vegas, he reminded himself. New York was home to his girlfriend, friends, and a rich array of cultural offerings. He commuted to Las Vegas for a while, staying in company hotels. As a consultant he was used to extensive travel; he took three to five flights a week. Yet the long commute to Las Vegas started to take a toll. Eventually he decided he wanted to live and work in the same place. He gave in and moved to the US casino capital. Breaking into social life in Las Vegas took some time, but the city was much cheaper than New York. He bought the McMansion of his dreams, a 4,200-square-foot house with a pool overlooking a golf course in a gated community. He parked a spiffy Audi A5 sports car in the oversized garage.

Kanter moved to Las Vegas as the company was consolidating its management in an effort to cut costs and make operations more efficient. Instead of duplicating marketing, accounting, and other functions in each region, statistics-loving executives in Vegas oversaw marketing initiatives from Mississippi to Indiana, from the New Jersey shore to San Diego.

The move marked a big change. For much of US casino history, local managers and their pit bosses had great autonomy over their operations. The dealer had a say in what happened at his table, the floor supervisor was responsible for his group of tables, and the manager oversaw his casino. James McElroy remembers well how things used to be. He has worked in Vegas casinos for forty years, climbing his way up from dealer to assistant casino manager at Caesars Palace. He

Joshua Kanter at Caesars Palace, Las Vegas. Source: Author photo.

nostalgically recalls the days when the dealer or supervisor had the power to dole out comps, including to friends or even to himself, to enjoy a steak dinner. "A lot of people were receiving comps that didn't deserve them," he says.

Today McElroy spends his days in the elegant Caesars Palace high-limit room, where players might wager $50,000 on a single hand of blackjack, and where those putting up $500,000 are escorted into a private gambling salon. But he cannot arbitrarily treat people to free meals. He must follow the same data formula that applies across the company.

The centralization of management gave executives like Joshua Kanter wide authority to set policy for all Caesars properties. But that did not make their jobs any easier. The real problem was that it was getting harder to lure gamblers into casinos. The massive cost-cutting that followed the recession made marketing more difficult. The total number of employees fell dramatically, from 87,000 reported in March 2008 to 69,000 two years later.[4]

Kanter remained optimistic, believing that even in slower economic times, when plunging staff rolls made the casinos a bit less friendly, Caesars' trove of personal data remained invaluable for targeting offers and encouraging client loyalty. Yet he thought the company could make better use of the data. In addition, he thought it prudent to expand the amount of information Caesars gathered—not only about gambling but about client spending and behavior more widely.

A lot had changed since the company had formalized its "no outside data" policy on clients in the mid-2000s. Many of the best insights were out in the open in social media, including Facebook.

9

The Puzzle of Your Identity

Six Degrees to Harry Lewis

During Gary Loveman's time at Harvard Business School, a respected computer science professor became dean of Harvard College on the other side of the Charles River. Harry Lewis was even more of a numbers nerd than Loveman, having earned a PhD in applied mathematics. A top expert on data, he has taught thousands of students about computer science. Like Loveman, he was very interested in what human insights can be gained from people's data. Because he had worked so long in computer science—starting long before the personal computer era—he was concerned about how much could be revealed about people by aggregating their data. Lewis did not know Loveman, but had heard of him.

One day in January 2004, not long after he stepped down after eight years as dean, Lewis received an email from an ambitious student. Bitter winter winds whipped off the Charles River that morning. Lewis had looked forward to starting a sabbatical, the magical bonus of academic life when tenured professors enjoy a semester away from their normal teaching duties.

The student had grown interested in how public information could link different people and reveal interesting characteristics about them. He had set up a website showing connections between people at the university and had mined the school newspaper, *The Harvard Crimson*, for the information. "Professor, I've been interested in graph theory and its applications to social networks for a while now, so I did some research . . . that has to do with linking people through articles they appear in from the *Crimson*," the student wrote. "I thought people would find this interesting, so I've set up a preliminary site that allows people to find the connection (through people and articles) from any person to the most frequently mentioned person in the time frame I looked at. This person is you.

"I wanted to ask your permission to put this site up though, since it has your name in its title."

The student called the proposed site "Six Degrees to Harry Lewis." The titled referenced a famous study by Stanley Milgram, who found that a random person could link to a stranger through people they knew using about six intermediaries.[1] Lewis reacted cautiously to the student, whom he knew from his course "Introduction to the Theory of Computation."

"Can I see it before I say yes? It's all public information, but there is somehow a point at which aggregation of public information feels like an invasion of privacy," Lewis wrote. "I am on sabbatical leave as of today, so you are catching me at a moment where I was about to relish some anonymity :)"

The student replied that he had already set up the site. He emailed the link. Professor Lewis replied with a few suggestions on how to improve it and gave his assent to going public: "Sure, what the hell. Seems harmless."[2]

Soon after, Professor Lewis, who had also taught Microsoft founder Bill Gates "Introduction to Combinatorial Mathematics" in the 1970s, said goodbye to another one of his brilliant students who decided to drop out of Harvard. A month later, the student, Mark Zuckerberg, built on that early experiment and created Facebook. In retrospect, Lewis's initial caution about aggregating public information has proven visionary. One can indeed learn a lot from many innocent facts about someone.

Ten years later, much as Zuckerberg briefly mined the *Harvard Crimson* to find trends, everyone from casino security officers to marketers and academic researchers regularly hunts for patterns in Facebook and other social networks. Often people find that sites like Facebook give away clues about us that we did not intend to reveal.

Consider, for example, the clues embedded in a person's "likes." In June 2007, David Stillwell had just finished college in Britain and had time to kill before starting graduate school in psychology. Facebook had about thirty million users at the time (it passed the one billion point in 2012). The social network had just started allowing outside developers to write applications that operated inside the site. Such apps could tap into profiles if users granted permission. Stillwell created myPersonality, an online test that allowed people to take a personality test that measures five main traits: openness to experience, conscientiousness, extraversion, agreeableness, and emotional stability.[3] Since then, nearly eight million people have taken the personality test, typically teenagers and twenty-somethings. Americans, Brits, and Canadians are the most active participants. Around 40 percent of those who took the test allowed Stillwell and other researchers to see their Facebook profiles.

In 2013, Stillwell and two other researchers published an analysis of what they could learn from the Facebook "likes" of 58,466 Americans.[4] In contrast to some of the more intimate Facebook preferences, likes are among the most innocuous and easily visible items. By default they are public. Just by looking at the likes—and not just obvious preferences such as liking a conservative political site or gay-oriented page—researchers could consistently infer intimate details such as sexual orientation, religion, political views, smoking, alcohol or drug use, and other characteristics. "If we can collect a few bits of data of a person, there is so much that we can predict," says study coauthor Thore Graepel, a Microsoft researcher. It may sound like a cliché, but the survey supported the idea that liking the musical *Wicked* or the singer Britney Spears was a good predictor of male homosexuality, much as the preference for rap group Wu-Tang Clan or basketball player Shaquille O'Neal suggested heterosexuality.

The study's third coauthor, Michal Kosinski, who works with Stillwell at the Psychometrics Centre at the University of Cambridge, is especially sensitive to government abuse of personal information because he grew up in Communist Poland. In fact, he considers himself a product of the martial law that sought to repress the independent

Solidarity trade union movement, which eventually undermined the Soviet-backed government. In 1981, when the Polish Communists imposed martial law, many couples opted to spend more time at home rather than go out on the town. Michal was born the following year. He says it might be unnerving for Europeans or Americans to be outed because of how they use the Internet. But it was far more dangerous for people in some other countries. "The same technology used in other countries is not unnerving, just directly dangerous," he says. "There are many worse things that could happen."[5]

"The first situation in which Iran will use big data to put some people in prison, it will have a huge backlash on companies like Amazon or Facebook or whichever company will be unlucky to have their data used against human rights," Kosinski says. Figuring out personality patterns from data is not difficult, he says. In fact, a high school student could write a Facebook "gaydar" application in an evening to out gay Facebook friends, perhaps to disastrous consequences. It could prompt suicides or other tragedies.[6]

It's one thing for an academic to unmask intimate patterns from Internet postings. But would a company actually seek to use such information for profit? Of course. Jim Adler, the former chief privacy officer at Intelius, says data brokers should be able to publish anything that people can see in public.[7] Such a standard, in Adler's view, opens the way to recording when people walk into gay bars, cancer facilities, or Alcoholics Anonymous clinics. Mass urbanization has created an expectation of privacy that did not exist before, Adler says. But the Internet is returning standards back to those of the small towns where people knew many details about one another.[8] "I really don't think we are violating people's privacy. I feel that there is an era of innovation that we are going through that is shrinking the world and putting us in public where we thought we were in private," he says.

Knowing someone's sexual orientation could prove valuable for Las Vegas casinos advertising drag shows or gay bars, for example. But targeted ads could also offend. Ads in gay publications or on Internet sites visited by people with such interests—the theme of Chapter 13, on

Internet advertising—may prove a more effective and less potentially offensive approach.[9]

*　*　*

Likes are just one of many ways to discern unexpected private details from Facebook profiles. The same year Stillwell set up myPersonality, a Massachusetts Institute of Technology master's degree student and an undergraduate senior wanted to see just how much they could infer about a person's sexual orientation even if the person did not disclose that information in public. Without Facebook's permission, Behram Mistree and Carter Jernigan used a computer program to harvest Facebook profiles of 6,077 MIT students. The automated process took several weeks. They noted sexual orientation for people who stated a preference in Facebook's "Interested In" tab, where one can list men, women, or both.

In their sample they found that a typical straight male had 0.7 gay male friends, whereas those who declared themselves gay males had 4.6 gay friends on average.[10] They created a logistic regression model and found that if more than 1.89 percent of a male's friends identified themselves as gay, the Facebook user who did not express a sexual preference was likely gay. They checked their finding against students whose true sexual orientation they already knew.[11]

"It's not so much that you are inadvertently disclosing things that you hadn't wanted to," Mistree said years later.[12] "It's actually that the locus of control for describing personal information about yourself using these social networks has moved from you to others. It's not your decision anymore. It's the decision of your neighbor. It's the decision of your basketball coach, all these people." Jernigan added, "It's not about what they post about you, it is what they post on themselves that then reflects on you."[13]

The same kinds of techniques that reveal intimate information from Facebook can help outsiders figure out who you are when you have not identified yourself. The vast proliferation of personal data as well as advances in computing power have made it harder to maintain anonymity. That's because some parts of a person's data could match with another dataset about them with more identifying details. It is as if several city maps had been ripped into pieces. An individual piece might not show enough to recognize the place, but a few pieces together would. In 1997 Latanya Sweeney, who in 2014 served as chief technology officer at the FTC, showed just how easy it is to identify someone with a few simple clues—even for a graduate student, as she was at the time at MIT.

One May morning in 1996, Massachusetts Governor William Weld attended a graduation ceremony at Bentley University, outside Boston, to receive an honorary degree. The event brought attention to a school often overshadowed by better-known area institutions such as Harvard, MIT, and Boston University. Shortly after receiving his honorary law doctorate, Weld collapsed and lost consciousness for about a minute. An ambulance took him to Deaconess-Waltham Hospital. The graduation ceremony proceeded, with the crowd pausing for a moment of silence and prayer for the governor. At the hospital, doctors announced that they had conducted an electrocardiogram, a chest X-ray, and blood tests on the fifty-year-old Weld. They concluded he had suffered nothing more serious than the flu. He recovered quickly.

The following year, Sweeney wanted to see if she could identify medical patients from anonymous records. The Massachusetts Group Insurance Commission (GIC), a state body that looks at health-care costs and treatment, released hospital exit records on state employees to researchers but without the patients' names. "I remembered Weld had collapsed and that's why I thought, 'Can I find Weld in the records?'" says Sweeney, who later became a Harvard professor.

She bought a copy of the voter rolls for Cambridge, the city where Weld lived. Those records contained the name, birth date, gender, and ZIP code for each resident. Only three men in the Cambridge area shared Weld's birth date, and he was the only one with that birth date in his ZIP code. Using that limited information, she pinpointed his hospital records.[14] Her study, published the following year, showed that just knowing someone's date of birth, gender, and postal code provided enough information to identify up to 87 percent of the US population. "You don't need very much information to reidentify people," she says.

In 2013 Sweeney, working with a research assistant and two students, tried to unlock the names of participants in an especially ambitious medical research study. That effort, called the Personal Genome Project (PGP), aimed to spark new discoveries. George Church, a professor of genetics at Harvard Medical School, says that advances in data and in medicine make it impossible to guarantee anonymity for most medical experiments. When he set up the Personal Genome Project, he made no privacy promises. In the interest of advancing knowledge of human health and disease, he posts the data for all volunteers on the Internet for any researcher to study. He does not list names, but many participants share intimate details: abortions, depression, sexual ailments, and prescription drugs are listed along with their DNA sequence.

Before accepting new volunteers, Church requires that they take an online exam about privacy risks. They must intimately know the details of the twenty-four-page consent form. "The Personal Genome Project is a new form of public genomics research and, as a result, it is impossible to accurately predict all of the possible risks and discomforts that you might experience," it says. Having someone identify participants is one of the listed risks. The exam does not pose a simple generic question such as "Do you understand the risks?" It lists twenty questions, and Church requires a perfect score. Potential volunteers can take the test as many times as they need until they pass. One person took the test ninety times before getting the required perfect score.[15]

Of course, almost no one reads privacy policies because they are so dull and obtuse. One study found that it would take between eight and twelve minutes to read a typical website privacy statement. The study's authors estimated that it would take a person between 181 hours and 304 hours a year to read all the privacy statements he or she came across over that period—well over a month of working hours.[16]

People likely read privacy policies about medical experiments more carefully, but Church says most studies are disingenuous in describing privacy risks. "This is one of the ways people get in over their heads in terms of personal data being exposed," he says. In fact, many surveys can expose personally identifiable information even if they say they are anonymous.

As of 2014, more than three thousand people had volunteered their data to the Personal Genome Project. Church would like to recruit up to one hundred thousand people, but he needs additional funding (it costs about $4,000 per person to take the DNA test and cover related administrative costs).

Every year the project hosts a conference where scientists and participants meet for two days of formal lectures as well as informal discussions. For the 2013 event in Boston, Sweeney set up a table in the hallway with her assistant to demonstrate that she could unmask the identity of many participants. Ahead of the conference she programmed her computers to collect publicly posted data on 1,130 of the volunteers. Of this number, 579 provided ZIP code, date of birth, and gender—the key information her 1997 study had shown could be used to identify large swaths of the US population. By cross-referencing the three pieces of information against voter registration records or other public documents, Sweeney identified 241 people, 42 percent of the total.[17] The Personal Genome Project confirmed that she had the names right 84 percent of the time, or 97 percent when adding nicknames and other variations on the first name.[18]

Participants at the conference reacted to Sweeney's findings largely by saying they expected one day to be identified. Gabriel Dean, who works at a telephone company, signed up after hearing about the Personal Genome Project on National Public Radio. He checked first with his siblings because he realized what he gave away about himself could reflect on them. As open as he was about his medical data, he remains concerned about revealing information on social networks, so he does not maintain profiles on Facebook or LinkedIn.

Throughout the two-day conference, study participants stopped by the table where Sweeney walked them through her website aboutmyinfo .org to demonstrate how easily she could identify them. She asked people to enter their ZIP code, date of birth, and gender into the site, which in turn told users if they were unique and thus identifiable. One

*Harvard professor
Latanya Sweeney
talks with her research
assistant Sean Hooley
at her office. Source:
Author photo.*

woman came up and asked in a somewhat feisty tone why she should care. Sweeney responded that, for example, a life insurance company could theoretically deny writing a policy based on personal data. The woman turned pale. "I was just denied life insurance," she said. The Harvard professor quickly replied that someone could be denied life insurance for many reasons and that it was far from clear that anyone had actually seen her medical data. But the woman did seem to recognize the potential danger from having such intimate medical details out there.

Many attending the conference embraced a let-the-world-know ethos. Steven Pinker, a well-known experimental psychologist and author of the 2011 book *The Better Angels of Our Nature*, stepped forward as one of the first ten volunteers in the study. He posts his genome and a 1996 scan of his brain on his website and insists even that amount of information does not reveal much about him as a person.[19] "There just isn't going to be an 'honesty gene' or anything else that would be nearly as informative as a person's behavior, which, after all, reflects the effect of all three billion base pairs and their interactions together with chance, environmental effects, and personal history," he says. "As for the medical records, I just don't think anyone is particularly interested in my back pain."

Sweeney's goal in publishing such findings is not to humiliate people by outing them. She believes that researchers with access for medical data on millions of patients may be able to find new cures for diseases or different patterns of effective treatment. Yet she wants to encourage people to find a better balance between sharing data and preserving some privacy. For example, people could list just their year of birth rather than full birth date, and just three rather than five or nine digits from their ZIP code. "Vulnerabilities exist, but there are solutions too," she says. "If they change those demographics, they can thwart that attack without losing research value."

Does someone need Sweeney's training, an advanced degree in computer science, to reidentify people from the Personal Genome Project? Apparently not. To test Sweeney's findings, I tried to find three participants who had especially detailed and lengthy medical histories. One profile listed an abortion, anal itching, constipation, marijuana use, urinary tract infection, and many other ailments. She gave her weight as 160 pounds and said she took medication for high blood pressure. I went to the site of a commercial data broker and entered the birth date of a woman in a certain ZIP code. Instantly two names came up for that birth date in that ZIP code, only one of which was a woman.

She turned out to be a professor and well-known scholar. She was surprised when I contacted her out of the blue. "I certainly did pay attention to the caveats about 'personal identification' when I signed up for the PGP, but didn't realize it would be so ridiculously easy to track down an individual," she said. "It doesn't worry me over-much, perhaps because I'm at an age where I'm not all that concerned 'what people might think' of various aspects of my history. I can imagine, though, that would not always have been the case."

Although she did not object to my using her case to illuminate the problem, I checked back several times. She works for a faith-based institution that strongly disapproves of abortion. The school staff handbook warns that engaging in conduct detrimental to the reputation of the institution could lead to dismissal. She said she was confident nothing would happen to her after serving as a tenured professor for decades. "It certainly isn't anything I hide (in fact, I use it as an example in class). That said, it might have made a difference many years ago, especially given that some former administrators were much more conservative than those we have today," she said. But in the end she did not want her name published—the details were just too intimate.

Another woman, sixty-eight, admitted on her Personal Genome Project survey to using cocaine and marijuana in the past and gave a long list of her ailments and the medications that she took. She also said she had suffered from child abuse from 1946 to 1963. For her birth date and ZIP code combination four or five female names appeared (one name was Lee, which could have been either gender). Yet the volunteer had also uploaded a genetic test to her profile that included her name. It took a little searching to find the phone number and email address for the woman, who had been involved in her high school's fiftieth reunion. She had left her web address details on a school alumni website, which in turn led to her email address.

The third volunteer was a seventy-two-year-old man whose profile listed alcoholism, bed-wetting to age twelve, bipolar disorder, cocaine use, depression, and many other ailments. Two men share his birth date in his Santa Barbara, California, ZIP code. One appeared to have moved. Searching the name of the second man led to a LinkedIn page saying he had gone to Harvard and had worked as a scientist. Fred Gamble confirmed he did indeed participate in the Personal Genome Project. He expressed surprise that someone had identified him, but not concern. He was retired and had become an active gardener. "Mine is detailed and there is some stuff in it that a younger person might not want broadcast, but I'm seventy-two and I don't really care," he told me.[20]

People volunteer for the Personal Genome Project because they are more open about their personal data in the first place. But not everyone wants to share such intimate data so freely. As a black woman who grew up in the South in the 1960s, Sweeney is sensitive to the potential for discrimination based on personal identity. She is also concerned about the vulnerability of anonymized medical data made public, which includes hospital discharge records released by most states. Such records exclude a patient's name, address, and Social Security number but still contain identifying clues. Insurance companies, labs, pharmacies, and various middlemen also have wide access to claims data related to medical conditions.

Selling deidentified data has become a multibillion-dollar business, even if such practices are largely hidden from the public. For example, when you fill a prescription, the pharmacy sells details about that transaction, earning about a penny. American pharmacies fill more than 2.5 million prescriptions every day, so over time those pennies add up. Nearly all of the country's sixty thousand pharmacies send out details of each transaction to companies that compile and analyze the information to resell to others. The data include age and gender of the patient; the doctor's name, address, and contact details; and details about the prescription.[21]

Despite assurances from the health-care industry, some privacy advocates say the trade in personal medical data will eventually harm people through reidentification. One prominent medical privacy advocate is Deborah Peel, a Freudian psychoanalyst. The first week Peel opened her practice in 1977, a patient startled her with an unusual question.

"If I pay you cash, will you keep my medical records private?"

At medical school Peel thought that mental health records could not be released without the patient's explicit permission. Yet she learned that records did get to employers who either fired people or demoted them. She agreed to keep records off the insurance rolls for cash. Over the years, she became ever more concerned about patient privacy. In 2004 she stopped taking new patients and set up the Patient Privacy Rights Foundation, based in Austin, Texas. "It's really hard not to come off as kind of a wing nut or separatist or I don't know what. But I'm just a doctor who's watched this for thirty-five years," she says. "With all this data out there, it's going to be the greatest source of job discrimination we've ever seen in this country, and it's going to start very early with your kid."

"The dirty little secret . . . whenever people talk about privacy rights, it always devolves to health data, and most lawyers and most of the public cannot believe that we have no control over our health data. But we don't! We fucking don't."

Good Data Intentions Gone Bad: Netflix/AOL Data Releases

In recent years, the ability to identify people thought to be anonymous has embarrassed well-known companies and institutions that have released data. One well-known incident occurred in 2006 after Netflix announced a dramatic contest: the company offered to pay $1 million to anyone who could improve its movie rating system by 10 percent. In theory, the plan would benefit everyone: predicting what movies would most appeal to individual subscribers could boost business and create a better customer experience. By outsourcing the effort to the public, Netflix could lure some of the best minds in data science and fill the wallet of a computer expert or team of researchers. "We're quite curious, really. To the tune of one million dollars," the company advertised.[22] The contest attracted wide attention. Hoping to snag the seven-figure payout, 51,051 people on 41,305 teams entered. Netflix released recommendations from nearly half a million subscribers, replacing the names of its customers with internal ID numbers.

The contest excited Arvind Narayanan, but for a different reason than other researchers. A University of Texas PhD student at the time, Narayanan did not aspire to win the million-dollar prize. Rather, he invented his own contest to reidentify some of the people whose names Netflix had removed when releasing the recommendations. He rushed to see his faculty advisor, Vitaly Shmatikov, a computer scientist with special interest in computer security and privacy.

Narayanan was convinced that Netflix was wrong in saying it could maintain the anonymity of customers in the released data. He felt confident that there had to be a way to identify some of them. If Narayanan and Shmatikov could succeed, they would demonstrate a major flaw in how companies approached protecting privacy as crowdsourcing became increasingly popular.

Both foreign-born, the student and professor had grown up in very different privacy environments. Narayanan hailed from Chennai, earlier known as Madras, a city of more than four million in southern India. As in other large Indian cities, surges of people crowded the streets and public transport, leaving little possibility for personal space. "I like to joke that it is not even feasible in India because if you insisted that everybody stay three feet apart from each other, you'd run out of space," he says. "When an Indian person applies for a job they put their date of birth and a bunch of other personal details on their CV, which is very jarring in terms of the kind of contextual boundaries that we have here."

Shmatikov, who came to the United States in 1992, grew up in Moscow during Soviet Communism's final years. The KGB and other state organs could monitor citizens of interest, but most Muscovites shuttled about the gray city anonymously, minding their own business among the masses. Muscovites could escape notice riding in the crowded Metro system or walking in Gorky Park. In some sense it was easier to be anonymous then because there was no massive data collection, and people weren't leaving digital traces all over the place.

"Of course, if they really wanted to track someone, they had no lack of manpower, they could always assign a man to follow you," Shmatikov says. "But you could do it for one person, for ten people, for a hundred people, you cannot do it for ten million people. So in that sense the vast majority of the population could be as anonymous as they wanted to be. Now it is all very different because now there really is technical capability to track anything anyone is doing anywhere."

At first glance, it might appear unlikely that two researchers could identify people who posted anonymous movie reviews on Netflix. Many people watch the same popular movies. Yet some people watch and review those popular movies in combination with obscure ones, creating distinct profiles. Another analogy: any two random humans share, on average, 99.9 percent of their DNA: all human variation (and identifiability) is attributable to the remaining 0.1 percent. Such combinations provide clues that can help unmask a person's identity, much as a contestant on the television game show *Wheel of Fortune* pieces together an entire message from partially revealed letters in a sentence. Some people in the Netflix prize dataset had watched and rated more than a thousand movies. Some had even rated more than ten thousand of the seventeen thousand movies then in the collection.

Narayanan came to learn that some cinephiles watch multiple movies a day and freely share their opinions on different sites, including imdb.com, where people often give their names when reviewing movies. Over the first eight days, Narayanan and Shmatikov worked feverishly into the night. By piecing together the names from IMDB with the same sets of movies in the Netflix prize dataset, they identified two Netflix subscribers by name, showing that they could solve the puzzle. They felt no need to go further: they had shown they could reidentify the movie lovers. "We were confident because there were no other matches that were even close," Narayanan said. "Out of all the other records in the 500,000 dataset there was one good match" for each reidentification. As a further check, they reidentified two colleagues who had shared their Netflix viewing data with them, so in those two cases they knew for sure that their method worked and that they had found the right people.

The findings illustrated the privacy dangers that massive amounts of personal data pose, even if stripped of names. Yet academics initially shunned their findings. Narayanan and Shmatikov offered a paper on their research to an academic conference and received a thumbs down. "It is well known that logs can leak lots of private data," one reviewer said in a rejection note. "It's not clear whether there is much real novelty/research in this paper."[23] A second conference also said no. Finally, a year later, the same conference that first rejected the paper accepted a revised version. This time, the study received wide public attention—although that did not lead to riches. The million-dollar prize went to a team of data scientists who had come up with a 10.06 percent improvement on the Netflix movie recommendation system—three years after the company first revealed the subscriber recommendations.[24]

The public attention to the privacy implications of the Netflix data eventually led to a class-action lawsuit. In that complaint, a lesbian said she did not want to reveal her sexual orientation or interest in gay-themed films. "On October 2, 2006, Netflix perpetrated the largest voluntary privacy breach to date, disclosing sensitive and personal identifying consumer information," the lawsuit said. "The information was not compromised by malicious intruders. Rather, it was given away to the world freely, and with fanfare."[25] Netflix eventually settled the case out of court. In 2010 it canceled plans for a second contest. Today the company would rather forget the whole episode.[26]

* * *

A few months before Netflix released its movie recommendation data in 2006, email and Internet pioneer AOL published the search histories of 650,000 users over three months—a total of twenty million searches. The company removed the IP addresses of the computer making the searches and instead assigned a unique ID number to each user so that researchers could follow the search patterns. Since users often look for information related to where they live and give clues about their identity over a period of time, two *New York Times* reporters succeeded in puzzling out the names of some of them.[27]

After a public outcry, AOL fired the official who released the data; the company's chief technology officer resigned. AOL quickly tried to remove the data, yet the company suffered a damaging blow to its reputation—and a costly lawsuit. Only in 2013 did a federal judge approve the class-action settlement, which cost AOL up to $5 million, plus $930,000 to cover plaintiff's attorney fees. People whose search data were released received $50 to $100.

Even today, one can still download the dataset on the Internet, again showing that once released, information can never be put back into the bottle. "It was a big reminder of the beginnings of what people now refer to as big data," AOL cofounder Steve Case reflected. "Data that was supposed to be helpful some people were able to use in a way that was not helpful. So it was a wake-up call to our business.[28]

"These issues are not new issues. What is new is that far more people are online, they are online far more habitually, far more networked, far more places, so therefore there is more tracking of data and more ability to kind of analyze it in ways that can be helpful and also ways that may not be helpful."

Unmasking sexual orientation or reidentifying people based on clues are obviously far from the business of running a casino, or luring guests into a department store, or any other business. The larger point is that many of the services we enjoy today in different areas of our lives collect data about us. Watching cable television, carrying a cell phone, using social media sites, or visiting a doctor all generate data that are shared widely, even if not with the person generating the data. Much of the information you generate is fairly innocuous. Your hobbies. Your favorite music. Your photos. Any one piece of data would not reveal very much. But continued advances in data mining have made small bits of personal data ever more revealing when combined—and ever more valuable to companies.

Sometimes, these clues lead all the way to the naked truth.

10

The Hunt for a Mystery Woman

Scanty Clues

A Yelp page reviewing Instant Checkmate, in a section called "about the business," showed the image of a smiling woman.[1] It described her as Kristen B., manager of Instant Checkmate, followed by: "I'm Kristen, customer relations director at Instant Checkmate. When I am not responding to facebook [*sic*] messages, tweets, linked in requests and such, I can be found blogging on various sites. I love my job at Instant Checkmate and I am proud of help [*sic*] our customers!"

In Las Vegas–datelined press releases and company blogs, the company seemed to leave the talking to Kristen Bright, described as a PR manager, public relations specialist, social media consultant, or spokeswoman.[2] Yet Kristen Bright did not respond to any attempts to contact her, either by phone or through email. Operators at the company's Las Vegas call center said they had never seen her. So I wondered: could a minuscule blurry photograph provide enough information to identify and locate the real woman behind the image?

I copied the photo and loaded it into Google's image search page. The results led to a photo of a woman on a boat with a bikini top stretched over significant cleavage. Someone had cropped the face from this image and put it on the Yelp page. Running a new search on the full photograph led to different pages with the same woman, photographed in a bikini or sexy underwear. On occasion she wore no top at all.

One view of the mystery woman I was trying to find. Source: Ann, surname withheld at her request.

The homemade, snapshot quality of the photos and a winning smile suggested a certain wholesomeness, even when she posed partially naked. Some tame family photos showed her with a boy, perhaps her son. A few bloggers had created pages in her honor, and admirers wrote in to compliment her beauty and curves. Some wondered where one might be able to find more images. Some blog comments referred to unseen explicit videos. The hunt continued.

The initial Google searches offered several names for the woman, with at least two surnames. Those names helped find other saucy images but no contact details, suggesting she used a stage moniker. The other images did not mention the name Kristen Bright. Searching through the new racy images did lead to a 2010 blog post showing her with a man who described himself as her husband, Tom. He said they were both thirty-eight years old and heading to a Jamaican resort for their twentieth wedding anniversary. For all these clues, the woman's real name and contact details remained elusive.

Then one day I conducted a search through a background data broker site used by lawyers, insurance companies, law enforcement agencies, and others. I found her stage surname embedded in a man's email address. That man, Tom, was then forty-one, about right for the husband if he had listed his true age in the Jamaica vacation posting a few years earlier. Tom had also filed a relatively recent Chapter 13 joint bankruptcy petition with his wife, whose name was Ann. Among the debts listed on the court documents: $131 owed to Victoria's Secret. Might the lingerie chain be the source of some of the skimpy garb modeled in the online photos?

Those documents led to an address and phone number in California. Still, additional proof was needed before calling. After all, lots of couples named Tom and Ann live in the United States. A call to the wrong couple asking about naked photographs might provoke a justifiably angry response. A search of Ann's real surname linked her to a Los Angeles–area high school where she had worked as a secretary. Deep within the school website lurked an old school newsletter with a photo of the support staff. Standing a bit shyly to the back of the group was a woman wearing a black vest over a white T-shirt. The face looked the same and the top-heavy body dimensions suggested she was indeed Ann.

I dialed a phone number I located for the couple and left a message, saying I was a fellow at Harvard University researching a book. An astonished Ann and Tom called back a few minutes later, wondering how they had been found. I told them about the Yelp listing for Instant Checkmate using her image. Had the website contacted her to gain permission to use her image as the face of the company? It had taken me a long time to find her. If she indeed worked for the data broker, the search would only have shown that she used a different name on the job. But she said not only did she *not* work for Instant Checkmate, she had never even heard of it or the name Kristen Bright. "Honestly, it's a little sickening," she said. Then she joked: "Geez, if they would have asked, I could have sold a better photo!"[3]

Ann's story shows that in the Internet era it is possible to piece together clues about one's true identity with just a little information. Her story turned out to be particularly saucy. Ann and Tom had tried to live a secret alternative erotic life on the Internet, a folly that ended up causing her great embarrassment.

* * *

One spring afternoon in 2011, a California high school principal called a secretary into his office. As Ann entered, she saw the school policeman, complete with gun in holster, seated with the principal around a large conference table. "This is kind of weird," the principal said. "I wanted the deputy here because I wanted someone else with me so that we wouldn't be alone in my office when I told you this."

The head of the school told her they had found a compromising video in which she appeared. "Well, you're not in trouble or anything. We are mostly concerned about how your son will react," he said.

The police deputy had a copy of an explicit video on his cell phone. "Would you like to see what video we are talking about?"

Ann looked around the room. She glanced at a picture of the principal shaking hands with Ronald Reagan and banners showing the school mascot. With horror her eyes fixed upon the wide flat-screen television mounted on the wall. She certainly did not want them replaying her exploits writ large. Her face flushed red, her embarrassment complete.

"No, my husband just called me and told me about it, so I know which video you are talking about."

It had all started out so innocently. In the early 2000s, Ann and Tom started posting family snapshots on the Internet for family and friends to see. They were slightly ahead of their time, posting on a public site a few years before Mark Zuckerberg talked to his Harvard professor Harry Lewis about building a prototype website for what became Facebook.

At first, the images portrayed tame everyday activities, some including their two children: the chili cook-off, an outing to a lake, a visit to Universal Studios, Father's Day. But in 2003, the images began attracting compliments from strangers on their online guestbook, especially those showing Ann wearing a revealing top or a bikini.

She and her husband decided to post more revealing images on a password-protected site, inviting their fans to take a peek—without family members stumbling upon the photos. Tom got a buzz from the attention Ann was getting ("I have a HOT wife," he boasted in

Ann posing for her husband. Source: Ann,
surname withheld at her request.

one post), and Ann enjoyed the compliments. "We'd both get a little turned on or whatever by what people said. So maybe if we did put racier pictures up it would be hot or it would be sexy," Ann says.

It excited her that unknown people far away found her sexy and attractive, and this unseen, remote enthusiasm sparked up their love life. "Sometimes we would read them together on the weekends. We'd sit down and go through them and, of course, it was sexually charging to do that, to see what people were saying," she says.

Fans would request specific images, and they would comply: "We'd get all excited and if the kids were not home, we would take more pictures here and go somewhere on the weekends and post them and wait to see what people thought, hear their comments."

Eventually family finances tightened, so Tom and Ann went a step further. Their best friends at the time, another couple, suggested the plan, but Tom and Ann became enthusiastic accomplices. They set up their own website at midnight, January 1, 2006, and, for the first time, posted self-filmed sex videos of themselves. The other married couple also posted explicit film clips of themselves. They invited fans to join the site for $24.95 per month, or $59.95 for three months. Within hours, $5,000 in subscription payments had poured in. They split the revenue with the other couple and celebrated their overnight financial success.

Eventually shooting video for the site made marital intimacy feel like a chore. They faced constant interruptions to adjust the lighting, make sure they exposed good angles, change positions, or check the camera. On top of that, they realized they could not prevent other people from reposting their images. Ann's popularity on the Internet was spreading too far, too fast. Without asking her permission, a dating site for those over forty used her photo, which annoyed her because she was then in her mid-thirties. One blog posted one of her images, apparently drawing the notice of a relative. "That would be my Aunt . . . kind of weird seeing stuff like this on the net," her niece wrote.

Ann began to feel self-conscious in public. Did others know about the videos? Did people in stores and on the street smile at her out of friendliness or because they had seen her naked? It was one thing to excite a remote unseen person. She found that arousing. But if neighbors, friends, or school colleagues were watching, that was creepy. Her husband, who worked in a professional services firm, also appeared in the videos but had hidden his face (other parts of his anatomy starred in the productions), so no one could recognize him. "I was naïve, and I thought nobody was going to notice. It became a bigger deal than I thought it would become, and I didn't like it," she says. "Back then, it still seemed like the Internet was kind of new. I'm a nobody—who thought it would spread?"

Within a few months, Ann and Tom decided to shut down their site. Eventually Ann got a job as a high school secretary, and her brief fling with explicit video faded from memory. Then over a lunch break during the late spring of 2011, a school guard saw an excited group of students huddled around a cell phone under a tree. She went over to see what was causing the stir and recognized Ann in a sex video. Word arrived first to Tom, and he called his wife.

Tom and Ann had devised a cover story in case their children ever learned about the explicit videos: the couple had sold a computer at a yard sale without erasing the hard drive. Someone had found the images and posted them online. In the principal's office, Ann carefully recited the tale to the two school officials. It was not clear if they were buying the story, but the principal did not take a harsh tone. He paused for a moment and asked her how she was doing.

"I just feel embarrassed, really embarrassed that this came out," Ann said.

"Don't be embarrassed. I have the utmost respect for you and your husband and your family, there's nothing for you to feel awkward about."

She asked the school to minimize the publicity. But it was already too late. Word about the videos spread like wildfire. She typically dressed fairly conservatively, but once students heard about her wild side, they wanted a second look. Boys, ignited by the fantasy of the sexually adventurous school secretary, peeked into her office, stared at her, turned, and left.

Ann felt so uncomfortable that she quit after the semester ended and transferred to another job. She became paranoid. It seemed that everyone knew about her past effort to lead a double life. Eventually she quit working entirely. "Back before, ten years ago, when you put pictures up on the Internet, there was total anonymity. But it's not like that anymore," Tom says. "You can see now you put a picture up on the Internet and you get a guy from Harvard calling you up on your cell phone."

More than a year after I first called them, Ann and Tom separated after twenty-four years together. She said their flirtation with an Internet double life was one of the reasons for the split.

Also many months after finding Tom and Ann, I received a telephone call from a Las Vegas–area number. The woman introduced herself as a former Instant Checkmate call center worker in Las Vegas. We had spoken months before when I called to ask the company to comment on my research. She had said nothing at the time. But she had kept my number and could speak openly now that she had been dismissed. She said call center workers routinely do not give their real last names.[4] "Any emails you've ever received from them, they are from employees, of course, but it's not their actual names," she said. "That's just the way they have it designed, it's always that way."

What about the name I had spent so much time hunting down? "There is no Kristen Bright," she confirmed.[5]

Kris Kibak, the founder of Instant Checkmate, later admitted the same. He said a third-party contractor helping his company with search engine optimization created the identities for Kristen Bright and Michael Smith, who was also quoted as speaking on behalf of the company. And he said call center workers did not give their real surnames. "As you can appreciate, some people aren't keen on having information about them—for example, an arrest record—available online and can get upset," Kibak says. "Because of this, I understand that the contractor used pseudonyms rather than actual employee names for reasons related to employee safety."

He said his company did not create or instruct anyone to create the Yelp page, and he said he had not known about Ann's photo being used without her permission.[6]

The hunt for the woman who was not Kristen Bright highlighted that in the Internet age, we all leave clues about ourselves—even when attempting to hide our real identities. You may not post photos of yourself in the buff as Ann did, but we all reveal details about ourselves by leaving naked data on the Internet and in public records. It took a while to find her using a mix of old-style detective work and technology. In the future, identifying people through photos or video images will be easier and faster. Casinos will be among the businesses pushing for more intelligent "eyes in the sky," and a lot of money is at stake.

11

Thousands of Eyes

Inside the Surveillance Room

It's a typical Friday evening inside the surveillance room of the ARIA Resort and Casino. The nerve center of an $18 million security system at a five-star facility, the room evokes a high-tech, sophisticated look. As at all casinos, the cameras record vast amounts of activity every day, but actually spotting suspicious activity falls to human surveillance and security officers. At a big casino hotel, three to six people per shift watch what is happening across the thousands of cameras.

They look for certain patterns of behavior suggesting a thief or a con, and rely on internal and external databases about people. They see all the joy, the foibles, the antics of hundreds of thousands of people coming through a typical large casino on the Las Vegas Strip every week. The overwhelming majority of these people are law-abiding, but a few regularly try to cheat or steal from the casino and its patrons. At the ARIA's surveillance room, two rows of large-screen televisions line a long back wall, and a third row continues along a bank of desks where three officials monitor the screens. A supervisor watches from a central desk at the back of the room.

A burly surveillance officer with a shaved head starts studying an incident brought to his attention by a casino staffer. A slot machine player sitting next to his wife asked a cocktail waitress to bring him a bottle of mineral water. The refreshment came free of charge, a regular perk for gamblers. He handed the waitress a bill and asked for change to give her a tip. When she returned with $20 in smaller bills, he complained that he had given her $100. The officer skips back the digital video. He follows the path of the waitress from the moment the gambler hands her the money. He sees her walk to the side of the room and place the bill into a change machine. It turns out the client is not always right. The surveillance officer could make out that the waitress had put a $20 bill into the machine. The staff tell the gambler what they had seen. He responds that he must have made a mistake. They take him at his word. They have captured his name from his loyalty card in the slot machine and they log the incident, in case he makes trouble in the future.

Another incident unfolds on a different bank of surveillance monitors. Again, it is not the fast action Hollywood viewers might expect from a movie such as *Ocean's Eleven*. It shows the day-to-day reality of what happens in a casino. A young man without a shirt or shoes reclines on the floor next to one of the slot machines near the lobby entrance. A slot attendant approaches; the man stumbles to his feet. The shirtless dude had clearly been taking advantage of Vegas's reputation for indulgence of alcohol. Several security guards try to escort him off the property. But the disoriented man does not comply. He throws up in front of one of the slot machines. Eventually, guards sit him in a wheelchair and roll him out the door. As a cleaning woman arrives to erase the unfortunate mess, the surveillance officer retraces the man's steps to see where he had come from. He suspects the man had been at the hotel's pool. The video shows he had wandered in shirtless from the street on a day when the temperature was above ninety degrees. The staff also logs the incident, cognizant that sometimes criminals plan such episodes as diversions for crimes elsewhere in the casino.

The security team quickly identified the first man from his loyalty card in a machine. In this case, they do not know if the drunk is a hotel guest—thus requiring a bit more delicate treatment—or an outsider who should quickly be shown the door. Finally they ask the drunk man's companion, who appears far more sober—at least he's steady on his feet—for a driver's license.

Security officer at work in a surveillance room at the ARIA Hotel in Las Vegas.
Source: Author photo.

The List

At casinos, surveillance starts from the moment one drives into or
arrives at the property. On each level of the Caesars Palace parking lot
cameras watch the passing vehicles, allowing license recognition technology to see if one has been reported stolen or is owned by somebody
of interest.[1] Another camera behind a black dome of glass atop a pole
shaped like an upside-down letter J looms above as people step out
of their vehicles on the top floor. As they walk down several flights of
stairs, yet another camera greets them at the bottom of every stairwell.

Toward the hotel's back entrance across another large open lot, a
camera atop the building records arrivals. As people enter the elevator,
digital video records the scene. Above the well-lit ground-floor hallway,

Surveillance camera overlooking the Caesars
Palace parking lot. Source: Author photo.

another camera captures the moment. Finally, at the turn into the actual casino, an especially large dome observes.

An estimated three thousand cameras peer down on the action in a typical large casino,[2] more than in any other place in the United States.[3] They record the handbag left beside a slot machine and the smart phone misplaced on a bar counter after a flirtatious encounter. Tiny pinhole cameras mounted inside bars of the cashier's cage see who is redeeming chips. Bathrooms and guest rooms are free of surveillance, but floor and elevator cameras see who is coming and going. Electronic key readers record the exact time someone enters or exits a room and elevator cameras see arrivals on each floor. Cameras above gaming tables show enough detail to make out individual cards or a suspicious signal from players engaged in a con.

Public surveillance cameras have never appeared as omnipresent as they are today.[4] Although casinos pack in an especially concentrated number into their establishments, ever more sophisticated and afford-able cameras watch us at every turn. Private businesses and govern-ment entities in the United States and abroad deploy them in growing numbers.

Cameras can record thousands of cars pulling into the lot every day and eighty thousand or so people milling around a casino. But without details on what they are seeing, such a vast amount of visual information is not tremendously useful. Security teams hope to link all these aspects of personal data together—so that they can use photo recognition technology to identify someone and then match him to a specific file of information.

Whatever device the security staff use, they need good information to ferret out cheats and swindlers. Before the days of sophisticated electronics, Las Vegas casinos relied on old-fashioned face books with profiles of potential troublemakers. The staff would page through a binder or folder stacked with the faces of individuals who might be a little dodgy. The most famous of these folders is the "black list," officially known as the Excluded Person List of the Nevada Gaming Control Board.[5] This document lists people so undesirable that they should not be allowed even to set foot inside a casino, let alone gamble there. They are barred completely. Today, the list excludes thirty-three men and one woman for life from Nevada casinos. Some are former mobsters; others are habitual cheaters. Most are in their golden years.

In 1967 Robert Griffin, a former Las Vegas police officer, and his wife, Beverly, started assembling a separate roster of slot machine cheat-ers, swindlers, thieves, and other undesirables casinos might want to exclude. Some on the Griffin list had not committed a crime but drew attention because of borderline illegal activities such as card count-ing, a skill that may prompt a casino to "trespass" or eject its practi-tioners. So-called advantage players became an ever bigger problem in the 1970s and 1980s. Griffin also offered casinos detective services to investigate such incidents.

Over the years the list grew into an essential reference book, and then a series of books with thousands of names. The Griffin Book included police mug shots, employee photographs, and any other images Robert and Beverly could obtain, plus basic characteristics of the people, such as height and weight and their suspected scam or talent that could put a casino at risk. The Griffin volumes achieved mythic status.

The Griffin Book. Source: Beverly Griffin (reprinted with permission).

William Hinkley worked his way up the ranks in casino security from a plainclothes investigator in the mid-1980s to top security official at a succession of popular hotels. He now oversees security at the Las Vegas Hooters Casino Hotel. For much of his career, the Griffin Book was important to his work. "Some people in the day interpreted Griffin as God," he says. "In the 1980s if you were in the Griffin Book, it was almost like the black book."

Griffin Investigations, the company Robert and Beverly founded in 1967, achieved its greatest success after its information helped uncover a group of blackjack card counters from MIT who had made millions in the 1990s, including from Caesars Palace. Their story later inspired the 2008 movie *21,* starring Kevin Spacey. Things came together in the case after Griffin Investigations received a key tip. One of the card counters had a spat with the others and telephoned one of the Griffin investigators. The source revealed some of the blackjack counters were coming to town and alerted the investigator to the disguises they would wear. Those clues were enough to break the case. The MIT group had operated for so long because they represented a new kind of threat: brain power applied to card counting. "A lot of them were brilliant minds to whom this was a simple thing to do," Griffin said. "And they differed from the old gamblers in that they were young Asians and young college students who had not before been a force in Las Vegas or other gaming areas."

The publicity from the MIT case made Griffin a well-known adversary for card counters and cheats. How-to books and websites on card counting regularly referred to the Griffin Book, and memoirs by gamblers boasted of how they avoided ending up on the list or how they bested the company's scrutiny. Richard Marcus tells the world on his website that he is the "World's #1 Casino and Poker Cheating Expert."[6] He portrays Griffin as a key adversary: "I myself was often under Griffin surveillance and spotted his agents staking out my Las Vegas house several times. Griffin and his detective agency were a major pain in my ass!"

Bob Nersesian, an attorney who defends gamblers accused of wrongdoing, also wrote about Griffin Investigations in his 2006 book *Beat the Players: Casinos, Cops and the Game Inside the Game*: "Amongst advantage and professional gamblers, few persons or companies are more vilified than Griffin Investigations. Simply, they are the bad guys. Griffin Investigations makes the lives of advantage gamblers miserable." Beverly Griffin disagrees. She says she only gives casinos information. It's up to the casino to decide the gambler's fate.

In recent years Griffin's business has struggled. First of all, it ran into legal and financial troubles. Two gamblers detained at Caesars Palace and at the Imperial Palace based on information in the Griffin Book successfully sued in 2001.[7] Beverly Griffin remains bitter that her company ended up in court and was compelled to pay $300,000 in legal fees. Griffin filed for Chapter 11 bankruptcy protection in 2005, the same year Harrah's bought Caesars Palace. She owed more than $100,000 to her lawyer and more than $100,000 to those who sued her, according to court papers.

The other challenge to the dominance of the Griffin Book has come from the explosion of information in the Internet age. Technology allows casinos to identify undesirables more easily than in the past. Many rely on their own databases rather than the Griffin Book. Caesars Entertainment and MGM Resorts—which together own a large chunk of the Las Vegas Strip—no longer subscribe, although some other casinos do.[8] Griffin says she still has many clients among casinos worldwide because it is harder for regional establishments to recognize cheaters and advantage players from Las Vegas or elsewhere. The worst may have passed for Beverly Griffin. Now divorced, she runs the business without her retired husband. She says she has paid off her debts after five years. Her service has moved to the Internet, and on the advice of her attorney, she has revamped its database to sharpen its accuracy. The problem in the past, she says, was that the Griffin Book might deem someone a cheater even if he had never been convicted of a crime. Today, her seven thousand listings are more cautious in terms of what they allege.

The threat of litigation has made security teams across the industry more cautious. In the days of mob influence in Las Vegas, security officials might have taken a suspected cheater or card counter to a back room to mete out a warning on the spot. It seems obligatory for films about Las Vegas to re-create such scenes. Griffin says such frontier justice ended in the 1970s. Nowadays, multimillion-dollar casinos would not risk losing their license to beat up a card counter.

With corporations trying to maintain a good public image, security officials do all they can to avoid lawsuits. They do not even like to accuse someone of counting cards. Likewise, security and surveillance officials are more reserved about swapping information with other casinos. They don't want to face lawsuits because of information they shared about a gambler. So even if there is more information readily available than in the past, the threat of litigation has tempered its distribution.

Video Recognition

In recent years, some casinos and other businesses have begun linking video recognition technology to their surveillance systems. Sure, a good surveillance officer can spot patterns of suspicious behavior and known troublemakers. Some remember faces from months or even years before. Yet with newcomers showing up every day, they cannot know the background of the overwhelming majority of the people on the casino floor. In the future, technologists hope, photo recognition will easily and accurately connect faces engaged in suspicious behavior with the names and files of those who have committed previous offenses.

Some security veterans look with awe at how such software has the potential to make their jobs ever easier. Yet in truth, the technology is still far from an all-knowing Big Brother. One leading company that sells photo recognition and security management software to casinos is called iView Systems. James Moore, the Canadian company's vice president, says facial identification correctly identifies 60–80 percent of people of interest to casino security teams. The problem remains a high rate of false positives—instances when the system thinks it recognizes a suspicious person but is, in fact, mistaken.

Using the iView Systems software, a typical large Las Vegas casino gets fifty to sixty genuine alerts a day. When such notifications produce a correct match in a database of people of interest, the security staff must decide what to do. The final decision is always made by someone who confirms the match. The computer also generates two hundred to five hundred false alerts per day, Moore says. That means for every ten alerts, only one may be of real concern. Part of the problem remains the quality of old photos scanned into the system. If a casino has only grainy images of people who have done something in the past, the system may not be able to recognize them.

Sometimes the technology is stunningly far off. Tom Flynn, head of security and surveillance at Caesars Palace, said he has seen photo recognition suggest a black woman as a match when he was searching for a white man. Such instances have turned some old-time security pros into skeptics. Dave Shepherd moved to Las Vegas thirty-five years ago to work for the FBI. He still maintains a no-nonsense manner befitting an official who once worked on cases against mob figures such as Frank "Lefty" Rosenthal. After leaving the FBI, Shepherd took a job heading up security at the Venetian Resort Hotel and Casino; he now works as a private security consultant. He is characteristically blunt when it comes to assessing photo recognition technology: "It doesn't work," he says. "Cameras can't recognize a typical person. The best way is still people on the ground."

Things may change, of course. Many companies are trying to develop more efficient systems. Some executives also believe photo and video recognition abilities could help improve service. If cameras could recognize the license plate number of a big roller driving up, the casino could promptly dispatch a favorite host. Such technology could alert department stores to the arrival of regular shoppers so that their favorite salespeople can be available to greet them. Stores are increasingly tracking shoppers electronically as they peruse the aisles. As with a lot of personal data, some people will welcome the attention while others will not. Many now accept that, whether we like it or not, giving away personal data in visual form is part of living in a modern society. Yet for others, the thought of being tracked by cameras, perhaps augmented by signals from a cell phone, is downright creepy.

A well-oiled customer service machine recognizing people in real time would require considerably more sophistication than is presently available. Not just a database with mug shots and detailed reports on tens of thousands of people of interest, a client-greeting system would have to incorporate millions of files. Also, it would need far fewer false positives to make sure the red carpet is rolled out for the right people.

Gary Loveman says it is useful to know when his best customers are at Caesars, and that they like to be recognized. But he does not see photo recognition playing a role for customer service. "I can't imagine in the foreseeable future that that would be better for us than lots of other things that we would want to do," he says. In any case, a casino usually knows when its best customers are arriving. Frequently the management has flown them into town for free, or sent a limo to pick them up.[9] At other times, high rollers announce themselves at the host office, or just hand in their elite-status loyalty card.

Ted Whiting, director of surveillance at the ARIA, says the dream of an all-knowing photo recognition system is still over the horizon, but it will come. "It's not as sexy as everybody thinks," he says. But he believes that as camera resolution improves over the next few years, security staff will be able to routinely recognize who's who on the casino floor. Then no one will be able to hide from the eyes in the casino skies.

Photo recognition technology could work best initially to identify staffers, who are well photographed and documented in advance. In addition to watching their clients, casino security teams devote a great deal of effort toward monitoring and nabbing their own staff members. In fact, casinos typically point more cameras on employees than on guests. Temptations surround workers at every turn: piles of cash and chips, mounds of expensive food, bars stocked with high-end liquor. A staffer may hope that no one notices when a few chips have been squirreled away or steaks stored in the freezer. Bartenders seek to boost their own tips by not so inadvertently forgetting to charge for drinks. The count room makes for some of the most monotonous watching, as staffers pile bills, and then more bills, and then ever more bills, into automated counters to determine how much cash is on hand. However dull the video may appear, the scene draws continuous monitoring, as does the cage where gamblers exchange chips for cash.

Mike Pfahler is director of corporate security and surveillance at Fifth Street Gaming. A former chief of police in a Pennsylvania town of three thousand, he has just 150 cameras in his small casino, the Silver Nugget. Located on the far north end of the Strip, beyond where tourists venture, it's a world apart from Caesars Palace, Wynn, Bellagio, and the other big hotels. The terrain up there looks more like a rugged desert landscape, and things can turn a bit rough. Over the years Pfahler has seen murders, drug deals, thefts, and other incidents at various casinos.[10] Crime also extends to the casino staff. On days when nothing else is happening, he goes into his surveillance room and watches staff members for suspicious behavior. "Nothing happens here that I don't see," he says.

Operating the eyes in the sky does not make Pfahler a popular guy, and his casino is small enough that everyone knows who he is. By 2014, the advance of connected technology made it possible for him to monitor all four of his company's casinos from his Silver Nugget office, receiving video images from three hundred cameras on his laptop or smart phone.[11] Even if he is further from some of the action than he once was, he still takes precautions. He carries a gun at all times, and worries that the widespread availability of personal information could put someone in his position at risk. He says it makes him sick to think that people can Google his name and locate his house. Some have threatened to kill him. "My kids often say to me, 'Dad, why don't you have any friends?' I get people fired, I get people arrested," he tells them.

But in the future, patrons and staff caught in the act of wrongdoing will probably have fewer people to blame when they are caught. Instead, they will curse the technology that leads to their downfall.

A Facebook Clue

Because cheats, thieves, and card counters often work in groups to outsmart casino operations, security officials have also embraced social networks to discern clues about suspects and their possible associates.

One day at the New York-New York casino in Las Vegas, a player at a slot machine caught the attention of a floor supervisor. The man placed his loyalty card into the slot machine. The card holder turned green, and the man entered in a PIN code. He selected the word "Freeplay" and used bonus points provided by the casino as an incentive to customers. After a while, he cashed out his winnings, then removed the card. He inserted another card and repeated the process, over and over again.

The supervisor stepped up to the machine. "Sir, let me see what you are doing," he said.

The man held a cigarette pack stuffed with twenty-two loyalty cards, each holding bonus credits allowing him to bet without paying any money. Because each player receives only one card, he could have no justification for possessing so many. The casino official led the man to a hotel detention room. Las Vegas police arrived and arrested him for theft.

The case puzzled casino officials at MGM Resorts International, which owns New York-New York, the ARIA, and many other casinos in Las Vegas. Searching a database of known troublemakers, they found nothing about the arrested man. The ruse involved considerable sophistication. The player had gained access to accounts with genuine Freeplay points. Betting the casino's bonus currency, he won real money. When another man bailed the player out of jail, a background search of that person still did not generate any red flags. Then security officials looked at the Facebook page of the man who had posted the bail money. One detail stood out in particular. Among several hundred Facebook friends appeared the name of Tony Ahn, an MGM database manager. Ahn had worked in the department overseeing Freeplay points for the company's customers.

Looking at Ahn's Facebook page, investigators discovered several friends who seemed familiar from the investigation. It turned out they were involved in the scheme. After police arrested someone in his team in 2010, Ahn told two others to go into the desert and bury a card encoder, counterfeit loyalty cards, and other evidence. The effort, almost a crime cliché in a city surrounded by desert, failed.

Police pieced together what had happened. Starting in 2009, Ahn had gained access to the Freeplay points a few weeks before they were to expire (like many airline miles and other reward credits, the points had a limited period of validity). He hoped that thousands of real owners of the points would not return to claim them. He allocated the points to blank cards he placed in the encoding machine and distributed the cards to his accomplices: twenty-two cards fitted into a cigarette pack.[12] The former MGM Resorts official was indicted in early 2011; the following year a judge sentenced Ahn, then twenty-nine, to fifty-seven months in prison and ordered him to pay $863,895 in restitution.[13] He is scheduled for release from federal prison at the end of 2016.

A lot of good old-fashioned police work went into solving the case. But the social network postings gave investigators the essential clue that exposed the conspiracy. "Without Facebook we probably would have never caught him," says Whiting, the surveillance director at the ARIA.[14] Tony Ahn learned the hard way that social network sites contain important clues about people and their behavior. Even innocent postings on Facebook can reveal surprising insights about a person, just as Harry Lewis had predicted when his student Mark Zuckerberg experimented with his first social network.

Surveillance cameras, photo recognition technology, social networks—all these things have given security teams new tools to discover people's identities and associations. Yet some old techniques remain a staple of their arsenal. For decades, casino security and surveillance staffs have kept mug shots of known criminals on hand—whether from the Griffin Book or police—to alert them to potential trouble. Police and security officials rely on them to recognize repeat offenders and process documentation. Today, mug shots also fuel a darker corner behind the data curtain. Entrepreneurs make money by publicizing the arrest records of millions of Americans. It's a shadowy world where the website owners do not reveal themselves to the public, fearing for their own safety. Yet one mug shot king was willing to share the often surprising behind-the-scenes story of his business.

12

Mugged

Mob Museum

After years of planning, in 2012 Las Vegas opened its Mob Museum, which chronicles the desert city's rich criminal past. Visitors start their tour in the mug shot/lineup room, where they are invited to step behind a one-way mirror. As they hold up faux police placards inscribed with numbers, friends and family members on the other side of the glass take photos. A sign above the lineup reads: "How did it come to this?"

Tourists find the whole spectacle highly entertaining. It's a joke they willingly engage in. But it's no joke when your mug shot is publicized for real.

The widespread availability of your personal data today means that others can find out not just about some of the happiest days of your life, such as when you got married or bought your house, but also the moments you would like to be allowed to forget. This latter kind of data has become more common as websites gathering and displaying mug shots have proliferated. In the realm of personal data, mug shots are especially powerful and damaging because they record what may be the lowest point of a person's life. Once upon a time, only the famous or the infamous would expect to see their mug shot turn up in public. Now entrepreneurs have found a way to make money from the arrest photos of ordinary people.

Police started taking mug shots as photography developed in the mid-nineteenth century. Since then, notorious criminals, as well as the

Tourists line up for mug shots at the Mob Museum in Las Vegas.
Source: Author photo.

rich and famous, have faced the constable's camera, including Michael Jackson, Mick Jagger, Frank Sinatra, Barry Bonds, Hugh Grant, Mel Gibson, and Martin Luther King Jr. On my last visit to Las Vegas, O. J. Simpson posed anew ahead of his latest courtroom appearances. Yet the vast bulk of mug shots one encounters on the Internet show ordinary people, many of whom have never actually been convicted of a crime.

How did it come to this?

Dispute Over $3.68 on a Restaurant Bill

One summer Saturday afternoon in 2007, Paola Roy and a friend joined a third woman for a late lunch at the House of India restaurant in Coral Gables, Florida. Roy had already eaten but wanted to keep her friend company, so she ordered a small $5.95 portion of spicy black lentils and naan bread. At the end of the meal she asked for a doggie bag. When the bill came the restaurant had charged her $9.95 for the larger portion of lentils. She refused to pay the higher amount and left $22 in cash on the table—$3.68 short of what the owner thought she should pay. He called the police.

The women left the restaurant and headed toward their cars in a garage. As she arrived, Roy saw a police officer on a bicycle dressed in spandex shorts. He signaled that she should approach him. Her heart pounded and she froze, prompting the officer to rush up a parking ramp toward her.

"I hear you skipped out on a check," he said.

"Well, someone lied to you," she replied.

She held a Styrofoam container with the extra lentils in her left hand as she explained the dispute. Several police cars arrived on the scene. One officer went over to interview the restaurant owner. Eventually the officer who had arrived by bike asked, "Are you going to pay the bill in full?"

"No."

"You are going to have to pay the $3.68 difference or I am going to arrest you."

"It was the restaurant owner's mistake. I don't feel I owe him the money, and I am not going to pay him. There is no reason for me to pay this bill."

He took out his handcuffs and grabbed her left wrist. Roy's friend yelled out that she would pay the difference. But Roy, angry about the way she was being treated, looked over at the officer's identification tag and read aloud his name.

"I want to see who is arresting me for three dollars and sixty-eight cents."

"Oh yeah? That's it, I'm taking you in."

He cuffed Roy's right hand and led her down the parking ramp, then into the backseat of a patrol car. She had never gotten in trouble with the law other than a few traffic tickets. As they drove to the station, Roy felt a moment of regret, then anger and defiance, as she replayed what had just happened to her. Police booked her and announced they would take her mug shot. She had come to the restaurant from the beach, so she had pulled back her hair and did not wear any lipstick or jewelry. The officer told her to remove her glasses and snapped the photo. She felt grateful that she might look a bit better in the image without glasses.

Some time later, officers removed her from the cell and drove her to a jail downtown, charged with "defrauding innkeeper." She arrived at 6:45 p.m., hours after her lunch, but the sun had yet to set. In the arrival area she saw a van of inmates arriving, many of the men unshaven and dirty, some with tattoos and holes in their clothes as though they had been fighting. She spent hours in a holding cell with other women who expressed amazement upon hearing how she came to be arrested. She was released from jail on bail at 5 a.m. the following morning. Prosecutors ended up dropping the charges soon afterward, and the matter seemed forgotten.

Starting a Mug Shot Business

The following year in Austin, Texas, Kyle Prall started a job as a financial analyst at Electric Reliability Council of Texas (ERCOT), which operates the electric grid for much of the state. He had gone through a lot of trouble as a teenager and young man, but those days were behind him now. He landed the position just before the financial crisis hit, costing millions of American workers their jobs. Las Vegas casinos were hit particularly hard; thousands of workers were fired as gamblers stayed home and saved their pennies.

Despite his relative good fortune in tough times, however, Prall remained restless. He found his finance work mind-numbing and meaningless. Around that time a friend told him about a Florida newspaper that published pictures of sex offenders. "That makes a lot of sense," he thought. "This is something I can do in my spare time." Prall's true calling was coming into focus.

Prall decided to publish a local newspaper that would display mug shots of ordinary citizens arrested for crimes both serious and not. For that he would need lots of images, so he turned to the local police department. Prall emailed the Austin police. He did not mention why he wanted the images.

"Hello Don, my name is Kyle Prall and I would like to inquire about an open records request for booking photos and booking information for every individual arrested for an entire previous week," he said in an email.[1] "I realize this is a rather large request, so I thought it would be a good idea to work out a couple details to make this request as easy for you as possible and as efficient as possible for myself as well.

"I would likely need to set this up on a weekly recurring basis."

Six days later Austin Police Department official Don Field wrote back. He offered a price tag of $1 an image—reasonable for a single image, prohibitive for a large archive of photos. Prall, after long hours researching the state's open records laws, filed a complaint. The police lowered the charge to 10 cents and then even lower, to about $90 a week for all the records he wanted. Neighboring Williamson County asked for $60 a week. He had obtained the first of what would eventually become millions of mug shots for his personal-data business.

Even as he gained access to the mug shots, Prall faced the uphill task of creating a traditional print newspaper at a disastrous time for the industry. Amid an anemic economy in 2008 and 2009, dozens of regional papers had folded. But more locals were committing crimes, giving the paper a steady supply of new faces. Initially, Prall hoped to do original reporting for the paper, which he called *Busted! In Austin*.[2] Eventually he settled on just publishing mug shots alongside descriptions of a few top crimes of the week. In May 2009, he printed two thousand copies of the first issue, and managed to get about seven hundred of them into stores. He had invested roughly $5,000 in the venture, and wondered if he was crazy to have done so.

Lured by the newspaper's subject and offbeat motto ("Getting arrested isn't funny . . . but the mug shots are"), people bought the paper—for $1 a copy. All the issues distributed to stores sold out. The next week stores took the full *Busted! In Austin* print run of two thousand copies. The new paper attracted a lot of attention. Local television featured it. Prall carefully remained out of the public eye, unmentioned in his own newspaper.

Within a year or two the paper hit a peak of about ten thousand sales of a single issue. In 2011 Prall bought the website domain bustedinaustin.com, the start of a migration online. In April, with the backing of new investor Ryan Russell (and after parting ways with his old partner), Prall launched another website—bustedmugshots.com— which posted mug shots from across the country. With the newspaper, a reader might randomly come across a friend, neighbor, or acquaintance whose mug shot appeared that week. Yet with about eight hundred thousand people living in Austin, most residents would never see the image, even if thousands read the paper every week. The Internet changed everything, because now anyone looking someone up would easily stumble upon his or her mug shot.

The wallop came from a few lines of code on each mug shot that ensured that the images would appear prominently in Internet searches for the names of those involved. Anyone clicking would be directed to bustedmugshots.com. The site declared it sought to improve public awareness of crime and perhaps generate tips to solve open cases.[3] But it stirred up great controversy because Prall decided to charge people to remove their images: $68 to erase an image within ten business days, or $108 to remove it within twenty-four hours. The idea of accepting payment to remove the booking photos, Prall says, was almost an accident—lawyers working for some of the people pictured in the mug shots started making demands and threats to get the images taken down, but one lawyer offered to pay $50 to have an image removed.

Ryan Russell reacted uneasily to the suggestion at first. "I don't know, guys, it doesn't seem right," he said. Yet the company was forking out thousands of dollars a month in legal bills to fight threats against the site, so Russell relented and embraced the plan. Prall saw the payments as a way to get the lawyers off their back. His site advertised the removal payments as "a reasonable fee that will cover our costs."

Anyone found not guilty of the charges could remove the images without charge. Officially, the company only allowed those arrested on nonviolent charges to remove their photos.[4] However, the company did not always follow this policy. When I called in 2012 to ask a call center attendant if I could remove the images of a man charged with murdering his father and brother and wounding his mother in Georgia, the attendant said yes. Prall says he has since retrained his staff to follow the firm's written guidelines on serious crimes.

A Bad Breakup

In late 2012, a friend called Paola Roy with an unusual question: "Have you Googled yourself recently?" She told Roy that her 2007 mug shot had all of a sudden started appearing prominently in search results. Roy worried that the image would complicate her efforts to find a new job. She seethed with anger toward Busted! and Kyle Prall. "It's not a public service to have others believe that I am some kind of a criminal," she said. "I should not have been arrested. I was not prosecuted or convicted of anything, so why is he ruining my life?"

Another whose images appeared on the site was Janet LaBarba, whose drunk-driving arrest came on a night of personal trouble. Over dinner and two glasses of wine in a fancy Dallas restaurant, the divorced wedding planner's boyfriend announced he was breaking up with her. They went home. She left her home and drove a short distance to visit a friend.

A driver who can make passengers uneasy even when sober in the light of day, LaBarba did not notice blinking traffic lights or the stop sign across the street from Whole Foods as she returned home around midnight.[5] A police officer whose flashing lights had not grabbed her attention as she drove followed her into her driveway. After she got out of the car he conducted a sobriety test.

She watched as the officer waved a pen back and forth. She then heard him declare that she exhibited slow eye movement. The officer hauled her down to the station, took her photo, and charged her with drunk driving. LaBarba already knew the drill: police had arrested her six months before for drunk driving, on another night when she had argued with her boyfriend.

The DUI arrests landed LaBarba in jail for a few days each time, and she had to wear an ankle monitor transmitting her whereabouts for five months. She also forked out $20,000 in legal fees. LaBarba's image appeared on bustedmugshots.com four times, even though she had only two arrests. By coding LaBarba's photographs, the site got them to surface at the top of online searches for her name. "It completely screwed with my life," she says. "People Googled me and it was very embarrassing."

For LaBarba, appearing on Prall's website has stung more than her punishment. She would rather have learned her lesson privately without the world knowing about her mistakes. She paid to make the photos go away.

The charges against Roy were quickly dropped, but Busted! twice refused her request to remove the image. Roy insisted she should not have to pay. "I can pay and have it removed and then it will pop up next year and I'll have to pay to have it removed and it will pop up another year, so I feel I could be doing this ad infinitum," she said. "As you can see I'm willing to go to jail for $3. I'm not going to let these people get away with this." She sent in her documentation a third time, and finally the site removed the image.

Whether they paid to remove their images or not, many who appeared on the site became angry when they learned that Prall himself had a long arrest record and troubled past yet seemed to show so little sympathy for their plights.

Restless Youth

A native of Bloomington, Illinois, the home of State Farm Insurance, Prall has held many jobs in his more than thirty years. As a boy he would occasionally help out on his grandparents' farm. In junior high school in the early 1990s, he woke before dawn to deliver the local newspaper, and later he added a second job serving food in a nursing home. With good grades at school and a father who worked as a local district court judge, Prall projected the image of an all-American boy.

He lived in middle-class comfort, yet he felt restless. In high school, Prall used his paperboy earnings to buy alcohol and marijuana. His clean-cut appearance impressed his dealer, who eventually suggested that he should try selling weed himself at his high school. The money was very good for a high school kid. He had earned about $100 a week delivering newspapers, yet he could make five times as much, sometimes even more, dealing marijuana. With a sharp mind for both schoolwork and entrepreneurship, Prall learned the new trade quickly. "After a while it became second nature," he said.

Prall impressed his peers and teachers as bright, and he maintained his good grades. He wasn't an athlete or a member of the popular crowd, but dealing made him a big man on campus. Everyone knew his name. The job brought the added advantage that he could smoke as much weed as he liked.

Over time, Prall expanded his reach to other high schools and even Illinois State University. A good friend helped out and encouraged him to present a tougher façade. When classmates' parents went out of town, Prall and his fellow dealers offered to sponsor parties at their homes. They would foot the bill for kegs and then take up residence in a corner, taking in hundreds or even thousands of dollars in a night in entrance fees. By promising to make the host kid popular overnight, they uncovered a steady stream of houses for their events.

The fact that Prall was up to something did not escape his parents' notice. His mother occasionally found large wads of cash in his room. She and Prall's father suspected he was running with a dubious crowd. At one point his father, who in his courtroom had seen what happened to kids who ran afoul of the law, confronted Prall. "I think you're up to something," the elder Prall told his son. "If you keep it up, you're going to get in trouble."

Prall ignored the warnings. He kept dealing all through high school, raking in tens of thousands of dollars. Still, when his friend branched out into cocaine, Prall stuck to weed. He feared trouble from the kind of people who bought cocaine. Good grades and a solid middle-class background helped keep Prall below the radar. Even with all the extra-curricular dealing, Prall graduated in the top 10 percent of his class. The University of Illinois at Urbana-Champaign accepted him, and he planned to matriculate in the fall and major in finance.

That summer, Prall moved out of his parents' house and into a cheap summer sublet he shared with some high school friends. It was a rite of passage for newly minted high school graduates in Bloomington, who got their first taste of living on their own by taking up residence in houses vacated by the city's college kids. One July day he was relaxing with a friend on the porch when plainclothes detectives arrived: "We're looking for Kyle Prall."

The cops told Prall they had to take him downtown because he had an outstanding traffic ticket. It wasn't the first time Prall had been hauled to the station. The previous arrests had all been for relatively minor violations too, like underage drinking. He always seemed to have a beer in his hand when police raided parties. But this time it was different.

He knew things were bad when officers took him through the back door. They took his mug shot and led him down a long hallway lined by holding cells. Prall recognized many of the shoes lined up outside the cell doors. The authorities had nabbed almost all his drug-dealing friends. But as Prall looked around the room, he noticed that one pair of shoes was missing. His good friend who had helped show him the ropes in the business had escaped arrest.

As he sat in his jail cell, Prall thought back to an episode that he now realized had led to his downfall. One cold winter day the previous winter, his pal had telephoned and said he had run out of marijuana and had to buy in bulk. Prall headed to his house, albeit a bit grumpily, as wholesale distribution meant far less profit than dealing to individual customers. A few blocks from the house, Prall noticed a Ford Crown Victoria parked on the side of the road. A man was sitting inside, reading a newspaper. "There is no way that guy is just sitting in his car reading his newspaper," Prall thought.

Prall called his friend and told him what he had seen. Perhaps he should not come over, he suggested. By that point in his dealing career, Prall had developed an instinct for signs of trouble. Yet he remained gullible enough to trust his savvy partner, who had already served time in juvenile detention. "It's okay, come on over," the friend assured him.

When Prall arrived, he found his friend acting a bit stiffly. Something was not right about the way he was talking when Prall handed him the marijuana he wanted to buy. "It's a quarter-pound, right?" he asked a few times. Prall didn't know it, but that was the day the other teen had become a police informant. That winter visit was one of four during which the friend gathered evidence against Prall using a wire taped to his chest.

The friend-turned-informant had grown up on the poorer side of town, and he had not received the same breaks in life. His father worked as a manual laborer, a world away from the courts of Prall's father. Prall knew his friend got along poorly with his father and step-mother, and he was always looking for a way to make a fast buck. At the Catholic school he attended, he stole lunch tickets and sold them to other kids for half price. He also pinched the answers to tests and made a tidy sum selling them. In fifth grade, his Catholic school kicked him out.[6]

Most of the students avoided the kid. But there was something about him that appealed to Prall, who had an innate rebellious streak. As he hit puberty Prall chafed at the well-off middle-class life he had enjoyed. His new friend, on the other hand, seemed to be the ballsy, live-for-the-day kind of kid Prall wished he was. Additionally, he used his outside earnings to dress flashily, and that appealed to Prall.

The two started out in business together in the seventh grade, when both took on newspaper delivery routes. On busy days they would lend each other a hand. They also got together after school to get into mischief. The friend seemed to bring out Prall's wild side. The two would go out and steal other kids' candy on Halloween or shoot wa-ter balloons, vegetables, and other objects at people with a powerful long-distance slingshot.

The friend typically led the way. In the summer before high school he started dealing small amounts of marijuana, charging $5 a joint. Over time Prall grew curious, and late in his freshman year he started smoking weed. The amount his friend earned from dealing began to impress him. It looked like easy money. Hardened by a tougher up-bringing, he schooled Prall in street savvy. Prall impressed his friend with how quickly he picked up the business. But the tougher kid couldn't figure out why someone with so much going for him would risk it all to sell dope.

"Your family's well-off," he said to Prall one day. "You're guaranteed to go to college. You're smart as fuck. Why in the world do you want to sell drugs and hang out with these scumbags?"

Prall had a ready reply: "Because it's fucking boring, dude. It's fucking boring hanging out with fucking dorks."

In December 1996, their son's senior year, the friend's father and stepmother discovered a stash of marijuana in their basement. It was the last straw after a series of troubling incidents. They had been trying to get him to shape up for years and worried about what would happen if he had to go to jail as an adult. They knew a detective and decided that their best hope was to try to work out some kind of a deal. Prall's friend was trapped. He had turned eighteen earlier that year. If he was arrested, there was no more juvenile hall. To avoid jail, he agreed to entrap other dealers by wearing a wire.

The friend-turned-informant recorded a series of conversations with Prall, and the evidence was irrefutable. Prall pleaded guilty to one felony count out of four original charges. The legal process dragged on for months, giving him enough time to finish his first term of freshman year at college before serving his time. That term Prall earned an A plus in a philosophy course on logic and reasoning.[7] In 1998, as his classmates headed off to their summer jobs, Prall turned himself in to the DeWitt County jail. After sixty days, he was set free. He also paid $1,550 in fines.

At the University of Illinois, Prall majored in finance and held part-time jobs delivering pizzas, working as a waiter, and helping at construction sites. Although he also got into several minor scrapes with the law, Prall graduated from college with an overall B-plus average. After studying with flash cards at the gym, in classes, and at coffee shops, he passed the Certified Public Accountant exam in 2002. With his criminal record, Prall did not find it easy to get hired, but a friend of his father's granted him an interview to work at his accounting firm. He started the job in the late summer after college, but quickly grew disillusioned with conventional work. "Absolutely hated it. It was mind-numbingly boring," he says.

In the years that followed, Prall drifted through a series of jobs. He analyzed credit reports for a Chicago-area bank, moved to Cleveland

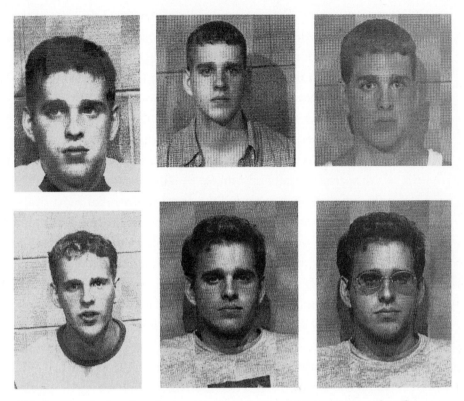

Kyle Prall's mug shots from his younger days. Source: McLean County Sheriff's Office.

and then New York, where he landed a job at a small investment bank specializing in bankruptcy restructuring. He was earning $100,000 a year, enough to afford a fifth-floor walkup apartment on Manhattan's Upper East Side. He met many clients and began to think big. "You know what? I could do what these guys do. Why am I not sitting on that side of the table?" he wondered. He decided to call it quits and moved in with a friend in Austin, Texas, looking for new opportunities.

Mug Shot Empire

Prall's personal-data empire lies in an office park overlooking downtown Austin, the Texas capital. The company does not list its address on its website or in local directories, and workers treat their location as a corporate secret. The sign on the door offers no indication of the company's business and could easily belong to a lawyer's or insurance office.[8] The desire for anonymity is explained by Ryan Russell, Prall's chief investor: "I'm tired of death threats. I've never dealt with something this controversial. I've never dealt with something that made me fear for my personal safety."

Inside, the atmosphere differs little from that of a typical startup. Computer engineers tap away on their keyboards in a large open space ringed by sparsely decorated offices. By 2014 bustedmugshots.com had gathered more than forty million arrest records. For most of the company's history it made money in part by charging people to pull their files from the service. That, understandably, outraged some of its targets, who think such a service is little more than an extortion racket.

Paola Roy and Janet LaBarba are just two of millions whose images appeared prominently in Internet searches thanks to Prall's company. Images posted by users on Facebook, Flickr, or other sites typically do not have the same sophisticated coding as Busted! uses, so they fall lower down in Internet searches.

Prall says he is performing a public service by publicizing the photos and helping those arrested on minor charges by allowing the removal of images. "We're not forcing you to pay for anything," Prall says. "To me it's not a dagger in the heart. It's a public record: it belongs to the public."

With twelve million to fourteen million arrests in the United States every year, most commonly for drugs, theft, and drunk driving, Prall has plenty of public records to chase, plenty of people to humiliate.[9] In total, the FBI maintains fingerprints and criminal histories on seventy-six million people.[10]

Prall defends posting images of people like Roy, even for such trifling matters. "We do not feel it should be up to us to decide which cases are worthy of meeting a nebulous standard of 'serving public good,' so we instead allow the citizens to make those kind of judgment calls themselves," he says. "Unlike the traditional media that cherry-picks the cases they cover based on their marketability, we make as much information as possible without filtering or putting an editorial spin on the incident. Of course, some cases will be more serious than others, but that is a very subjective standard that we do not feel is our place to define."

Why do local agencies provide Busted! any mug shots at all? Government bodies have long distributed public records in an effort to provide openness about their activities. Each US state and court system maintains its own open records rules, but for many decades they have collected an increasing amount of personal documents and typically made them available to the public.[11]

Before electronic records, obtaining a personal record or a mug shot required going down to a city office or courthouse to fetch the record manually, or making a request by mail, a process that could take weeks. Nowadays, many of these documents are instantly available.

Prall has developed a routine to vacuum up mug shots. Using a polite tone, he demands that local police departments provide him photos. If that fails, he drafts appeals and complaints to supervisory state boards. His relentless requests irritate many. "I deal with a lot of distasteful people, and he's right at the top of that list," says Les Moore, legal adviser to the Irving, Texas, police department. "This guy's been a pain in my backside for a number of years." Bustedmugshots.com tells visitors that it is "a valuable asset to local law enforcement" that has led to breakthroughs in crime investigations. Many local officials disagree. They object to the site's profit motive. And though they do not show much sympathy for the lawbreakers in their jails, they do not necessarily believe in public shaming either. Mostly, however, they don't believe the site offers much of a public service.

Like others in the Wild West of the Internet age, Prall is testing the limits of the business of personal data, where secrets are harder to keep than ever before. "I wonder what Kyle Prall tells his family and friends that he does for a living. Does he tell them that he deliberately tries to hurt others so that he hopes to profit from the pain he induces?" wrote Eric Turkewitz, a New York lawyer who maintains a blog on legal issues.[12]

Legal experts say future court cases and legislation may curtail some of the traffic in personal data. Claire Dawson-Brown, assistant district attorney in Travis County, Texas, where Busted! is based, says she is concerned that criminal data sites sometimes have incorrect information and are not forced to comply with state expunction orders to destroy certain cases from the criminal records. "If you get arrested for a felony offense, it can ruin your life," she says. "Now that this information is out there, it is ever more horrific for people to get their lives back together. . . . How do you get this garbage out of there?"

Although he is open about his criminal past, Prall understands the sentiment. He is sensitive to the impact of his own checkered youth. In 2010 he asked the Illinois governor for clemency regarding his drug felony conviction. "My felony conviction has made it very difficult for me to obtain a job in many areas of business that I am trained for, and also hurts my chances for future advancement in my career," he wrote in his petition.

Prall's high school friend-turned-informant shares similar concerns, albeit in more colorful language. He condemns Prall for shaming people on the web. "He could fuck with people's careers. Come on, you could have a job for ten years and then all of a sudden his mug shot pops up and they did not know about it and they lose their job because of it," he says. "I've got a kid, I've got a job. I don't need my job knowing that I was arrested. I mean, I lose my job, I lose my house, you know? How am I supposed to support my family now because somebody wants to blackmail me with putting my shit up on Google? I mean, it really is unethical, it really is."

Anyone can sell personal information on the Internet and affect millions of lives. With few regulations governing their activities, entrepreneurs have set up a number of mug shot sites in recent years. Busted! has become a leader in a field where the major players typically stay hidden, their stories unknown. Prall at least had the courage to tell his story in depth and in plain sight, unlike most of the others who traffic in damaging personal data.

In business terms, Prall has succeeded in gaining attention and building a base for the future. Already by late 2012, he said people were clicking on the site two million times a month, and more than one hundred thousand subscribers paid $8.99 a month.[13] Prall was spending $15,000 a month just to operate a call center in Costa Rica. The company also employed seven people in the Austin office.

Prall and Ryan Russell said they would like to transform their company into a major source of citizen tips to help solve crimes, a sort of Internet version of John Walsh's television program *America's Most Wanted*. To this end they created a new website, bustedgrid.com, which advertises itself as a "crime information network" allowing users to look up arrest reports and related information such as criminal incident maps of neighborhoods and sex offender alerts. "The mug shots are a hook to get the public interested," Prall says. "There's got to be some kind of hook."

Prall nonchalantly ignores criticism and ridicule of his work. Russell, however, admits to being less thick-skinned and more worried about transforming the firm into a more useful criminal data site. "In a perfect world we wouldn't remove anybody," he says. Russell thinks Busted! is a cut above the other mug shot websites, of which there are quite a few. "Did it begin as something that was lowbrow? Yes, we did. Can we transform it to a beacon of integrity? I think we can," Russell says. "I don't think we are in the mug shots space. We're in the criminal data space.

"In five years you'll see Kyle's name more in the lights of John Walsh rather than—what's the name of the guy at *Hustler*?—Larry Flynt." Walsh, the father of a boy who was brutally murdered in 1981, says his long-running television show has led to the capture of more than 1,200 fugitives.

After I met Prall, officials at the Las Vegas Metropolitan Police Department showed me around the booking station, where they process arrests. A steady stream of detainees, each with hands cuffed to a chain around the waist, arrived in a corner of one room. A police official in front of a computer captured the images with a mounted digital camera. Three bright lights on the ceiling illuminated the scene. One man had no previous record but was caught driving with a suspended license. Others had extensive drug and criminal records. A captain in the central booking bureau emphasized that his department does

Kyle Prall at the state capitol in Austin, Texas, in front of portraits of state legislators. Source: Author photo.

not cooperate with Busted! Staff provide mug shots only to recognized media outlets on a case-by-case basis.[14] He made it clear he found such online businesses distasteful. At least as far as mug shots are concerned, what happens in Vegas really does stay in Vegas.

In late 2012 Prall traveled to Las Vegas. Like so many others, he was hoping to realize a dream. For him the goal was not winning in the casino but gaining respectability by attending a Crime Stoppers conference. He met with law enforcement officials to convince them that Busted! could help in the fight against crime. He left the event so enthusiastic that he issued a press release. "Our participation in the event was a great experience. Crime Stoppers understood the Busted! Grid vision and fully embraced what we are doing," he wrote.[15] Soon afterward he started calling Busted! "the premier crime information network."[16]

Despite the upbeat words, 2013 turned out to be a rather difficult year for Prall. Class-action lawsuits against mug shot websites gathered force.[17] Leading credit card companies said they would stop processing payments to remove mug shots, and Google changed its search results to give less prominence to these images. The long-running tabloid television show *Inside Edition* hunted Prall down in Austin to confront him about his website.[18] During this whole time, Prall was mostly silent. He had always kept a low public profile, but in 2012 he had agreed to share his story for this book. He had visited me at Harvard that year, and we had participated in two public lectures together. I had also visited him in Austin. But in 2013, he went incommunicado except for an occasional email. Finally, at the end of that year, he got back in touch.

Busted! had changed its policy, he said. The company would display all new mug shots for fifteen days; those of violent or serious offenders would stay up for thirty days. After that, people could opt out of having their records appear in search engine results free of charge, although subscribers to Busted! could still view the record.

"We made the change in part for the merchant processing difficulties we were experiencing, and the frivolous lawsuits," he said, referring to the credit card payment issues and legal challenges. "The decision was also based on the fact that this has been our plan all along, to stop charging for removals." Prall had told me that was the long-term plan when we met in 2012. Along the way, he had tested the limits of personal data on the Internet and caused a lot of pain. But in at least one regard, he had succeeded: his job was not boring.

13

Internet Advertising

The Stranger from the Land of No Advertising

The unflattering photographs and arrest details form both the core product and advertising content of mug shot websites. Most businesses embrace a far subtler approach toward personal data. On the other end of the spectrum, Internet advertisers often ignore names and customer profiles, and focus on trying to figure out what groups of people should see their messages. This field, known as "online behavioral advertising," is grabbing an increasingly large share of the hundreds of billions of dollars companies spend annually urging the masses to buy.

In recent years the field has attracted experts with deep knowledge in harvesting and interpreting personal data—people like Claudia Perlich. Her upbringing seemed especially unlikely to land her at a New York advertising firm at the center of this revolution in advertising. She grew up in Gera, a rail junction town more than 120 miles southwest of Berlin, on the closed side of the Iron Curtain.

When she was just a year old, East Germany's socialist government did away with advertising altogether. The country did not want to promote the crude consumer culture of the West—and in any case, it did not have the consumer goods to fulfill public demand. In 1976, after tantalizing viewers with offers for everything from denture cleaning products to automobiles, the German Democratic Republic aired its last television commercial.[1] Even by the austere standards of the Soviet Union, East Germany set a restrictive example.

Growing up, Perlich viewed notices of upcoming cultural events but nothing that would encourage citizens to buy anything. In a country where citizens had to wait for more than a decade before they could purchase a hard-plastic Trabant car, ads made little sense. "There was no need for advertising because there was a very simple decision process: you either bought what was available or not," she says.

One day in 1989, when she was fifteen, Perlich learned on television that authorities had opened up the Berlin Wall. East Germans could travel freely for the first time. A few months later, Perlich and her family made their maiden journey to West Germany. She walked amazed through giant malls in Cologne, a rich city of pedestrian shopping streets—all that enclosed space, endless rows of consumer products, and escalators that transported visitors into wide open areas!

Many middle-aged East Germans lost their jobs and suffered through a difficult transition in the following years, but Germany's reunification gave Perlich a wealth of new opportunities. She went to university in the western half of the country, near Frankfurt, and stayed with a relative to save money. Although she had been learning Russian since third grade, she later switched to English, which she mastered well enough to receive a PhD in information systems at New York University.

Perlich developed a passion for analyzing huge quantities of data to make sense of the world: "I love playing around with data," she says. "I don't care if it is yeast genomes, movies, or people's browsing histories." As an IBM researcher from 2004 to 2010, she studied patterns for a range of projects, helping to better predict breast cancer, identify pneumonia patients, and develop predictive models of what movies people will like. Her data-mining work earned her a series of prestigious prizes. All these projects relied on using large amounts of data to predict what would happen in the future. The data scientists at Caesars in Las Vegas use a similar approach to study gambling habits and spending patterns to craft offers luring people back to the casino.

"I always need examples first. I can't find terrorists unless I've seen five thousand first. I'm only as good as the data," she says. Piecing together clues like Internet use and other habits, she can easily puzzle out personal attributes such as sexual orientation. When too many factors are uncertain, her models break down. She cannot predict whether you are going to eat pizza next Friday, nor does she know what the stock market will do in the future.

In 2010, she took on the full-time task of improving advertising delivery, the very embodiment of the consumer capitalism so conspicuously absent from her childhood. That year she became chief data scientist for Media6Degrees in New York, one of dozens of new advertising technology companies that have emerged in recent years.

Targeting Ads

Media6Degrees, which became Dstillery in September 2013, analyzes how people surf the Internet to target the right advertisements to the right people at the right time. The firm's clients include Kraft, CVS, Wendy's, HP, Sears, Tropicana, Hertz, Kellogg's, Domino's Pizza, Microsoft, Toyota, and Saks Fifth Avenue.[2] If the company is placing ads for a shoe store, it studies what sites the best shoe buyers visit. Staff may detect a pattern among certain fashion and beauty blogs and other shoe-related sites. Personal details such as household income and geographic location, key to direct marketing, do not matter in this context—the only thing that's relevant is how people surf the Internet. "If you do something that other people who bought lipstick do, I'll try to sell you lipstick. People's actions speak a lot clearer about who they are," Perlich says.

To deliver ads, Perlich has computers follow what millions of Internet users do, score their behavior, and decide whether to serve them ads on particular topics.[3] This machine-based analysis of vast quantities of data lies at the heart of the fast-growing field of online behavioral advertising. How exactly does Perlich know what anyone is doing on the web, let alone those visiting any one of a hundred million web pages? Through the magic (or, some might say, sorcery) of transparent one-pixel images, sometimes called web beacons, which are embedded into web pages. Such images allow companies like Dstillery to store a simple file called a cookie on your computer with a random number they have assigned you.

Only the website you are visiting has the ability to save a cookie on your hard drive. If you read the *New York Times* online, only the NYTimes.com server can store cookies (unless you set your browser settings to refuse them). If you go to eBay, eBay and perhaps others working with the site will store cookies. The sites will also ask your browser for their own cookies from past visits, but they cannot get access to cookies from other websites.

Dstillery can join the action only if it is working with the website. Then it can look for past cookies it recognizes on your computer and save what is called a third-party cookie. The third-party cookie allows Dstillery to recognize the same browser if the user goes to sites with which the firm has data partnerships, as well as to marketers running ad campaigns with them.

Much like a person looking at the windows of a house across the street, the technology allows Dstillery to see only some of your Internet activity. One might notice the person in the house in front of the right window on the ground floor, then some time later see him pass a window on the opposite end of the house, and then perhaps upstairs. The outsider would not know what the house dweller did between the times he or she passed by these windows. Similarly, Dstillery does not know when Internet users surf to the many sites with which they do not have data-sharing arrangements. But Dstillery can view ten million websites, as if peering into many different buildings with thousands of windows each. Typically, Internet users have no idea what companies are able to see when they visit a page. However, some browser plug-ins allow the data hunted to find out who the data hunters are. For example, a plug-in called disconnect.me shows a series of circles around each website representing ad firms such as DoubleClick, Facebook, and many others. It is often surprising how large this cluster of circles around the site turns out to be.

The cookies allow Dstillery to record the sites you visit until you delete them, something some users never do (although browsers and plug-ins such as disconnect.me allow users to block cookies all the time

When you visit this
site, the following
sites are informed:

- www.google.com
- ajax.googleapis.com
- kaltura.com
- 3lift.com
- taboolasyndication.com
- doubleclick.net
- criteo.com
- tynt.com
- quantserve.com
- llnwd.net
- fishwrapper.com
- 2o7.net
- youtube.com
- ytimg.com
- zergnet.com
- taboola.com
- scorecardresearch.com

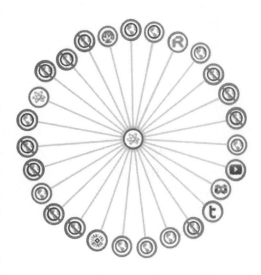

Graphical view of all the companies following a user on the site TMZ.com.
Source: Graphic from browser plug-in disconnect.me (reprinted with permission).

if they want). Perlich says her company can reliably track about half
the US population that actively uses a desktop or laptop computer,
seeing their cookies for an average of ninety days. The company has
gathered data showing users looking at a product and perhaps eventually buying, as well as a trail of some of the websites visited beforehand.
By analyzing such trends, Dstillery uses predictive modeling to assign
scores to every browser in its system. That score, in turn, determines to
whom they will try to serve ads and when.[4]

Dstillery also buys tracking data from outside firms, including from
a company that provides a popular toolbar that allows people to share
content on Facebook, Twitter, Pinterest, or other sites with just a click.
That means that even if Dstillery does not have a direct relationship

with the company operating the website, it can see data on people visiting that site if it has the social toolbar installed there.

Perlich can learn even more about people's patterns of Internet use through the ad networks that her company uses to place advertisements. Dstillery uses real-time bidding (RTB), a process in which companies decide in fractions of a second whether to place an ad targeted to a specific visitor. Dstillery, in effect, asks the RTB network to let the company know when a certain user appears. For example, if that user goes to the *New York Times* website, the RTB asks Dstillery if it wants to bid to place an ad. Even if it doesn't buy an ad, Dstillery has gained new information about that user's pattern of site visits. Dstillery creates a unique twenty-digit number for the people it tracks, but then encrypts the data it gathers so that the information would prove meaningless to outsiders. The company says it does not collect personally identifiable information.

Tracking has become increasingly common in recent years. Many online advertising firms collect information to target their ads, and many well-known firms use web beacons and cookies to gather data on users. Typically they reveal the tracking only in the fine print of their privacy policies, so the process is invisible to almost all users. A sampling of such companies includes Yahoo, Facebook, eBay, HP, American Airlines, Nokia, the Vanguard Group, Microsoft, GE, the New York Yankees, Playboy, Target, Pfizer. Even the Internal Revenue Service makes use of tracking. Also using web beacons are smaller sites such as those of the Nebraska Game and Parks Commission, rasushi .com (a chain of sushi restaurants), and 007.com, the official site of James Bond.

User opinions vary greatly about online tracking, whether through cookies or other means. Some appreciate tracking because it allows advertisers to target messages of interest; others find it sinister. Dstillery CEO Tom Phillips, who cofounded the hip satirical magazine *Spy* in 1986 and later worked for Google to help the company make better use of its data for advertising, scoffs at criticism of targeted ads. He says people make a big fuss over nothing. "Who cares what advertising they show?" he asks. "What is all of this hullabaloo? It's just advertising, who cares!"

He contrasts online ad targeting with traditional direct marketing, which relies on a person's name, address, and other information. He says such ads, addressed to you by name and delivered by mail, email, or telemarketing, are much more personal than messages coming via the Internet and mobile. With Internet and mobile ads, "they can always clear the cookie, not pay attention to the ad. They can be in control." In fact, in the short term, the biggest threat to Dstillery and the industry overall came not from public outcry about tracking but from a pattern of deliberate deception that Perlich and other data scientists at the company discovered.

What the Hell's Going On?

Doubts nagged at Perlich. She feared that somehow she had messed up. For months she had noticed patterns of data on her Dell laptop that did not make any sense. Her computers showed a stampede of interest in obscure sites. She feared her computer models had somehow failed, perhaps because they were recording the wrong data. "We found our models doing extremely well, too well for a data scientist's liking," she said.

Perlich enjoys the freedom to work from home or from the office. She wanted to talk about her doubts to colleague Ori Stitelman, another bespectacled PhD computer whiz, in person. She took the train to the office in Lower Manhattan and arrived at their open work area in front of a massive whiteboard typically filled with mathematical formulas. They reviewed a checklist of potential flaws in their work. Could their models introduce errors as they measured how people navigated the Internet? Then, as Perlich sat in her beloved Ikea Poäng chair, with its curved back and footrest, a flash of intuition seized her. Someone had deliberately created an Internet illusion, hoping to lure money from some of the world's biggest advertisers. She told Stitelman: "This has to be fraud!"

A few days later Stitelman walked past the ping pong table near his desk and climbed the narrow stairwell between the two floors of company headquarters. He set his sights on Andrew Pancer, Dstillery's chief operating officer. To maintain a startup vibe at the young company, Pancer and other executives sit side by side with the rest of the staff, undivided even by cubicles. He looked up and listened as Stitelman and Perlich told him what was on their minds. He reacted sharply. "Oh, shit, there's a problem," he said. "What the hell's going on?"[5]

Within a day the company's management realized that click fraud could jeopardize the very survival of their startup. It was hard enough to explain to companies how online behavioral advertising worked. They feared their clients would flee altogether if they learned that fraud polluted the whole sector.

By following the one-pixel images they had placed on millions of computers, Perlich and Stitelman discovered previously obscure websites scoring remarkably well, suggesting that many people were visiting clusters of these sites before moving on to better-known retail sites. Their models showed thousands of websites they had never heard of, including Iamcatwalk.com,[6] therisinghollywood.com,[7] parentingnews .com,[8] and womenshealthspace.com,[9] scoring better than any other sites, representing a sort of online stampede to unknown pastures. Such patterns ordinarily would suggest that companies should place their ads where the stampede was taking place.

But were these ghost visitors? The people visiting many of these websites seemed to have utterly unconnected interests. Of those who visited parentingnews.com, 80 percent would also go to ChinaFlix .com.[10] "Why would all these parents want to watch Chinese videos?" Perlich wondered. Then ChinaFlix would send heavy traffic to well-known websites such as chase.com or nike.com. Could it be that people visiting ChinaFlix.com were much more likely to apply for a credit card or buy running shoes and pizza than other Internet users?

The data scientists tried to figure out the relationship between the different sites and found that many visitors were going from one to another in fractions of seconds—at speeds that were impossibly fast. The traffic was automated somehow. It was mechanized, not human.

Claudia Perlich at work. Source: Author photo.

Stitelman, who earned his doctorate in biostatistics in 2010 at the University of California, Berkeley, worked until late in the night to try to understand what was happening.

In some cases, Perlich and Stitelman detected patterns in which a cookie traveled back and forth among seven hundred websites for a millisecond each, suggesting that a single Internet user had clicked to different pages ten thousand times in one day. The heavy traffic among the sites made them seem like key nodes on which to advertise.

Click fraud presented a dilemma for a firm competing in a tough business.

Overall, the new sites represented as much as a fifth of the total inventory of some online advertising networks, meaning that a fair chunk of advertising did not encounter humans at all. Although the data scientists had produced some scientifically fascinating results, their findings pleased nobody. They meant Dstillery, as well as its on-line advertising rivals, were sometimes buying ads that no one would ever view.

If Dstillery quietly cleaned up its models to avoid the suspect networks, rivals might show better numbers in delivering ads to wider audiences. The executives were unsure how to react. Across the online advertising ecosystem, people made money by not rocking the boat.

Stitelman said some media buyers at companies buying the ads asked them to turn the click fraud back on after they learned what had happened—their numbers looked worse without the fraudulent hits. Without the numbers, their annual bonuses could suffer. "The sad thing is that everyone is incentivized to sort of ignore it," he says. "Even though we know it's all fake! I don't know how people look in the mirror."

The ruse relied on hijacking the computers of thousands of users, who did not realize that their Internet browsers were reaching out on their own to these little-known sites. Often this hijacking occurred after an Internet user visited a porn site. As the Internet browser displayed erotic images, malicious software known as malware would secretly launch a second browser. The malware running the second browser would then visit hundreds of sites, suggesting that the user might be interested in getting a credit card or buying sneakers. But all the user wanted to do was watch porn. Dstillery eventually created a "penalty box" system to remove suspect traffic from its systems, at least on a temporary basis. "We don't want to dilute the models with signals from people who watch porn," Perlich said. The porn sites may have had their own legitimate advertising on their pages, but Dstillery wanted to stay away from those murky waters.

At least initially, Dstillery's honesty hurt the bottom line. "A couple agencies told us we put you up against this other vendor and they are beating you solidly," Phillips said. Overall, Dstillery fell short of revenue projections for the year, displeasing its three main investors. Phillips said most of the twenty online ad exchanges where he places ads are polluted, some severely.

"Everyone out there does shady stuff, sometimes inadvertently," he said. Either sloppiness or deceit lies behind the click fraud. "Benign neglect—it's not so benign—they are neglecting that they are buying shit. I'm not saying that they know. Part of what I am doing in keeping that dialogue open with competitors is, I want to let them know that we know what they are doing."

The Dstillery data scientists found that some of the sites with the hyperactive traffic were owned by AlphaBird, a San Francisco–based company that operated more than seventy websites, such as wellhabits .com, brilliantriches.com, fundwiser.com, and fulloffashion.com. The company advertised that it "guarantees targeted, engaged audiences for online video" and said it had "delivered tens of millions of engaged viewers for publishers, agencies, studios and Fortune 1000 brands."[11]

Chase Norlin, AlphaBird's CEO, initially declined to talk about his company, but he later agreed. He said he was not aware of the traffic patterns Dstillery had found, and said that even if some dubious traffic entered into online advertising systems from time to time, his company made an active effort to weed it out. "You have to remember that when you buy media, sometimes crappy stuff does get in there and our system is designed to filter all that out. Sometimes stuff does get through, and this could be one of those occasions, but it is usually caught pretty quickly because we have to catch it or the clients catch it," he said.[12]

Norlin stressed that any company seeking to operate a business based on fraudulent traffic would quickly be discovered and would not be able to attract clients. He added that his company ran sophisticated real-time filters against automated, nonhuman bot visits to its site. "If what you are describing is accurate, we would have been shut off a long time ago. We wouldn't be a business. It's literally that simple," he said. "We're a vertically integrated digital marketing company. We are about a hundred people. This is not some, you know, two-person shady operation in Eastern Europe."

Norlin asked for evidence of unusual activity Dstillery had found. One spreadsheet I sent him showed the journey of an Internet cookie bouncing among several AlphaBird sites on May 22, 2012. A video also showed that typing in one web address oddly kept leading back to two AlphaBird sites.[13] Some time later, Norlin wrote back saying he would not comment anymore.

I wrote Norlin again, telling him I had planned a trip to San Francisco, AlphaBird's hometown. He agreed to meet, but the day before our scheduled meeting he canceled the appointment and said he would want me to sign a nondisclosure agreement or he would not talk again.

Two days later, an AlphaBird official wrote saying that Norlin, company president Alex Rowland, and chief operating officer Justin Manes wanted to talk. They had heard that several articles were going to appear the next day and had become alarmed about the negative publicity it could generate. Somehow they thought I was behind the articles (I wasn't). In the following days, a series of articles was published on fake botnet traffic, some naming AlphaBird as one of the problem sites.

AlphaBird said the secret to its ability to attract Internet visitors to previously unknown sites lay in "buying traffic." Although buying an audience might appear to be a daunting task, an Internet search of "buy Internet traffic" leads to sites offering to bring visitors to any web page. For example, maxvisits.com sells one hundred thousand unique US visitors for $114, or $94.98 per hundred thousand visitors from forty-five countries. The company promised "real and unique human website traffic, no bots." It also offered traffic from web browsers that "pop under" the browser a web user is looking at. Upgradevisits.com said: "Using our own proprietary software, we are able to 'push' visitors that have landed on one of our affiliates directly (or through redirection) to your website."[14]

Manes explained how AlphaBird did this. "It is really easy," he said. "You put your money in the machine and you buy visitors and visitors come to your site."[15]

Rowland said his company paid others hundreds of thousands of dollars to deliver visitors to AlphaBird sites. "We do that at massive scale. We're also looking at this and saying, 'Well, we figured out a model in which we can basically buy audience to come into the site, and even without a high degree of return rates, we still make money, so why would we not continue to do that?'"

Some of the services selling traffic do acknowledge techniques that raise ethical questions. For example, Fulltraffic.net offered to generate a million worldwide visitors for just $190 when I first looked, a number that increased to $450 at the start of 2014. The company tells potential clients: "Be warned that this type of traffic may not be delivered in the form of full page (visitors may leave your site before the entire content is loaded). Be also warned that these visitors ARE NOT IP Unique, which means that the same person may load the same page SEVERAL TIMES and each of those times will be counted as a 'VISITOR' by FullTraffic."[16]

The team at AlphaBird, which advertised that it had offices in San Francisco, Los Angeles, New York, and Sydney, said that if some of the companies they had used to deliver visitors deployed botnets or other fraudulent methods, they did not know about it. They portrayed a thriving business, but some months after we last talked in 2013, the name AlphaBird had flown. Its website redirected to a different company. Many of the AlphaBird websites—such as Iamcatwalk.com, which had once showed surges of traffic—also no longer operated by the end of 2013.

A California business filing showed AlphaBird had changed its name to Emerge Digital, whose website listed Norlin as its CEO and Rowland as its president.[17] Its home page boasted that *Inc. Magazine* named Emerge Digital as the fastest-growing advertising and marketing company in Silicon Valley and placed it at number eight on a list of five thousand companies overall in the United States. In 2014, Norlin said his business was thriving, although he had closed down the various websites in 2013. He added, "We were never proven guilty of anything. . . . Owning websites and driving traffic to them is common business practice. Regardless, we exited that business after all the negative publicity, but this is still happening widespread across the industry. Hopefully the Interactive Advertising Bureau or other governing body will come up with a set of standard practices that companies can follow so that the industry as a whole can improve and provide more value."[18]

In the big picture, Perlich says click fraud continues more or less unabated. In fact, the deceptions have grown more sophisticated, although companies such as White Ops have emerged to help advertisers eliminate bot fraud. Their message to marketers is simple. "Sophisticated bots act like people, but they don't follow your brands or buy your products, and they are diluting your metrics and the effectiveness of your campaigns," it says on its web page.[19]

The click fraud issue came to light because Dstillery did not target individuals by name; it had stripped out personal data at the heart of traditional direct marketing. The company does not know who you are and has not linked someone's details to an Acxiom or other company database on hundreds of millions of people.

By contrast, service businesses want to know as much as they can about each individual patron. Caesars executives think a lot about how to gather data on their customers while behaving in a responsible way, a recurring theme in the next four chapters. They have seen that through clever use of incentives, companies can influence what people do and how they share data. They put those insights to the test when they ushered in a major change to their loyalty program, one that risked alienating their best customers.

14

Seeking the Goldilocks Balance

Fostering Loyalty

The best businesses give consumers a choice whether or not to share their data, and offer benefits in return. The trick for executives is to strike the right balance when offering incentives. Big data helps companies such as Caesars tweak their formulas to best influence customer behavior.

People will share information for discounts or rewards, a trend that has accelerated in the Internet era. For example, some car insurers offer better drivers lower prices if they allow monitoring of their driving habits. So motorists agree to install a telematics device in the car's dashboard, which sends back information such as what time of day the person drives, how fast he brakes, and other characteristics. At a company like Progressive, about two-thirds of drivers in the program get a 10–15 percent discount. So far, the company has avoided charging bad drivers more because it has been encouraging people to sign up. But in the future, bad drivers will have to fork out perhaps a 10 percent premium.[1]

At Caesars, data from loyalty cards set the reward levels to motivate how people spend money. That's why Dan Kostel received an offer for $1,000 in free chips and a free room and meals at Caesars Palace. It seemed he had hit the jackpot even before crossing through the casino's always-open doors. It wasn't, however, a case of good luck.

Caesars singled out Kostel because he looked like the kind of player who would spend a lot and because he appeared receptive to their offers. They looked at a dozen or more characteristics such as how far away he is from Vegas, his average bet, his favorite game, the things he charges to his room, and how often he comes. If he has not come in a while, he may get a particularly enticing promotion. Once he starts coming regularly, the offers may diminish. If the company calibrates its offers properly, both Caesars and the customer end up happy.

Kostel estimates that he lost a total of about $5,000 at the black-jack table during his first year as a Caesars regular. He knows that gamblers sometimes underestimate their losses and concedes the same may have happened to him. In any case, he says the casino gave him at least $5,000 in free rooms, food, drinks, and other perks, so overall he is satisfied—as is the casino. CEO Gary Loveman said Kostel likely helped the casino's bottom line, even though he received many freebies. "It is very unusual that someone whose actual loss in gaming is $5,000 or perhaps a bit more, for that not to be profitable to us," Loveman says. "That's how it should work: we should be able to give you things that you care about—not have you littered with things you don't care about—and have it work out profitably for us."[2]

Learning More About Customers

Customers today may allow an electronic "little brother" in the car or carry around loyalty cards in exchange for discounts, but once upon a time, people held their personal information close. They warily eyed merchants who seemed too nosy and asked too many questions. Businesses got used to learning a little about customers and then supplementing their files with outside data.

Veteran marketer Barbara Eskin has noticed a shift in the public's willingness to share information. She started her career in 1979 at *Ladies' Home Journal.* Back then the magazine found subscribers by renting subscriber lists from rivals such as *Good Housekeeping* and *Family Circle.*[3] "People were much more cautious about the information. It wasn't as easily accessible and, moreover, people thought it should be their own personal information," she says.

Over the years, Eskin saw growing sophistication in how much marketers could learn about customers. In 1983, the US Postal Service introduced ZIP+4, which gave marketers far more precise information than before, sometimes pinpointing a single large apartment or office building. Marketers started mapping out micro-neighborhoods with customer information that became easier to buy over time.

More recently, Eskin worked as director of the loyalty program at high-end chocolatier Godiva.[4] Like Total Rewards at Caesars, Godiva's program offers incentives to tease out customer information that could help drive more sales. Godiva offers a free piece of candy every month just for signing up, which initially meant volunteering basic details such as name and email. Members can collect their rewards, worth $2.25 to $2.50 retail (although it costs just a fraction of that to manufacture), at any US or Canadian Godiva store. More than five million people joined in the first few years after the program's 2009 inception. Yet it did not work as widely as Eskin had hoped. Many did buy more chocolate, but 1.1 million signed up and then disappeared. The company needed more information to understand the people who were interested enough to sign up but who did not become good customers.

Eskin discussed Godiva's mixed success with other marketers at a Direct Marketing Association training seminar.[5] Godiva could ask for more information at sign-up, but Eskin did not want to deter people from joining by demanding too many details.[6] Seminar leader Devyani Sadh, CEO of the marketing firm Data Square, suggested big data could help. Godiva could learn a lot more about an email address by buying supplementary personal information from data brokers. She paused for a moment and then described the type of companies Eskin should seek out: "reputable." Everyone chuckled. The field has a mixed reputation, even as data appending has become increasingly commonplace.

Data appenders vary in size and stature, from massive data brokers such as Experian and Acxiom to mom-and-pop startups. Acxiom says such data make a big difference. Placing ads in the right context—for example, showing shoes on a fashion page—boosts sales 32 percent. Demographic information such as name and address can boost performance more than fivefold. Adding behavioral data such as what sites people are looking at in sequence to determine their likely buying habits (the focus of Chapter 13) lifts responses more than twelvefold. Adding all this information together rockets response rates fifty-five times more than untargeted media, Acxiom tells clients.[7]

Chicago-based Rapleaf is an example of a smaller data appender. For a penny per piece of information, the company adds age or gender to an email address, or other details such as location, income, marital status, presence of children, homeowner status, or a person's areas of interest or past purchases. Some marketers send in lists of as few as a thousand emails, says Rapleaf CEO Phil Davis. Others send millions. When we last spoke in 2014, he said the company had handled more than three billion emails over the past quarter.[8]

Davis gave an example of how additional data might help a website offering daily deals. For a special on manicures and pedicures, just knowing age and gender could shape a different appeal to married men. "They could say, you know, 'If you are like most men, you're going to screw up and your wife is going to get mad at you. Next time don't give her flowers, have this mani-pedi ready for it. Oh, by the way, don't be a Neanderthal, your wife might like it if your nails looked good once in a while,'" he says.

Davis admires how Gary Loveman and his team at Caesars Entertainment use personal data to target offers, showing the company's impact far beyond casinos. "Caesars is awesome," he says. "It is one thing to single out one data field and one result, but they put it into an algorithm. I think frankly that analytics is a really cool thing. Take lots of data, put it into an algorithm, and come up with a better recommendation. So now the recommendation could be a specific club. Here's the good club on Tuesday nights you should be going to."

Caesars, whose casinos include the Harrah's, Bally's, and Horseshoe brands, extending as far as Britain, Egypt, and South Africa, have detailed insights on likely customer spending because they track not just betting but hotel stays, meals, and many other things for which the more than forty-five million loyalty members have spent money.[9] Over many years, Caesars and rival casinos have figured out someone's likely future spending by simple math: average bet, multiplied by bets per hour, multiplied by total time gambling, multiplied by the house's mathematical advantage in the gambler's preferred game. That equation means a slot player betting the same amount over the same amount of time as a good blackjack player may be more valuable because the odds are worse on slot machines. At Caesars, about 85 percent of gambling revenue comes from Total Rewards members, making the loyalty program what Loveman calls "the big dog in the company."[10]

By profiling their best customers, Caesars want to find more people like them. Who is the next Dan Kostel, ready to travel from Los Angeles to Las Vegas once a month to gamble thousands of dollars? Who are the New Jersey retirees who might visit Atlantic City dozens of weekends a year? For some companies, identifying likely customers is relatively easy. A manufacturer of cribs and diapers looks for new parents. Landscapers, alarm companies, and Internet and cable providers rent lists of people moving into new homes. Other goods and services, such as gambling and fine chocolate, are harder to target. Caesars executives long felt they possessed the most relevant information to boost their business by watching what customers do in their hotels and casinos. But the financial crisis of 2008 jolted their forecasting models. A financial crisis makes people think hard about how they spend their money. Some changed long-established habits.

"Let's imagine Adam Tanner used to be part of a segment of people that behaved largely the same way—guys your age—buys the same sorts of things at the same rate. Since the crisis the divergence of behavior in your group has gone way up," Loveman says. Once-similar customers were no longer acting in a herdlike manner. "So if you were selling pools you'd find a guy who bought a pool and you'd go to other neighbors and say, 'Look, the Tanners have a pool, you've got to have a pool.' What we observe recently is that it is much harder to predict what similar people will do after the crisis."

Changing the Magic Balance

Caesars had another problem. Company executives felt they were, in effect, paying too much in perks and benefits for customer data. Caesars give back about $25 in perks such as free rooms, food, and chips for every $100 of profit. Of that amount, about $2.50 funds points that a customer can redeem for free play, food, entertainment, and hotel stays. That's the advertised part that gamblers know they will be getting. On top of that, the company allocates an average of $22.50 per $100 profit for unpublished targeted offers and comps—such as the free chips offered to players like Kostel.[11] Those offers are not democratically distributed. Valuable players may receive freebies worth $40 per $100 of company profit. Others might get just $5—based on what Caesars believe will generate the best return.

Caesars gave out a lot of free food and drinks in their loyalty club lounges, but fretted some people stayed too long and consumed too much given how much they spent over the course of the year. Behind their backs, staff dubbed such guests "grazers." One homeless man spent much of his $1,400 monthly disability check at the Harrah's in Kansas City to earn Diamond status so he could eat every meal there for free. He was eventually kicked out after, in effect, figuring out how to squeeze the maximum value of the loyalty program to his benefit.

Because of tougher times since 2008, fewer Caesars clients were working their way up the tiers of Total Rewards. Caesars hoped their members would aspire to move up from entry-level Gold to Platinum, Diamond, and then Seven Stars status—and spend more throughout the process. But the progression wasn't happening the way it once did. The slow economy was not the only problem. At the start of Total Rewards, Caesars had unmatched technology and expertise. Over the years, rival casinos introduced their own popular programs. Some of Loveman's math nerds defected to the competition.

Caesars had to rethink their approach, so they decided to change the parameters of Total Rewards. It was the type of adjustment airlines have embraced from time to time. Other programs are also constantly tinkering to find the "Goldilocks balance": enough free chocolate, flights, meals, hotel rooms, and other perks to keep people signing up with their personal data and coming back for more—without hurting the bottom line.

Total Rewards chief Joshua Kanter worked throughout 2012 on the program's most significant revamp in more than a decade. The new plan required more points to reach the next level but gave bonus points for big spending on any single day. By raising the lowest-level elite Diamond threshold from eleven thousand to fifteen thousand points, the company hoped to thin the ranks of grazers. Kanter calculated that 10 percent of Total Rewards members would fall to a lower status. Yet perhaps 25 percent fewer people would crowd the elite lounges, creating a more appealing atmosphere and saving the company money. He felt overrun in the Diamond lounges, the second-highest level in the Total Rewards program. Sometimes twenty-five people were lining up to get into the elite lounge—hardly VIP service.

* * *

On a fall afternoon in 2012, Kanter took some deep breaths ahead of the first in a series of conference calls in which he was to explain the changes to top management across the country. Although he kept his feelings to himself, he had mixed emotions. He had good reasons to tinker with a successful formula, but he knew any change risked inciting a New Coke debacle. "In one ear I have operational leadership saying . . . 'I need your help to focus our property operations on the very best customers,'" he said. "In the other ear, I've got general managers from across the network saying, 'I can't believe you are doing this. You are going to completely piss off my best customers, who come every single day.'"

Kanter was still relatively new at Caesars, but he had been around long enough to know that the changes would bewilder some managers. "Any time there is change there are people who freak out because it's too much change, because it's too confusing and they don't think we can execute on it," he thought. "And then there are other people who will say, 'It's not big enough. Why are we going to go through all this trouble?'"

Kanter dialed into the conference call and started his presentation. Managers reacted cautiously at first. Gradually, one after the other aired concerns about the impact on the eight million active Total Rewards members—the core audience vital to the company's future.[12] Darrell Pilant, a vice president of operations and marketing in San Diego, worried about how the program's best customers, its Seven Stars members, would react after learning they would need 50 percent more points—150,000 points from 100,000—to qualify for that top-level elite status for 2014. "I'm just thinking about the difficult conversation," he said. "The 50 percent increase is going to be a slap in the face."

John Koster, the regional president of Harrah's in northern Nevada, later outlined his concerns in an email.[13] "Our competition is not raising the play bar to maintain loyalty program status," he said. "They possess newer products with excellent locations (Indian Gaming) and aforesaid aggressive reinvestment. Add to that the rotten economy . . . and this is certainly somewhat of a risky initiative. Loss of Tier Status is 'loss of face.' Customers don't take kindly to that and tend to show their angst via lost trips and play, or complete defection."

Kanter's direct boss, Tariq Shaukat, the executive vice president and chief marketing officer, thought the internal unveiling did not go as well as he had hoped. He believed they could have done a better job of explaining why they were making the changes. Over the next week Kanter held another five conference calls, talking to a total of a few hundred people. Each time, he grew better at explaining the complicated changes. Calming fears of both Caesars staff and Total Rewards members was so vital that both Kanter and Shaukat—who, like Kanter, joined Caesars from McKinsey & Company—personally drafted the message to Total Rewards members.

Another problem threatened before the announcement went public. Some of the management team were sharing details of the upcoming changes with customers. Partial leaks appeared on blog sites. In early December the company sent around a stern warning: "We put ourselves, our players and this great program at risk if we do not roll the information out properly," Brandi Ellis, senior vice president of VIP marketing, wrote in a memo.

The Carrot and the Donkey

Loveman was not involved in the day-to-day changes, but he watched from the sidelines. He knew moving the goalposts would make some people very unhappy and spark debate inside the company. The people who faced the greatest challenges were the casino staff who had to explain the changes to guests. "These are huge high-volume operating businesses, so when you mess with something like Total Rewards there's going to be thousands of people coming to our staff in the property with an issue," Loveman said. "If you get it wrong, you make their life miserable."

People did complain. Rodney Holland, a regular video poker player at Harrah's in Kansas City, reacted warily when he first heard about the changes. "They had better not move the carrot too far ahead of this donkey, because then this donkey may not come at all," he huffed. Holland had been frequenting Harrah's Kansas City since it opened in 1994. He did not spend huge amounts when he gambled—typically $189 on average. But he came at least once a week, sometimes four or five times in one week, enough to earn him 138,000 tier points by late 2012—well clear of the old 100,000 level that bestowed Seven Stars membership, but short of the new level of 150,000 points.

A few months into 2013, Loveman thought the Total Rewards revamp had gone fine, although some officials remained worried. Clients were changing their behavior, which was the goal in the first place. They gambled more on the days they came, because the new rules gave players bonus points for spending more on any given day. Yet since customers spent more when they came, they were coming less frequently. Average daily spend went up, but the number of visits went down. Overall, they spent about the same amount of money as before, although some key clients spent more.

"That is actually what we had designed the strategy to promote, and that is, in fact, what we are seeing," Kanter said. Yet the decreased frequency of visits alarmed some company officials. "Now we've got people who are freaking out around the company, about, 'Oh, my God, visitation has gone down, what am I going to do?'"

The company demonstrated that incentives in the data-intensive loyalty program could shift how customers behave. That was great. However, with billions of dollars in debt to pay in the coming years, it still needed to do more to boost its overall revenue. It needed more customers, and more insights on its regulars. Caesars, as well their rivals, looked for more data from beyond the casino walls.

15

New Frontiers in Customer Data

Following the Money

For all the transactional data Caesars capture, they do not know what might be the most valuable personal data of all: how much customers spend in rival casinos. Like a jealous lover peering into the bedroom of an unfaithful partner, they would love to know what is happening when the client is out of sight. At first glance, it might seem unlikely that casinos could find out what people do away from their establishments. But in recent years they have been able to buy information showing how much money clients obtain in other casinos through credit and debit card cash advances and check cashing.

Data on what gamblers do elsewhere are hard to come by, and especially valuable, because casinos remain one of the last strongholds of cash (along with flea markets, tag sales, and underground businesses such as off-the-books labor and drug dealing). With the exception of higher-end players who wire in money ahead of their visit or receive a line of credit, most gambling takes place in cash. Some people arrive with a stack of bills, but many want more during their stay. When gamblers reach the daily limits on their ATM cards, they may cash checks or get credit card advances.

In 2013, a publicly traded company called Global Cash Access (GCA) dispensed $20.2 billion in cash at more than a thousand casinos, accounting for an estimated two-thirds of all the cash distributed inside casinos.[1] Gamblers in aggregate draw between 60 percent and 70 percent of cash at casinos through ATM withdrawal, credit/debit card, cash advance, or check cashing, says Scott Dowty, GCA's executive vice president. The company says it has personal information on more than nine million gamblers' credit cards, debit cards, checks, and, in some cases, ATM withdrawals. Through a service called Casino Share Intelligence (CSI), introduced in 2010, the company allows casinos to see how much cash specific clients have taken out elsewhere.[2] "You will finally be able to see beyond your four walls," a company promotional video says.[3] "Before CSI you'd have no way of knowing where John was when he wasn't with you. . . . This robust tool can even identify the top players in your market—and analyze how much cash they're withdrawing in your casino compared to your competitors," GCA advertises.[4]

Harry Hagerty, who served as GCA's chief financial officer from 2004 to 2007, says such information could prompt a casino to boost its offers to a gambler: "A property might say, 'I've got a guy who's taking out $1,000 in my various properties through cash advance, so there's a good customer.' But we could go and show, 'Hey, that same guy is doing $5,000 a month in other casinos.'" GCA does not share which other casinos the particular gambler went to, but provides an overall amount of withdrawals in all other casinos.

Was GCA concerned about the privacy of gamblers who might not be aware that their transaction data would be sold? "We are doing what they [management] thought would be useful and valuable to our customers, who are the casinos," says Hagerty. In all likelihood, gamblers do not fully understand that GCA shares information about how much cash they take out because the details are in the fine print. Dowty points out that customers sign their approval when completing their transactions, essentially opting themselves into the program. He adds that customers can also call the company's toll-free number to opt out of information sharing.

Caesars executive Joshua Kanter says that Caesars once shared data gathered through ATM machines but quit years ago. Some other companies have also stopped participating, he adds. "Our customers really don't expect that that information would be captured," he says. "It's not appropriate for us to be giving a third-party access to information about our customers." GCA staff confirmed that MGM Resorts did not share data with them—so two of the major players in Las Vegas were nonparticipants. "It was a nice loophole business for a while, but I suspect it's had its day," Kanter says. "That loophole has been closing consistently over many years. Good for them while they made money off of it. It's kind of like those guys when the Internet first became a big deal in the late '90s, those guys who bought burgerking.com and for a little while there was this opportunity to act on something before everybody got wise to it. I would put this in the same category."[5]

The Troubles with Cash

Casinos and other businesses may be able to learn more about customers as mobile and other electronic payment methods become more common. That's because debit and credit card transactions, and most online payments (excluding virtual currencies such as Bitcoin), show your name as well as that of the bank or institution that handles the transaction. In recent years a series of companies have made deals with card-issuing banks (including Bank of America) that allow them to offer targeted discounts to certain customers based on their purchases. Under such programs, called merchant-funded rewards, a store such as Sports Authority might offer a special deal to all those who buy a certain amount of equipment at a rival every month.[6] Those not deemed to be regular buyers at rivals would not receive the offer. Caesars also began learning more about how customers spend their money outside their casinos when they introduced the Total Rewards credit card in 2013.

For the time being, however, casinos still do much of their business in cash, following routines established decades ago that they would be happy to do away with. They spend a lot collecting, transporting, and guarding it. Clay Behrman, who oversees Caesars' cage operations, says a midsize regional casino might keep $12 million to $14 million in cash on hand at any given time. The labor cost of handling that amount of cash would be $1.5 million to $2 million annually. At Caesars Palace alone, sixty-five people work in the cage areas and fifteen to eighteen in the count room (the place you always see in the movies where stone-faced workers are counting the cash). Hagerty calculated that one casino company had $350 million sitting in cash across all its casino floors at any one time. Over a year, the company's cost of borrowing and handling all that money would be $35 million, he estimated. Cash is expensive. Because it is so obviously stealable, special provisions are in place to secure it. These include steel boxes and secure rooms. Beyond a mantrap corridor with a double series of doors that open only one at a time lies the count room, where workers typically stand at transparent tables, drink from transparent water bottles, and wear smocks or jumpsuits without pockets.[7] Surveillance cameras watch carefully.

From there some of the cash goes to the cage; the rest goes to a vault room. The vault has thicker walls and wire mesh protection against break-ins, as well as security features such as biometric entrance codes. When casinos want to deposit cash in a bank, an armored car service enters the building through a secure indoor location or a gated back area. All these operations impact the casino's bottom line.

Because most casino jurisdictions do not allow credit cards for gambling (a precaution against incurring debt in a moment of vulnerability), Hagerty's company, Sightline Payments, has spent years trying to usher in what it calls a prepaid cashless revolution in casinos. The company proposed introducing prepaid cash cards that could be branded like a loyalty card from a casino company such as MGM Resorts or Station Casinos, which runs ten casino hotels in the Las Vegas area typically catering to locals. The cards would fund wagering accounts for casino and online gaming and work only in the casino branding the card. People could add money to the cards online and, for nongaming purchases, use them anywhere Discover cards are accepted. Casinos could also see what other kinds of things customers buy using the card. "Stations previously had no idea what I was spending off their properties," Hagerty says. "All the casino knows is what you do within the four walls of the casino. Now they can know more about what their consumer really values."

A slot machine player at Caesars Palace. As of 2014, gamblers in Nevada can use prepaid cash cards. Source: Author photo.

He gave an example of someone who buys ice cream from Cold Stone Creamery with a Sightline cash card. Once the casino knew that the person was a fan of those desserts, it could target a promotion giving a free sundae or store coupon as a reward for gaming. Sightline Payments needed a change of regulations to introduce the card in Nevada, and after a long effort, it succeeded in February 2014. It hopes customers can start using its cards in Nevada casinos in the second half of 2014.[8] The company is working on getting rules altered in other states as well.[9] Another new frontier in gathering customer data from gamblers was opening up.

Cell Phone Apps

Another tool that could help casinos know when loyalty club members are acting promiscuously comes via its cell phone apps, which use GPS tracking to determine where clients are located. Caesars' apps for Las Vegas, Atlantic City, and Lake Tahoe, as well as for Total Rewards, allow visitors to receive offers via text messages based on their location. Other casinos also advertise cell phone applications that send geo-targeted content. "Enjoy location-specific content that changes depending on where you are. Unlock special offers once you're within a few miles of The Mirage or actually at the property," MGM Resorts advertises.[10]

As marketers and data brokers seek ever more information for insights about prospective customers, they salivate at the possibility of new insights from mobile data. The use of personal data coming from your mobile phone and other devices will continue to generate debate as more and more people acquire mobile technology. Because few rules limit gathering personal data other than in areas related to medical, financial, and hiring records, business executives are cautiously exploring how far they can go without setting off a public backlash or government intervention. "Personally identifiable information versus no personally identifiable information is the red line that may trigger Congress," says Jack Feuer, founder of Digital Marketing Works, a consulting agency specializing in digital advertising.

Jorey Ramer, founder of Jumptap, a leading mobile ad company, says it is possible to market to mobile devices respectfully and effectively by sending out messages that people actually want.[11] His Boston-based startup buys aggregated data from companies such as Acxiom to deliver ads not to individual names but rather to broad groups of people sorted by interests, such as business travelers and suburban moms. Like many advertising executives, he points out that the commercial message allows you to get a service for free, such as access to a sports or news site. "I see digital advertising—in particular mobile, where consumers will spend most of their time—as simply the opportunity for companies to build their own roads to make it easy for the right consumers to visit, at lower cost than any previous method of customer acquisition," he says.

"We believe we are on the right side of privacy," he says. "Jumptap does not see information that would allow a person to be identified in real life such as a name, phone number, email address, or street address. Companies that do see such information require special care."

Some companies are taking a more direct approach and advertising to mobile phones on a one-to-one basis, meaning that you may see a different message from your neighbor because of what they have deduced about you. For example, Catalina Marketing, which advertises that it collects "purchase histories of more than 75 percent of U.S. shoppers and 128 million health consumers," delivers personalized mobile ads to seventy million households.[12] The company gathers data on more than one billion transactions per month, giving it a lot of information to personalize digital media and target mobile ads.[13]

At a Harvard Business School conference for students hoping to become successful digital marketers and entrepreneurs, one industry official let his guard down when talking about his industry. "We thrive on what a lot of people consider to be invasive, trying to track what kinds of websites people go to," said Daniel Ruby, suggesting firms had gone too far into people's private spheres in the name of marketing. He worked at the time as director of online marketing at Localytics, advising companies on using mobile phone location data. "The public doesn't like that. Nobody likes that."[14]

Gary Loveman embraces tailored cell phone messages based on knowing where you are, provided the marketing does not cross certain boundaries. "For example, when I am carrying this stupid thing around and when I land in Hong Kong I immediately get an offer of different types of services in Hong Kong through SMS [text message]. Usually it's a ferry service or a trip to a sightseeing venue or something like that," he says. "And the worst case is that you just delete it. I don't think anybody finds that too troubling. And we're not using that to call their spouses and tell them they are in Las Vegas at the moment, which I suspect might be disturbing."

Yvette Monet, a spokeswoman for MGM Resorts International, says her company does not target based on very precise location, although such ability exists. The casino chain's technology notes what ZIP code users are in, not exactly where they are. Thus it might send an offer to everyone in 89109 around the Strip, not just to people in a rival casino. "We are in the process of expanding our property Wi-Fi capabilities so that we can send to people within our properties some offers, but we're not there," she says. "With Wi-Fi, for example, if I go to the swimming pool and then leave the swimming pool to go somewhere else in the hotel, the hotel knows I've been at the pool and they'll send me an offer to lure me back to the pool." Or perhaps the hotel would send a message about a restaurant special or casino tournament, all aimed at keeping customers engaged and spending at the hotel. Joshua Kanter says Caesars have similar plans and adds that every self-respecting marketing company will do the same.

From a business perspective, knowing more about clients can only help, whether from smart phone GPS information or commercial profiles bought from data brokers. Yet such data gathering raises privacy sensitivities. Unlike the loyalty card data, which customers willingly exchange for rewards, mobile technology allows companies to collect a lot of data about customers without their active knowledge.

Rich Mirman helped fine-tune what was then Harrah's data collection on its clients. But tracking consumer location through mobile phones makes him uneasy. "Now, to me it seems a little bit unethical in terms of watching their movements without them knowing that you are watching their movements," he says. "There is a big difference in me pulling a card out of my wallet, either handing it to the pit boss, handing it to the waitress, or putting it in the slot machine—that's a deliberate act that says I want you to know something about me."

Walter Salmon, the former Harrah's board member who is now in his eighties, also has concerns. He says he'd rather that a competitive company not know the very moment that he is shopping in Best Buy, even if the rival is sending a promotion for a better offer. "I think there is a line there because I think it's disturbing my privacy," he says. "What if someone went to a house of prostitution?"

As with many areas on the frontier of the business of personal data, Caesars are struggling to find the right mix of advancing their business interests and giving clients something of value in return. "We don't want customers to feel that we are Big Brother, but there is value in having access to that kind of information, so we are trying to find the right balance," Kanter says. As for Salmon's comment that companies could know that someone had visited a house of ill repute, Kanter replied curtly: "That would be useless information to us because it is so unrelated to our business."

Making real-time use of data from clients' smart phones remains difficult, but businesses are moving in that direction. Caesars are now beginning to think about how to collect that data at vast scale and interpret it in real time.

Personalizing the Slot Machine

Some insiders believe that the real long-term problem facing casinos is not marketing but demographics: many people weaned on video games and the Internet are not as interested in today's casino games as their parents or grandparents. Kanter, part of a demographic of players in their thirties and forties vital to the future of casinos, admits it took him a while to understand the appeal of slot machines, the big money makers at American casinos today. When he first started at Caesars he just did not see why anyone liked them. "The odds are against you, you're going to lose, why would you do that stupid thing?" he thought. Then he started playing Slotomania, an online slot game Caesars own and market widely across the Internet, Facebook, and iTunes. He began to appreciate the rhythm: long lulls of losses punctuated by thrills of big wins. "It's restful and entertaining at the same time," he says. "There is something Zen-like about being there."[15]

Slot developers hope their games of the future will not be an acquired taste but a compelling pleasure. Adding personal data to the mix may help. Patti Hart, CEO at International Game Technology, a leading slot machine manufacturer, says her machines may one day make more use of personal data, welcoming regulars through retinal scans, face or voice recognition, or fingerprints. "I can personalize this slot machine to be the Patti slot machine," she says. "It has my family pictures, it has my music, it has, you know, my friends and whatever. I can send a Facebook notification to my family that I just won $300 at the Elvis machine."

"The only impediment for us is not technology; it's regulation."

Hart says she is sensitive to privacy concerns, although she believes the issue will fade over time. Some people will not want to be tracked, she says, but she expects such sentiment to diminish. "I think the world has moved to a place where people are saying, 'I want personalization and in order to get personalization I have to give you data,'" she says.

John Acres, the innovator who devised the first slot player tracking systems in 1983, says slot machines of the future must incorporate far more personal data and involve friends to make them more social. He wants to take data he can instantly glean from third-party sources, such as income level, age, gender, and club memberships, and adapt the machine to suit the player's profile. The overall plan is to change the machine characteristics based on what it perceives about the user.[16]

Acres has done well as an entrepreneur over the years. He says he sold his last business for $143 million. His share was about $50 million. He has spent $23 million, about a third of that from his own pocket, in recent years trying to revolutionize casinos. His slot machines of the future would introduce bonus rounds and winnings based on who the player is. So the basic cycle of spins would still have the same odds as before and would not turn a winning spin into a loss. But he would supplement the natural cycle with player-specific bonus winnings built into the natural cycle of the game. "Gary Loveman is going to mail you $100 in free play. So I'm saying, 'Why do we have to pay homage to the postal service? Why don't I just give it to you right here?'" he says. Both cases constitute marketing costs by the casino; Acres thinks his scenario will engage gamblers more.

Authorities would have to change the rules for Acres to realize his vision. He fully realizes he may fall completely flat on his face. "I claim that I can see the future. The difference between being a visionary and being delusional is impossible to tell without seeing how the future unfolds. It could be absolutely delusional," he says.

Acres's vision of the future is intriguing. With white hair, white beard, and powerful biceps, he has the aura of a prophet—a data prophet. He wants to learn even more about customers by purchasing large amounts of information from data brokers. Might gathering all that data to operate a casino game appear a bit creepy? "It's

John Acres at his Las Vegas office in front of some of his casino innovations, including Madame Fortuna. Source: Author photo.

absolutely creepy. It depends on how you use it," he says. "If I creep you out or discourage you from a relationship with me, I've crossed the line. If I have encouraged you or improved the relationship with me, I haven't. . . . We will never have the anonymity that we once had. That is part of the price of living in modern society. It's not an option," he continues. "Creepiness changes with time. Over time you will come to accept it. It's not going away."

16

Casino Adventures in Three Cities

Your Casino Dossier in Real Time

The day before Christmas is another busy day for Tom Cook, manager of Harrah's in North Kansas City. Unlike in Las Vegas, where people journey specifically to gamble, casinos in smaller cities rely on locals to fill the seats at slot machines and gaming tables. Keeping regulars happy is vital to Cook's business on the banks of the Missouri River.

He scoops a smart phone out of his pocket and launches an app called RTCM—real-time casino marketing. A stream of emails starts arriving, telling him intimate details about his best customers playing at that moment, including exactly where they are sitting scattered among 1,600 slot machines in the cavernous casino.

The first email updates the manager about Richard. The gambler has gathered 165,000 loyalty points for the year—equivalent to roughly $82,500 in annual spending. He is one of just three hundred or so top-level Seven Stars members in the Kansas City area. Such players make up the top 0.5 percent of gamblers at the world's largest casino company, but they account for $1.3 billion of Caesars Entertainment's more than $8 billion in annual revenue. The company rewards such top-tier members every year with a complimentary dinner worth $500 and a cruise ship voyage, along with access to elite lounges.

On this day so far, Richard has cycled $4,940 through the machines. Since Harrah's Kansas City sets the machine to keep an average of 10 percent of slot bets, he should have lost $494 by now. However, the email tells Cook that as of 12:05 p.m., Richard is down $688. On his last visit four days before, he lost $1,390. The update also reminds the manager of Richard's birth date and year, and notes he lives in the Kansas City area.

Cook navigates toward Richard between the long banks of slot machines. An orchestra of sound pours forth, a chorus of *ka-ching* and excitement emitting from the bellies of the machines. Themes and catch phrases from old television shows and movies compete for attention. The manager arrives before an unusually complex series of spinning video images called Li'l Red. There he greets a solidly built man sporting a white mustache and a long-sleeve T-shirt. The two chat amiably, although Richard keeps playing most of the time. He says he has lost about $200 so far—a far rosier assessment than his real loss. Cook does not correct him. They trade stories of gym routines, diets, and a new food delivery service. Richard jokes that he likes the Li'l Red machine because the female cartoon character on top has larger-than-average breasts.

Management wants to keep a balance between showing special friendliness to big spenders and not bothering them too often. So after the conversation, the casino manager sends a quick email to the system noting that he has spoken with Richard. The rest of the staff will now wait at least a week before singling him out again for a special greeting. Cook then moves to say hello to Janet, playing at machine CC02. She typically loses $600 a day, but today she is up $286. Her profile also says she has accumulated $455 of freebies—for items such as show tickets or meals, to which casino hosts can throw in another $33 at their discretion. By the time he arrives, Janet has moved to machine GD03. Although the machines are all wired, they transmit data on a low-speed network, so it can take a few minutes for the email to arrive in Cook's phone. Another email soon shows her latest location, but by the time Cook arrives she has risen from her seat and is briskly walking away. Rather than stop her midstride, he says nothing.

The next email gives a profile on John at slot machine UB01. He has to accrue just a few thousand more points to remain a Seven Stars elite member for the following year. "I'm sure that's why he's here," Cook thinks.

When the manager arrives to say hello, John barely glances away from his slot machine. They exchange few words; the manager moves on. Cook knows that many players just want to zone out and escape into their favorite machine. He carefully gauges who is talkative, who loves bawdy jokes, who prefers a quick hello. He knows John is a man of few words, and besides that, he knows John is enjoying a good streak: he is up $59 although the odds suggest he should be down $145 by then. And he is enjoying an especially good day compared to his last outing, five days before, when he lost $772. A three-letter "behavior segment" code in the email also shows that John has been coming less frequently than he had in the past and has been spending less.

Cook comes from the old school of hospitality championed by Las Vegas pioneers like Benny Binion, who wandered through his casino wearing a wide-brim hat from his native Texas as he glad-handed his guests. Cook, who earlier in his career worked at casinos in Atlantic City and Arizona, says hello to pretty much everyone even as he makes a special effort to linger with his top customers. He does have one limitation different from most casino managers: he cannot offer his guests free drinks because he is barred by Missouri gaming regulations.

The staff at Caesars' headquarters love Cook's devotion to customer service and to his employees and have used some of his innovations elsewhere in the company. They appreciate his plainspoken opinions, which often contain a lot of wisdom, but sometimes dissent on important issues. Cook feels that headquarters—mostly staffed with people with elite university degrees—does not always appreciate the wisdom of a manager in the trenches or the value of the human touch. He once thought the attraction of being a general manager was making big decisions about how to run and promote his property. But that time has passed; data crunched at a central location now dictate strategy. "We've lost that creativity, that uniqueness, because we are trying to do things across multiple properties," he says. "I don't begrudge the brainiacs at all that are up there, but the arrogance that their work is more important."

Such attitudes have created some tensions with high command. Back in Vegas Loveman has supported Cook, even when they have a difference of opinion. He knows that Cook has an MBA from UCLA, and recognizes that local executives pick up on trends and insights about gamblers unseen in raw data. "That's all true and that's a perfect tension," Loveman says about Cook's "brainiac" remark. "You never want that tension to go away. That's hard for people to get their head around." Loveman knows that Cook and his fellow managers have to deal with thousands of people every Saturday night at midnight. "The propeller heads that are working around here are pushing ideas out at Tom, and Tom is pushing back saying it's impractical, it's not fast enough, it's too hard to execute. That's where the magic happens, that's exactly what we want," Loveman insists.

Dan's Big Night Out

In Vegas, Dan Kostel had started going to Caesars regularly after they sent him an offer for $1,000 in free chips. He kept getting similar offers for a while, until the figure went down to $300. He stayed away for five months, hoping Caesars would increase its offer. After some time the amount did rise back to $1,000. When I met him in June 2013, he was ready to collect $850 in free play and a free room at Caesars Palace.

I invited Joshua Kanter to join us that Friday evening. Quite busy beforehand, Kanter had recently committed most of his free time for the next two years by enrolling in the Wharton MBA Program for Executives in San Francisco. Encouraged by Gary Loveman, he would travel there every two weeks for two years of weekend classes. He spent his evenings and weekends studying, and on that Friday was already en route to San Francisco. He conceded his work-life balance was, as he put it, overdeveloped in one aspect and underdeveloped in the other.

Before starting the program, Kanter allowed himself one indulgence: a weeklong cruise. The Total Rewards chief oversees the Caesars partnership with Norwegian Cruise Line that includes free annual trips for Seven Stars members, so he wanted to experience it himself. He had just broken up with a girlfriend after a year, so he went alone.

Reflecting on the cruise, he said a David Foster Wallace essay he had recently read pretty much summed up his feelings: "A Supposedly Fun Thing I'll Never Do Again."

I met Kostel not at Caesars Palace but at the Cosmopolitan Hotel, two mega-hotels away. The Cosmopolitan had offered him a free suite for the weekend, so he actually slept there (he would do some gambling there too, hoping to be comped in the future). The hotel draws a far younger and hipper crowd than Caesars. Women in short, formfitting dresses wandered through the lobby. The elegant suite consisted of two bathrooms, a bedroom, a living room, and a super-modern kitchen. A long balcony overlooked the massive fountains of the Bellagio and Caesars Palace. From the balcony, Kostel noticed a woman on the balcony of the parallel tower performing some kind of intimate dance for a seated man. It was all very Vegas.

To receive his $850 in chips, Kostel had to appear to be staying at Caesars. Hotels reckon you gamble more if you sleep there. It would have been a ten-minute stroll from the Cosmopolitan, but with the temperature outside hovering at 119 degrees, at least according to my car's thermometer, we drove over. He checked in at a special reception area for Total Rewards Diamond-tier members, just a notch down from the top Seven Stars status. They gave him a large, well-appointed room overlooking the Bellagio fountains and the Cosmopolitan Hotel beyond that.

Later that night Kostel met an acquaintance, another blackjack player who had accepted free rooms in three separate hotels, taking advantage of various offers intended to lure his business. Such antics illustrate that by putting point values on everything people do in the casinos, Caesars and its rivals have conditioned people to seek freebies at every turn. Gamblers are always bargaining for perks—demands some frontline staff sometimes find a bit tiresome.

"They think they shouldn't have to pay for their hotel room; they think they should eat at the steakhouse, not the buffet; they think they should have free drinks, not paid drinks; they should get four tickets to Celine, not two tickets; and they are always talking to our people about this," Loveman says. "That's been in the industry for a long time at the high end, but we certainly made it a pervasive notion that every-body has something available to them, and people are naturally always pressing that envelope."

Kanter, hearing about Kostel's multiple rooms, affirmed that Caesars did care if comped clients do not spend the night. It means that they spend less: "When someone stays in our hotel versus visits us from another hotel, on average the difference in their play is something north of 30 percent," he said.

After checking in at Caesars Palace, Kostel stopped by his room for a brief visit. A housekeeper knocked at the door, carrying a fancy box of gift nuts, a recognition of his Diamond status. After an appointment at the hotel spa, he was ready to gamble. He stepped up to the cage off the casino floor, where, after a small delay, he received a series of computer-printed paper tickets worth $850. Usually Kostel prefers to play in the high-limit room, which offers slightly better odds and rules on blackjack and a more elegant ambiance than the expansive casino floor. With the better odds, he says the house has only a 0.26 percent advantage over the player, meaning that over 1,200 hands of cards he had a 46 percent likelihood of emerging as a winner. "I believe that I have a reasonable chance of leaving a winner," says Kostel, who earned an MBA in Spain.

He strolled past a series of blackjack tables in the high-limit room that required a minimum of $200 per bet, above his comfort zone. So he proceeded to a table with a lower limit outside the high-limit room. His luck was out at first—it seemed like he might quickly cycle through the $850 in voucher tickets and end up with nothing. But then he won a series of hands, and by the time he had used his last voucher, $800 in chips sat in a pile before him. He promptly returned to the cage and cashed in. So far he had received a free room, some gift nuts, and $800 from Caesars.

On his last visit to Caesars Palace Kostel had seen a pair of Prada sunglasses in the Forum Shops. Now he decided he wanted to buy them. The shops are not owned by Caesars, but when he mentioned he was a Total Rewards member, he received an unadvertised 15 percent discount. As he paid, the manager asked him to fill out a form giving his address and email for the store's marketing list. He volunteered just his email and clicked a box asking not to be sent offers.

Before dinner, Kostel stopped by the sports betting desk to wager $90 on the Belmont Stakes the next day. He did not give his Total Rewards number, because he did not want Caesars to know he would still be in town the following day. The program rates you on each day of play, and just picking up any winnings without doing any fresh gambling could lower the daily average Caesars uses to calculate future offers.

We dined at the Mesa Grill Southwestern Restaurant, one of his favorites, where he had reserved a table. When the waiter arrived, he asked, "Are you joining us for the first time?" Kostel was annoyed. "The whole personalization thing does not work as Gary Loveman tells you it does," he said. "It makes me feel like I'm some dumbass that has never been here before." About eighty thousand people come through Caesars Palace in a day, creating a daunting task for the staff to greet even their most valuable Total Rewards members at every turn. "I'm highly demanding, I get that," he said.

After dinner Kostel returned to the high-limit room. The minimum blackjack bet remained at $200, not the $100 he had hoped to find. At $200 a hand, he realized he could lose the $3,000 he was ready to risk in just a few minutes. But he liked the ambiance and the odds there. Even though it was more than he wanted to spend per hand, he asked a supervisor for the $3,000 in credit. The supervisor checked his credit history and returned with a pile of $100 chips.

By this point of the night Kostel was more animated, having started with rum and coke in his room and progressed to a couple of margaritas at dinner. "Bust!" he cried out a few times, wishing the dealer would draw cards putting him over twenty-one so Kostel would win his hand. Other times he called out the card numbers he hoped to receive. Yet he remained sharp in his play. Over twenty years, he had learned the mathematical odds for when to take a new card depending on what he had and what cards the dealer showed. One other gambler at the table, playing two simultaneous hands of up to $800 each, said little during the play.

Kostel's luck started strong and continued. After about half an hour, he picked up his chips for a break. He was $1,000 ahead, and also had the $800 in cash he had won earlier. So far he had spent $200 on a pair of sunglasses and signed a $70 dinner bill to his room. We sat down in a nearby lounge. A man without a shirt on wandered by. Others wore shorts or frumpy clothes. Some giddy bachelorettes sauntered past. The Cosmopolitan, where he was in fact staying, had a more elegant crowd, he thought. But he wanted to continue playing that night at Caesars Palace, hoping that Caesars would send him generous offers for free play in the future, and comp his meal and visit to the spa that afternoon. For Kostel, winning comps was part of the overall game.

He returned to the blackjack table for a few more hours, playing until after midnight. At the end, his total blackjack winnings reached $4,700. The next day he learned that his horse bets—a sport in which he says he has little knowledge—had hit big. He had placed three $20 bets on a long shot called Palace Malice to win, place, and show. The horse won, transforming that $60 into $475. He also placed another three $10 bets for a different horse to win, place, and show. It came in second, winning $80 from a $30 wager. He picked up his winnings anonymously so that Caesars would not know he had stopped by without placing new bets.

Overall, it was one of those trips where everything went right for Kostel. At the end, Caesars even comped him for the meal, spa visit, and drinks he had charged to his room. After such a winning streak, his incidental expenses would not have made a dent in his total winnings. But the casino wanted him to leave on a high with a strong desire to return. Caesars succeeded on that score. They know in the long term the odds are on their side to gain back anything Kostel won that night.[1]

"If they didn't have a system of marketing to you, I'd never be there. I'd be at the Wynn or Bellagio," Kostel said. "I would never be here if they were not offering—not some stupid reward like a bowling tournament and a banquet—but $850 or $1,000 in free play." Although far from flawless, Caesars' mining of personal data had worked. By knowing a lot about Kostel, they had kept his business.

Opening Night

On a late winter's day in 2013, Loveman, Kanter, and other top officials traveled to the Midwest to attend the opening of the latest property in the Caesars family, Horseshoe Casino Cincinnati. Before the mayor and local dignitaries arrived to inaugurate a twenty-four-hour establishment that, short of natural disaster or emergency, would never close again, staffers anxiously prepared for zero hour. Uniformed poker dealers, most of whom had not worked in a casino before, crowded around tables to play one another in final practice rounds. They wagered play money.

Inside the cavernous open casino floor, cleaning staff dusted off the two thousand slot machines, each costing as much as an economy car and collectively worth tens of millions of dollars. Eager patrons would soon spin them about seven times a minute, and, by the law of averages, 9 or 10 cents of each dollar bet would disappear into the machines. Melissa Price, the company-wide vice president of gaming, toured the floor. Experience told her each machine would bring in about $350 to $400 a day in revenue. The Horseshoe Cincinnati faced a major obstacle: Ohio bars smoking on casino floors, and many slot players like to smoke. Jamie Papp, who bought and set up the slot machines, said gambling, smoking, and drinking were all habits that went well together. He said slot revenues at casinos without cigarettes typically fall short of revenues at smoking casinos by 15 to 18 percent.

Behind the scenes technicians checked the flow of data through more than three hundred miles of Ethernet cables—enough to stretch from Washington, DC, to New York and beyond—linking every slot machine spin and transaction to a basement IT server room. A long array of tubes and vents kept servers cool, and backup power stood at the ready, just in case. Even bartender stations were wired so staff could rush drinks ordered directly from slot machines.

Security guards placed their thumbs onto an electronic reader to gain access to the surveillance room. There, four guards sat side by side behind four computer screens each. A supervisor at a fifth desk watched them watching the others, as well as his own cluster of computer monitors. They faced thirty large television screens on the wall in front of them, clustered nine at each end and twelve in the middle.

One security guard peered into the action in the count room, where women broke open one stack of $20 bills after another and ran them through bill counting machines. If anything suspicious caught her eye, the guard could zoom the ceiling camera to focus so closely that she could read the quantity of bills spitting out of the counter. Another bank of monitors focused on card tables, ready to watch the action in a few hours' time.

A steady stream of staffers arrived through the back entrance, showed ID cards, then punched in to a time clock—all the movements were captured by the casino's computer system. Some of the staff headed to an automated dry-cleaning rack. They entered in a number, and their cleanly pressed uniform appeared behind a slot large enough to pull out a suit on a hanger. Minutes later they emerged from changing rooms—male dealers in bow ties, waitresses in sleeveless tops pressed tightly against cleavage.

Two employees punch in ahead of opening night at Horseshoe Casino Cincinnati. Source: Author photo.

A supervisor called out the evening assignments for dealers lined up in the high-limit room. Most were excited, and some were a bit nervous.

When the VIP opening hour came, the staff created a meandering gauntlet across the casino floor. As the guests arrived and made their way to a ballroom for the opening reception, the staff cheered wildly to welcome the visitors. Kanter, dressed in an orange tie to match the Total Rewards logo, wandered behind the line and applauded enthusiastically.

After the invited guests enjoyed some drinks, food, and live jazz in the ballroom, management tried to hush the crowd to thank city officials, investors, and staffers who had made the opening of a new casino possible. Loveman used humor to quiet down his audience. "I want to remind you that I am a casino boss. You've seen all the movies and you know what I am capable of," he said. "There are a lot of big guys with Italian names waiting for instructions." To each side of the stage, a showgirl, imported from Las Vegas for the event and clad scantily in feathers, smiled perfectly throughout the presentation.

A little later, I met Loveman in a small conference room off the high-limit room. For all the celebration, for all the customer data analytics Loveman had pioneered, his company continued to face tough times. A week earlier, the company had reported a 2012 loss of $1.5 billion. The year before that it had recorded a loss of nearly $700 million, and things would only get worse in the future. In both years the company paid more than $2 billion to service its debt alone. The *Wall Street Journal* dubbed Caesars "wobbly." Even with its carefully tended client data, the heavy debt load threatened to become the storm that ravages all.

Did data analytics represent an elegant sandcastle that a rising tide of debt would wipe out? "We're not going bankrupt," Loveman said. "We show a loss because of things like interest expense and write-downs on depreciated assets and things like that. But the operations of the company are highly profitable and very successful, so the company last year made right at $2 billion operating its casinos around the world. That's an extraordinary number—very healthy number."

A performer tethered to the ceiling pours champagne for guests on opening night at Horseshoe Casino Cincinnati. Source: Author photo.

In 2013 that number was to stay largely the same, coming in at nearly $1.9 billion.

He noted the company had a low level of debt until it was privatized. "It was an overt decision by its new owners in 2008, and that's what the burden has been. It's a financing decision, not the operation of the business that's the problem," he said. "The measure of Total Rewards is how it competes against its local and regional competitors every month. What goes on the balance sheet is not indicative of that at all."

Loveman's case was that there is a difference between the company's overall loss under rules known as generally accepted accounting principles (GAAP) and the day-to-day profit it makes from running its casinos. He said the company makes money virtually every day virtually everywhere it operates. But the expense of the debt, write-downs of old buildings in Atlantic City, and other things make the GAAP-reported number a loss.

Loveman said the company could ease its debt load by selling new shares to the public, but he did not want to do that. He said he could raise billions of dollars that way, which would lower debt and increase profits. "But the problem with that would be the existing shareholders,

Gary Loveman at the opening of Horseshoe Casino in Cleveland, 2012. Source: Jason Miller, courtesy of Caesars Entertainment.

including myself, would be diluted terribly by the number of shares that we would have to give to do that and none of us wants to do that," he said.[2] Loveman does find it frustrating that the debt issue casts such a long shadow over his company and its innovations using customer data. "It's a huge challenge. We've been working on it for a long time. The company was financed in a certain way because everybody thought the world was going to be better, better, better, and almost immediately after it was financed in this way, the world got worse, worse, worse," he said.

And things got even worse in 2013, a year in which the company reported a $2.9 billion loss, nearly double the loss of 2012. By then, Caesars had not recorded an annual profit since 2009, which itself followed a year in which it lost more than $5 billion. By the start of 2014, Caesars faced a total debt of $23.6 billion—more than the annual GDP of dozens of smaller countries.[3] Randy Fine, Loveman's former Harvard Business School student, ended up working for him as the first vice president of Total Rewards. Now he is critical of his former boss. Fine expects that Caesars will one day have to declare bankruptcy. "There is no question that the company chose to take on too much leverage," he says. "Debt can't be serviced because revenues don't support it, and revenue is driven by customer management." Yet many investors disagreed, and the stock price of Caesars Entertainment had about doubled in the year after the opening of the new property in Cincinnati. Optimists thought that if anyone could extract themselves from such a debt, it would be Gary Loveman and his team.

Visitors saw no clues of any of this uncertainty about the future on the casino floor that night in Cincinnati. As Loveman spoke, thousands of people lined up to try their luck in the new establishment. When they finally got in, many headed first not for the gaming tables or buffet restaurant, but for the Total Rewards lines to get their loyalty cards. In the Cincinnati area, about sixty thousand people already had rewards cards from visits to other Caesars casinos. A few weeks earlier management had ordered 197,000 entry-level Gold cards to distribute to new customers ready to share their personal data in exchange for rewards. On opening night 1,825 people signed up before swarming the casino floor. "You can get a free trip to the buffet," said Edward Willis, sixty-six, a local who recently retired. "I'll take free food."

Asked what he thought about sharing his personal data through the program, Calvin Daniels said he was anxious to collect his rewards and winnings. And besides, he added, "I've got nothing to hide." By the end of the first week, 17,770 new people had volunteered to give away their data by signing up for Total Rewards.[4] The opening night was not just a flash in the pan. Within the first year of operation, nearly five million people had visited the Cincinnati casino.[5]

17

Embracing Outside Data

The Path to the Sunshine Test

Tariq Shaukat inched up Las Vegas Boulevard in bumper-to-bumper traffic after leaving a meeting. As the chief marketing officer at Caesars, he worked out of a luxurious office in Caesars Palace near Gary Loveman. Yet much of his marketing team occupied space south of the airport, six miles away. He had come to know the route back to his office intimately, skirting past the airport, then the massive Mandalay Bay complex to his left, followed by the glass pyramid of Luxor. Next came the faux Big Apple skyline of New York-New York and the massive fountains in front of the Bellagio before he arrived at Caesars Palace.

In all of Gary Loveman's time there, Caesars had just once strayed from their policy of only using personal data they had collected with the customers' consent. That had been a typical Loveman experiment. The company knew that many people visited Las Vegas who were not Total Rewards members. Perhaps if Caesars could identify some of those visitors, they could convert them into long-term clients? So they bought outside data, sent out promotions, and waited to see the results. Pretty soon, it became clear the effort was a dud. The failure loomed large in the internal corporate lore. Sometimes executives would float a new thought to supplement their information on clients by buying from data brokers such as Acxiom only for the past failure to be recalled, and the idea would be discarded, both on practical and philosophical grounds.

Yet as the capture and interpretation of personal data continued to grow more sophisticated, Caesars risked falling behind as rivals gathered as much information as possible, from any possible source, often with great success. Early in Loveman's tenure at the company, using outside data had seemed unfair, something clients did not expect. Since then the practice had become commonplace across many industries, even if most clients did not know about it.

Even the way Caesars handled and processed their impressive amounts of data appeared a bit dated in the era of cloud computing. That's why Joshua Kanter, joined on the line by the company's IT director, called Shaukat that late summer day in 2012 as he was driving back from the airport-area office. They wanted to cast aside some of the past restrictions on how the company processed customer information, including a ban on storing data on external servers owned by other companies. Shaukat listened attentively. At one point he asked how the company could expand its understanding of customers by gathering information about them not provided directly to the company. When Kanter reiterated that Caesars did not allow any use of such third-party data, and did not approve of storing their own data on external or cloud-based servers, Shaukat asked simply, "Why not?"

With that, Shaukat and Kanter started plotting a data revolution—a revolution at least by Caesars' cautious standards. They would use outside data and find more efficient ways to process and store that information. Neither man had been around in the mid-1990s when the company first embraced its "no outside personal data" policy. Nor were they present when Harrah's bought Caesars Palace and reconfirmed the restriction in the mid-2000s. But both felt it no longer made sense to embrace a blanket ban that predated even Loveman's arrival at the company. Too much had changed in marketing to customers not to take a different approach. Also, as long as the customer data could be securely stored elsewhere, it did not necessarily have to stay in Vegas.

A policy change on this scale required Loveman's buy-in. Shaukat brought up the issue on the weekly senior management call. Loveman knew the marketing team wanted to beef up the company website and create a greater online presence. Shaukat referred to such efforts when he brought up the issue.

"By the way, Gary, one of the things that we are looking at is third-party data. For example, as we get more into digital, what types of third-party data are we open to using and not?"

Shaukat was new enough—a recruit from the world of consulting—that he could still question where the policy had come from in the first place without seeming unprepared. "There is a rumor at least that you said no third-party data under any circumstances can be used. Is that still true or not true?"

He waited for Loveman's response. The future of the company's marketing direction rested on it. Loveman, whose deep voice gave a powerful impression even through the tinny speakers of a conference call, replied, "I don't remember ever saying that, but we are absolutely not going to use data on personal, private information, such as information on assets, finances, and health care."

Many data brokers try to piece together clues about how well-off people are financially, what assets they own, and what they earn. That information was too personal, the CEO said. But he opened the door on other fronts: "We are absolutely not going to use that sort of data. But using data like some of the demographic data that's out there, some of the social data that's out there, I'm open to rethinking where the right line is."

Shaukat told Loveman that he would send suggestions on how the company should update how it used technology to handle customer data. They had moved the line.

Shaukat, Kanter, and others, including from the legal team, started a formal revamp of the policy, emailing back and forth until they hammered out a document cautiously embracing outside data. Caesars could use third-party services like cloud-based computing to handle customer data. They could turn to outside data brokers like Acxiom for more insights on customers, provided they secured the right confidentiality agreements and security controls. The executives remained mindful that they should still approach outside data with sensitivity. The last thing they wanted to do was alienate loyal customers.

"Data-driven marketing is so core to what we do that we have to make sure that we are preserving the trust and preserving our ability to actually use data to drive our relationships with customers. That's the DNA of the company," Shaukat later reflected. "We no longer have to reject out of hand, without even thinking about it, policy around using third-party data. But we will always want to be several steps on the right side, on the correct side of that line. . . . If there is a gray area we generally try to stay on the whiter side of that as opposed to getting into the gray."

Caesars needed to understand better how clients spent money beyond the casino floor, on things such as entertainment and dining, increasingly important slices of the Las Vegas casino revenue pie. Figuring out who the potential gamblers are based on personal data has always proved rather difficult. The only broad personal data category predictive of potential gamblers is small businesses owners: entrepreneurs have a risk-reward profile similar to those willing to wage an all-or-nothing bet at a gaming table. But entertainment is another matter. Kanter started exploring partnerships with companies such as Ticketmaster, the ticket distribution and sales company, which knows what kinds of shows people like. If you have bought tickets in the past to concerts of '80s rock bands, for example, Ticketmaster's data may prompt the casino chain to recommend Caesars shows in that genre, much as Amazon and Netflix do for their users. Or maybe more information about dining habits would allow Caesars to better target their many culinary offerings. Part of the value of a partnership with a concert promoter was finding new customers, appealing to Ticketmaster customers who were not Caesars regulars.

Behind closed doors, executives spent many hours considering how they might use personal data from social networks such as Facebook. They wanted to make the Total Rewards website more social so that guests could share with friends the news that they had just booked a room at the Flamingo Hotel in Las Vegas or that they were redeeming points for a gift in their merchandise store. When a customer signs in to the website via Facebook, the casino company can also see much of the data on the customer's Facebook profile. As shown in earlier chapters, outsiders can infer a great deal of intimate information from Facebook, including from simple things such as "likes" and friends.

"If our hosts get access to that information, for example, as they are dealing with a customer, does the customer sort of recoil with horror that they actually know that?" Shaukat asks. "Or do they say, 'I logged in using my Facebook account—of course they know that'?"

For now, the company has decided to limit how much Facebook data it will use. It will steer clear of certain personal information such as sexual orientation, even if such data might help sell tickets to certain shows. "The last thing I want is for customers to say, 'You know what, you guys are creepy, you're invading my privacy,'" Shaukat says. "I draw the line when the stuff is very personal." He also emphasizes that Caesars protects privacy by not selling data about Total Rewards clients to others, although it sometimes sends promotions from other companies. Such promotion partnerships often make good sense, such as when an airline wants to fill its seats to Las Vegas by advertising deals on flights.

As the head of Total Rewards, Kanter was on the front lines of data-gathering about customers. He wanted to know all he could about his clients. But he did not want to strip them naked through the most aggressive, cutting-edge possibilities of data aggregation. He sought to bring more customers through the door but also hold his head high and believe that he was doing the right thing. As he considered new data, he applied what he called the Sunshine Test: "If all the information were out there in the light of day, would our customers understand and be okay with what we are doing, and is there some kind of commensurate value that they are getting?"

Of course, anyone can gamble or visit a casino hotel without being tracked if they decline to join the Caesars loyalty program. But Loveman believes customers will continue to share data if they get something in return. "If you prove to the guest that you use that information productively, they tend to be quite generous with it," he says. "If you prove to them on the other hand that you are a dope and you don't listen to them, then they are going to get pretty frustrated with it. For example, if you go to a grocery store and all your grocery purchases

*Joshua Kanter of Caesars advocates a "Sunshine
Test" when it comes to using personal data.
Source: Author photo.*

are scanned and you're a lifelong vegetarian but every week you get an
ad in the mail for meat, that pretty much convinces you that nobody
is listening."

Data's Blind Spot

For all their power and potential, big data and data analytics, whether
about specific individuals or broader business trends, are not all-powerful and do not always produce the right answer. For Gary Loveman,
data's limitations in forecasting the future failed him when he most
needed insight.

In 2006, rival casino innovator Steve Wynn offered to sell him a
subconcession to operate in Macau for $900 million. Harrah's had al-
ready passed on an opportunity to buy into Macau in 2002. That year,
the government there ended a decades-old casino monopoly and auc-
tioned off three licenses, opening the market to foreign operators. Executives involved in the decision say Harrah's worried that association

with Macau's unsavory reputation could complicate their standing with US gaming regulators. Several years later Harrah's had a second chance when three more sublicenses went on the market. By then it was clear that gambling in Macau was growing dramatically every year and nearing Las Vegas in gaming revenue.

Loveman, his chief financial officer, and others delved into their spreadsheets and conducted their usual vigorous analysis. Could their mathematical models justify such a high price tag just for a license to operate in the former Portuguese colony? Looking at statistics from 2005, the math nerds saw that all of Macau earned casino revenue of $5.7 billion in 2005, up from $5.1 billion the year before.[1]

A few weeks later, Loveman called Wynn with his conclusion: "Steve, it's too expensive. We don't believe that we can sustain that number."

"That's my price," Wynn replied. "If you don't want to pay it, I'll find someone else who does."[2]

Wynn found a buyer at his full asking price almost immediately. The buyer's confidence in untested potential trumped rational analysis. Macau has since become the world capital of gambling, dwarfing Las Vegas, with about seven times more gambling revenue than Las Vegas in 2013. Chinese players have emerged as the world's biggest whales— mega-gamblers who wager millions of dollars a year, and they love Macau. Loveman looks back on that decision as the biggest mistake of his career.

"No one had ever paid $900 million just for a license—not a building or a business," Loveman says. "The tremendous accumulation of wealth in coastal China, the desire of folks in that market to gamble, the quality of the facilities themselves to be built—there was no precedent ever in the history of the industry that could anticipate such a thing. So as a result the methods that we used, the kind of conventional analytic methods that we used—they just can't foresee that kind of thing adequately. So as a result we underestimated the value. . . . Even the most optimistic people—including Steve, who I consider to be wildly optimistic—could never have imagined that that market would be $35 billion in 2012, and that's exactly what happened." By 2007, Macau was nearing Las Vegas in overall casino revenue; it surpassed

Vegas in 2008. Revenue continued to soar in the following years as Vegas went into a deep slump, and in 2010 Macau made $23.5 billion, more than double the casino revenues in all of Nevada.[3] Total Macau casino business had about doubled again by 2013, when it recorded $45.2 billion in revenue.[4]

Wynn and Sheldon Adelson, the owner of the Las Vegas Sands Corporation, whose properties include the Venetian, both jumped at the chance to expand into Macau when licenses were first awarded in 2002, cementing their reputations as casino visionaries. Conventional wisdom had underestimated both men before. Many predicted Wynn would go bankrupt after he opened up the $630 million Mirage casino in 1989. "He's such a genius that I'm not sure any analytics could trump his intuition, so he's actually a little bit of an anomaly, I think," says Patti Hart, CEO of slot machine maker IGT. "Steve has a very sophisticated analytics business. The problem is his ideas are always better than the analytics because he has just great intuition." Conventional wisdom also expected Adelson to fail after he opened the Venetian in 1999. Both instinctual investors defied the skeptics.

Another example of the value of instinct played to the company's advantage over the long run. After Harrah's reached a deal to buy Caesars Entertainment in 2004 for $9.4 billion, Caesars Palace executives briefed Loveman and top managers on their deal with singer Celine Dion. She had agreed to anchor their new four-thousand-seat Colosseum starting in 2003, performing two hundred shows a year for three years. Many at the time thought a single headliner could not command big crowds like larger productions did.

Caesars Palace officials told Loveman and marketing chief Rich Mirman that the Celine contract had proved vital to reviving the Caesars Palace brand. The Harrah's financial team had looked at how much they were going to pay her and thought the deal made no sense. But in the first months after the show opened, on days when Dion performed, the hotel and casino showed additional income of $200,000 from more gambling and food and drink revenue.[5] "You know, we never in a million years would have done the Celine Dion deal, not in a million years. But yet it was the key to their success," Loveman told Mirman as they left the meeting. It was another case where a company experiences intangible benefits that did not show up in the numbers. Celine Dion remains a leading performer at Caesars Palace.

Caesars' Influential Shadow

Even using extensive data from its Total Rewards system, Caesars can sometimes be clueless in reading the intentions of their clients. David Schwartz, director of the Center for Gaming Research at the University of Nevada Las Vegas, is a Total Rewards member who receives a stream of what he considers mistargeted offers. The author of three books on gambling, Schwartz cites as examples discounted "insider" rates to stay at the company's hotels in Las Vegas ranging from $20 a night at the Quad to $94 at Caesars Palace, under email headlines such as "Wish You Were Here . . . "[6] He gets offers to visit Atlantic City, an unlikely lure for someone living in Las Vegas. And to attend an overnight party celebrating the 2009 comedy film *The Hangover*. Schwartz is married with children and says the latter offer does not appeal to him.

"What was the reason that the ultra-sophisticated Total Rewards system is sending a Las Vegas resident emails telling him that 'the Sin City sunshine is calling your name again?'" he asks. He is skeptical about the extent to which there is any loyalty in the gaming business and says customers just go where they get the best deal.

Total Rewards head Kanter says the company is not mindlessly spamming local residents. The company knows that if a local does not have to drive home, he or she might gamble longer, generating more revenue. "He may not appreciate that logic, but it's naïve to think that we did not intelligently arrive at the decision. Out of a hundred people that look like him, we'll get a few of them who will respond and at the segment level it's a good decision," Kanter says.

Harrah's Kansas City manager Tom Cook says the company often falls short of using the personal data on gamblers to make very specific targeted offers. Loveman is surprisingly receptive to such criticism. "We may not catch that as well as I claim to catch it. He's quite right," Loveman says. "The problem is that when you go onto the system and try to do it, it's really hard and time-consuming. So pulling the data list and segmenting the data list geographically turns out to be a bitch, and so we don't do it very well, in fact, so we wind up messing that up."

The CEO says the company does not react quickly enough to details of a customer's visit, and sometimes does not anticipate well enough what customers are doing. But overall, Caesars' deep dive into personal data has long paid off. "Certainly by any measure it is tremendously effective," Loveman says.[7]

Over time, clever use of personal data has dramatically improved Caesars' bottom line in the Loveman years. When he joined Harrah's, clients spent just 36 percent of their gambling budget with them. Today, customers devote more than 60 percent of their gaming spending to Caesars. VIPs spend nearly 80 percent with the company.[8] Microtargeting clients made his company a leader in the industry and cemented Loveman's rise to CEO in 2003. During his regnum Caesars became the world's biggest casino company, running more than fifty casinos,[9] up from fourteen, in seven countries.[10] When Loveman arrived they operated only in the United States. Now they employ sixty-eight thousand people, up from fourteen thousand.[11]

Rival casinos have embraced loyalty programs and gather granular data on wagering and other spending. Some gamblers belong to so many programs that they keep a stack of loyalty cards on a keychain ring. The forgetful among them attach a string from their pants to the ring as a reminder to remove the plastic slab before getting up from a slot machine. "What our marketing is intended to do is to give us an extraordinary share compared with what our position would normally provide, and that's how we measure ourselves," Loveman says. "And we exceed our fair share in every market but one, I think, across the country."

For years, casino rivals ridiculed Loveman and his management team as "casino nerds." Go ahead, call him a nerd, propellerhead, or geek—he doesn't mind. "There are traditionalists in the business who view that as a pejorative notion. They say that with disdain," he says. "But the industry has really come along in this direction."

As Caesars embrace outside supplementary customer data, it is likely that other companies inside and outside the world of casinos will continue to do so. You may not visit casinos at all. But rest assured that those credit card offers you get in the mail, the frequent flyer and loyalty club offers, as well as other solicitations are based on sophisticated guesses about what kind of customer you are and what you might be interested in. Even businesses as diverse as the Walt Disney Company embrace the data-driven approach championed by Loveman and speak in similar terms. "What we say at Disney is that there is never too much data," says Leon Gantt, manager of Disney World's information technology. "We want to have enough information to understand what they want beforehand and anticipate it." The beloved company faces the same puzzle managers face across the economy: "We have these mountains of data . . . how can we use it without alienating clients while maximizing revenue?"

Opening the Secret Files

Things become more complicated with third-party data. From a consumer standpoint, the problem with such information has long been that these files constitute a black box. As with the Stasi files during the days of East Germany, the ordinary person has no hope of seeing the totality of what commercial data brokers such as Acxiom and Experian have assembled.

For some years, people could request to see just that part of their Acxiom file gathered from public documents, showing less interesting information such as their address and phone number. Yet almost no one was able to surmount the firm's onerous requirements to see even this fragment. The process required sending Acxiom a Social Security number, date of birth, driver's license number, current address, phone number, and email address, as well as a $5 check—and then waiting two weeks. From 2009 to mid-2012, between seventy-seven and 342 people per year had asked to see their files, with just two to sixteen annually providing enough information to get access, the company told a congressional panel.

Yet even then, the commercial dossier remained off-limits. That part of the file includes a description of one's general family and financial situation. It might list race, ethnicity, religious affiliation, education, political affiliation, occupation, and hobbies. Acxiom, as well as other leading data brokers, might know what credit cards you use, as well as some health topics of interest to you such as diabetes or arthritis. Knowing that all of that information exists in unseen vaults at companies people had no relationship with made a lot of them—at least those who knew about it—rather uncomfortable. And the mounds of data continue to grow: in a typical week, Acxiom processes a trillion transactions—twenty times the number of searches conducted by Google.[12]

In 2011, Acxiom embraced a change in direction by hiring a new CEO, Scott Howe, a former Microsoft executive whom Gary Loveman had taught at Harvard Business School. In interviewing for the position, Howe preached a new direction for Acxiom. The world was moving toward increased transparency and consumer control, and companies that ignore this trend would do so at their peril, he said.[13] He got the job leading 6,200 people and moved slowly but deliberately toward cracking open Acxiom's doors to the public. After about a year and a half of internal reorganization Howe kicked off plans to allow people to see a part of their files instantly online. "Long before I came to Acxiom it had always bugged me that I did not know what data was collected about me," he said. "I think it is bad business that companies lie or exploit or obfuscate the truth from their customers. That's not the kind of company that any of us want to work at."

Some of the old guard at Acxiom scoffed at Howe's push.[14] They recognized the pressure from privacy advocates and the threat of future government regulation. They had experienced similar spurts in the past and thought the scrutiny would pass. They saw no reason to change how things had always been done. But Howe pressed on. "I just could not work at a company, quite frankly, that it felt like we were not doing what was ethically right," he said. "I couldn't feel good about coming to work every day and being branded as the biggest company that no one's ever heard of or, you know, the commercial equivalent of NSA or the supersecret spy guys."

Scott Howe, CEO of Acxiom.
Source: Author photo.

In September 2013, Acxiom launched AboutTheData.com, a web interface that allows the general public to look up their data instantly. Howe knew that even after Acxiom spent millions of dollars on the project, the site could still be improved. But he thought it was best to go live quickly rather than wait years for engineers to design a perfect system.

Thousands went online to meet their digital doubles. What many consumers found was often not an all-knowing Big Brother but a world of imperfect replicas, sometimes as odd as the flawed Bizarro world of Htrae (read that backward) of Superman comics, where things are the opposite of Earth.

Rich Mirman, the first data guru hired by Gary Loveman, remembered how Acxiom had long tried to sell data during his time at the company. He and others at the time were never convinced of the utility of such information, and seeing his own file did not change his out-look. Acxiom had accurately listed many of the kinds of things his household buys, but they completely misread who he is, saying he is single with no kids and a dial-up modem harkening to the Internet's earliest days. "How many single men without kids own a minivan?" he wondered. "They should have figured out that I was married with kids—the dial-up modem is just silly."

Joshua Kanter found that Acxiom knew about his hobbies, pur-chases, and home, but a lot of the small details were wrong. It knew that he owned his beloved 2011 Audi A5, but it was way off on his income. Overall, he thought, his profile looked as it might have two decades earlier, when he was running his college painting business.

Acxiom thought Kyle Prall, founder of the controversial site bustedmugshots.com, was still a student and that he had a child. In re-ality, he had left school more than a decade before and had not brought any offspring into the world. Claudia Perlich, the East German–born data scientist who was too young when the Berlin Wall fell to have had a Stasi file, looked herself up only to receive a response that "we were unable to verify you." I found that same response on my own file.

For casino entrepreneur John Acres, who wants to reinvent gam-bling by using personal information to make games more responsive to individual preferences, Acxiom knew nearly the correct square footage of his house, but his file was wrong on his household income, his ve-hicles, and the value of his home. "Nothing in there was very informa-tive," he said. "It was still pretty worthless."

It's not that the emperor has no clothes. But the attire is more piece-meal and ragged than many had feared. Acxiom CEO Howe said his own file had six or seven mistakes, but noted that the errors come from data wholesalers supplying Acxiom with the raw material for what might be two thousand data points in an individual file.

Before going live with the site, Howe had worried that many us-ers would opt out entirely, leaving Acxiom with less comprehensive files. But something surprising happened as people reviewed their AboutTheData.com files. Eleven percent corrected inaccuracies in their files (with political party the single item changed most often), leaving

Acxiom better, more valuable data to sell. Fewer than 2 percent of the half a million people who visited AboutTheData.com early on said goodbye for good. Howe had forecast that as many as 15 percent of visitors would use the new site to opt out.

"Managing your data or your preferences or your permissions should be something you think about as often as managing the maintenance of your car, or managing your yard, or managing your health care," Howe predicts. "It is just going to be something that is part of everybody's routine because those that do it are going to have better experiences. They are going to have better offers, they are going to get unique content, they are going to get better information."

Many users corrected their files for free. But what if consumers received cash or compensation in exchange for their information? Marketers would get the most accurate data because no one knows you better than you. Under such a system, companies would offer money, status, or special offers to make it worthwhile to share personal data. In the last few years, a number of companies have begun embracing such a model to empower consumers. Some of their founders have dramatic stories of their own.

18

The Not-So-Enriching Business of Privacy

Profiting from Privacy

Shane Green nervously unveiled his startup's website on November 11, 2011, at exactly 11:11 a.m. Place your private information on Personal.com, he told the world, and eventually companies will pay for access to your information and to market to you. Not pennies, but real money—at least $1,000 a year for the average consumer. On the day the site went live, Green felt pangs of doubt. "Oh, my God, do we really know what we are doing?"

Some Internet entrepreneurs and commentators thought he was committing a major blunder. Not only could he not safely store personal details such as passport information, medical records, passwords, and alarm codes, but what he was doing was potentially reckless, possibly vulnerable to hacking, the naysayers said. Things did not turn out as either Green or his skeptics thought they would.

Since the 1990s, a series of startups have sought to create tools to help consumers navigate the data-hungry world with greater privacy. With so many people accustomed to receiving free Internet services, these entrepreneurs have struggled to sign up paying customers. Several of these businesses have gone under.

By 2014, the market was becoming more receptive after Edward Snowden's revelations about the US government's gathering of vast troves of personal data. "People are going to be more conscious of the fact that what they do put out there is going to be public, and therefore I would say their online behavior will be altered," says Emanuel Pleitez, chief strategy officer at data broker Spokeo, who also ran for mayor of Los Angeles in 2013.

The public is also slowly becoming more aware that firms gather and store as much personal data as they can. "Unfortunately this type of data collection—we're at the very beginning of it," says Dan Auerbach, formerly of the Electronic Frontier Foundation, a privacy and consumer rights advocacy group. "We're kind of entering a new era where data can just be stored forever. Back in the old days you might be able to leverage this data for a little bit and then have to throw it away because, oh, there is just too much data to keep. But now it is really realistic to suggest companies can do this forever."

These factors created opportunity for Personal.com and other privacy companies. But Green struggled to interest investors. Early on, the entrepreneur twice met Esther Dyson, a journalist-turned-investor whose many life adventures include training to become an astronaut in Russia. She had served as chairwoman of the Electronic Frontier Foundation. Dyson said she was fascinated with the idea. She told him that she and others invested in a number of privacy startups that never really got off the ground, often after burning through millions of dollars. "Everyone who ever became good at this idea of empowering people with their data ended up going to the dark side," she said.[1]

Reputation.com

Out in Silicon Valley, another firm with the same goal of setting up a personal data vault, Reputation.com, took a different path. First it learned how to make money—then it set its sights on empowering people with their own data.[2] It spent millions of dollars a year advertising in newspapers and on radio.[3] Set up by Harvard lawyer-turned-entrepreneur Michael Fertik, Reputation.com built its business around removing or obscuring damaging Internet information and reviews.

A typical client might be a lawyer, doctor, or independent contractor who fears that a negative review could harm business. Fertik cites the example of a builder who does a subpar job once every few years and then faces unrelenting Internet criticism from a disgruntled customer. Or an employer who fires someone for stealing and then is accused of racism. Reputation.com seeks to make some of the negative postings fall lower in Google search rankings by adding more positive posts about the client, such as on a blog site or LinkedIn profile, or by collecting real reviews from real customers. Prices range from less than $1,000 to $6,000 for such help. "Our product is not perfect," Fertik says. "If there are a hundred [negative] data points out there, we can probably put fifty back in the tube."

A man possessing seemingly unending energy and opinions, Fertik grew up on Manhattan's Upper West Side and attended private schools. His father directed commercial and documentary films; his mother worked as a psychotherapist. After attending Harvard College and Harvard Law School, Fertik set up ReputationDefender.com, which became Reputation.com after he bought the domain name for $200,000. At his office headquarters in Redwood City, in California's Silicon Valley, Fertik works from a standing desk in front of a MacBook Air laptop. Sometimes he wears a weighted jacket that provides exercise as he moves.

What really excites Fertik—and he is often quite excitable—is the idea of allowing people to make money by creating their own data vaults, something the company has worked on for many months. On a recent afternoon, engineers in their twenties and thirties, from places as far afield as Russia, Brazil, and India, are sitting around a conference table. They're watching a projection at the end of the room as they try to put the final touches on their latest innovation.

The team has assembled public information on tens of millions of Americans, and is fine-tuning a software program that scores everyone's lifetime earning potential. They factor in details from résumés and online sites such as LinkedIn, which lists education, past jobs, and geographic location. Such data will enable Reputation.com to tell advertisers who has the potential to make, say, $500,000 a year in the next ten years.

With these scores, Reputation.com is hoping to allow people to sell their information to the highest bidders. If, for example, you share that you travel a few times a year to southern Florida, stay in upscale hotels, and spend your holidays playing golf, various businesses may be willing to pony up cash for the opportunity to market directly to you. Or perhaps they will offer bonus points or status in their loyalty programs or other incentives. To make such a system work, Fertik says he needs data on tens of millions of people, insight about customers that makes them interesting to marketers, and user permission.

"The big open secret about the Internet is that it's a cheat. The people are constantly being exploited without their knowledge or permission," says Fertik. "The Internet companies that tout the value system of being transparent rely, fundamentally, on being completely non-transparent with you when it comes to your information."

Data-gathering has become commonplace for all transactions beyond forking over cash at a store—even if the vendor says it really cares about privacy. For example, Adam & Eve, a company that sells sex toys and adult videos, also rents address lists of its customers so that other marketers can contact, for example, women who have bought porn in recent months. Chad Davis, the director of marketing for PHE Inc., which owns Adam & Eve, says, "We really do take our customers' privacy very seriously." The company does that by screening the clients who rent its lists—to ensure appropriate marketing use of its data—but not by keeping that data private.[4] Like others that rent mailing lists, the company also seeds its lists with a few false addresses so it can see if those renting the lists market in the way they have said they would.

Those who read Adam & Eve's fine print learn that the company does rent postal addresses to other companies, although it allows customers to opt out.[5] Some have complained that they did not know their data would be sold. "I ordered some fun bedroom items for my wife from adam&eve.com," one man wrote on reddit.com. "Biggest mistake I've made in a while. Since my single, one-time order, I have received *DOZENS* of graphic pornographic catalogs showing up in my mail."[6]

Allowing consumers to profit from their data remains a difficult business proposition. Reputation.com, Personal.com, and others seeking to create data vaults face a chicken-and-egg dilemma: What marketer would pay substantial money for personally curated information when so few have signed up? And how could the data vault induce consumers to join without real benefits?

Reputation.com tried to get around this problem by quietly scraping public data off the Internet on millions of people. "We are gathering data without people's knowledge right now in order to learn and get information, but we are not sharing it or selling it," Fertik says. "Unless you get enough data, you don't have enough insight. And if you don't have enough insight, you can't actually get the vendors to sign up. And if you can't get the vendors to sign up, you can't get the consumer to sign up."

That a privacy company assembles profiles on millions of people without their knowledge is a bit surprising. "I don't think it is creepy because we don't plant any cookies. . . . We basically find stuff that is on the open Internet about people," he says.

To fund the effort, the company relied on revenue from its businesses to improve online reputations and its service that removes details about individual clients held by data brokers such as PeopleSmart, featured in Chapter 6. "I could have gone and tried to raise $100 million on this theory that there is a data privacy vault thing in the future and what happens is you end up with a complete bereft piece of shit," says Fertik. "Would you spend $10 million if you have no revenue, no real customers, no real user base? That's an 'If you build it, they will not come' story."

When Identity Meant Life or Death

Personal.com, however, took this riskier path, creating a personal data vault with the hope of figuring out how to make money. Direct experience with how personal information can determine a person's fate bolstered the company's conviction. Two of the founders, Tarik Kurspahic and Edin Saracevic, grew up in multiethnic Sarajevo. For centuries, Muslims, Orthodox Christians, Christians, and Jews lived side by side, sharing cafe tables along pedestrian streets, joking, gossiping, flirting, and enjoying life. Then in 1991, Yugoslavia started collapsing. Ethnic identity—Muslim, Orthodox Serb, and Catholic Croat—became a matter of life and death.

Kurspahic was a classic Yugoslav mix: son of a Belgrade Serb and a Bosnian Muslim. As war spread elsewhere in Yugoslavia, some warned that the ethnic groups in Sarajevo would fight. "There's no way, no chance that that will happen here," Kurspahic thought. In April 1992, two days before his eighteenth birthday, thousands marched through the streets in a peace demonstration. He joined a crowd in front of the Parliament building. Later, a gunman fired into the crowd, killing two women. Like other hotheaded eighteen-year-olds, he just wanted to find the guy who fired the shots and "toss him out of the window."

The longest siege in modern history was about to start. Kurspahic and Saracevic, who had worked as event planners, did what they could to survive. Neither was particularly religious, but society marked them as Muslims—their names gave them away. Both served with local neighborhood defense forces. Kurspahic fled Sarajevo later that year and moved with his family to the United States.

Some years older, Saracevic remained for another two years in the besieged city. When he was growing up as the child of Muslims, the national government promoted "unity and brotherhood" of all its ethnic groups. Saracevic thought of himself as a Yugoslav, not a Bosnian or a Muslim. Just before the start of the war he and an ethnic Serb business partner had finished building three sandwich shops, sort of like McDonald's but in the shape of windmills. With the warmer weather of spring approaching, it seemed like a great time to open a sandwich business. He had planned to install the first windmill in just two days. He lost his entire savings.

During the war, Saracevic continued his entrepreneurial activities when possible. At one point he printed more than two hundred T-shirts embossed with the slogan "United Colors of Bosnia." Within hours, he sold all of them to foreign journalists covering the war. In 1994, he produced the movie *Misaldo* (which, spelled backward, means "I am leaving" in Bosnian), a series of satirical commercials about the war. One for Nike sneakers showed people running for their lives in Snipers' Alley. The film gained him an invitation to the Berlinale International Film Festival. The United Nations escorted him out of the besieged city. Saracevic then moved to the United States.

Shane Green watched the Bosnian war from afar, outraged that the West waited years before intervening. His interest in global affairs had blossomed during a 1987 high school trip to Europe that included a day in East Berlin. When his school group arrived on the western side of the Berlin Wall, he stepped too close to the imposing structure, a few feet inside East German terrain. A Communist guard, shouting through a loudspeaker, ordered him to step back.

Later that day he visited East Germany's largest department store and chatted with a sales clerk. The conversation aroused the attention of a security guard who demanded to see his passport. Green's chaperones had warned him to avoid exactly such a situation in which an East German official might take away travel documents. He felt helpless and angry—he did not want to conform to such a system. After he left East Berlin he burst into tears. These experiences inspired Green to become an evangelist for the individual's right to control his or her own data. "I've learned from my whole life experience to be suspicious of institutions or even people who have power and use it in ways that are not transparent," he says.

After the Bosnian war ended, Green traveled to Sarajevo several times to rebuild playgrounds and render other help. In Washington, DC, he met Saracevic and Kurspahic. Together they created the Map Network, a company making digital and print maps for special events such as the Super Bowl. The founders, who owned about half the shares, sold the business in 2006 for $37.5 million but continued to work there. Nokia, in turn, bought it the following year.

With 1.2 billion people owning Nokia devices at the time, Green saw the staggering potential of big data generated from cell phones. He suggested that Nokia allow users access to their own data. "The amount of data that was able to be captured kind of blew my mind," he says. The company was not interested in that vision. Green and his Bosnian partners began to ask, "What would it look like if we turned this whole model upside down and built a platform for individuals to become the ultimate gatekeepers, controllers of their own data?" The idea for Personal.com was born.

Slow Start

Green, Saracevic, Kurspahic, and two others founded Personal.com in 2009. For the first two years they designed the site and the software behind it, which encrypts user data and promises never to share it without permission. People can upload personal documents and information such as house and car insurance policies, credit card and frequent flyer numbers, alarm codes, bank accounts, tax records, medications, passports, and other ID details—even clothing sizes and other minutiae of daily life.

By the end of 2013 Green had raised $20 million, including from AOL founder Steve Case, who now leads investment company Revolution.com, and Ted Leonsis, the majority owner of several Washington, DC–area professional sports teams. By contrast, Reputation.com raised $65 million in capital over several rounds.

In his pitches, Green—whose rimless glasses, trimmed beard, and short hair recall one of the best-known photos of a middle-aged Steve Jobs—stressed that his company would establish a fair market value for personal data. "We believe the average U.S. consumer can earn $1,000 or more annually," he told potential investors.

His pitch cited car buyers as an example. "Declare your intent to purchase a new car, add relevant criteria to your existing car data and let the world compete for your attention and your business," his investor prospectus said. Marketers would gain direct access to customers just as they were ready to buy; he cited, as an example, "213,000 consumers with luxury cars whose leases expire in the next 90 days." Another projected use would enable people to advertise their travel plans and allow marketers to send them discounts ranging from 10 percent

*Personal.com's cofounders, Edin Saracevic, Shane Green, and Tarik Kurspahic
(from left), at the firm's Washington, DC, office. Source: Personal.com (reprinted
with permission).*

to 30 percent. The company expected to make money by charging a
10 percent commission.

Personal.com's initial investment did not translate into many customers after its November 2011 beta launch. Fewer than six thousand
people signed up in the initial months, and many who did found it
daunting. Those who persevered needed hours to enter all their data and
documents, a process as satisfying as sorting bills into an accordion file.

Personal.com received a fair amount of media coverage, but some of
the articles set unreasonable expectations that users would soon be able
to cash in on their self-curated personal information. "Unless you have
millions and millions of users, no one cares about you—and, in fact,
they scoff at you," Green says. "It hasn't always been easy: there have
been some really rough ups and downs." Part of the problem stemmed
from their inability to make users money. "I was more bullish at that
time than was warranted about the willingness of partners to work with

us," Green says in retrospect. "That was a miscalculation on our part. And [we] never ended up launching that side of the business."

With relatively few users signing up, the Personal.com team discussed more than a dozen other ideas to attract more interest. One idea proposed using information from a person's vault to fill out forms when buying airline tickets or prescription eyeglasses, or when registering on e-commerce sites. Green initially resisted, as did his technology guru, Kurspahic. "When you look at cool tech companies and the kind of stuff that they do, this does not sit at the top of the food chain. And from that perspective that wasn't appealing to most of us. We all want to do supercool stuff," Kurspahic says.

But people who saw demonstrations of the feature really liked it, and Personal.com launched "Fill It" in 2013. For the first time, entering all their data into the encrypted vault directly helped users. Personal.com started signing agreements with entities such as Geico insurance, schools, and the Department of Education, which placed a copy of users' insurance information or student loan details into the vault. The idea was to get businesses to pay the $30-per-user annual subscription as a service to attract customers. Another company called FileThis connects data from users' bank accounts, credit card statements, phone bills, mutual funds, and other merchants, and places a copy directly into their Personal.com vaults. Slowly, the service was coming alive.[7] By spring 2014, one hundred thousand users had signed up for Personal.com. The company also created a second site, fillit.com, to help promote the service, and it continued to map thousands of website forms every week to expand its capabilities.[8]

Out in California, Reputation.com, focusing on its core business, delayed launching its own data vault, with Fertik hoping it would go live later in 2014. Other companies with similar ideas—such as mydex.org, ownyourinfo.com, qiy.nl, myinfosafedirect.com, and datacoup.com—have not taken the world by storm. In 2014, datacoup.com actually started paying people for their data, but it has struggled with the same chicken-and-egg problem that has vexed others. Datacoup.com offered as much as $8 a month to users, but on average paid just $1.56 in February 2014 as it sought to find buyers for the data.[9]

Selling other people's data with or without their knowledge remains far more profitable than protecting and selling data on behalf of consumers, at least for now. Yet the ideas are intriguing and may continue to evolve into an empowering solution for consumers. In 2014, even Acxiom was talking about the possibility of paying users for their data, especially to know when they were in the market for a car or other big-ticket items, a move that could herald a major transformation of marketing and advertising.[10] Because it already has hundreds of millions of files on people and many clients, a data broker like Acxiom could overcome the chicken-and-egg dilemma.

Todd Cullen, a former Acxiom vice president for global data products, is convinced the balance of power will ultimately shift to consumers, away from anonymous data brokers and middlemen. He says companies such as Personal.com will crawl, walk, and then run, meaning it will take time. "The model today is completely backwards," says Cullen, now the chief data officer at advertising firm Ogilvy and Mather. "Consumers are beginning to realize data itself has value."

That's the way it should be. Customers should have the final say in how and with whom they share their data. Privacy tools can help, but they are only part of a solution that protects consumers against possible abuses. Companies have to be open and responsible about what personal data they gather, and government rules may be needed to assure certain intimate data are not abused.

19

Empowerment

Insiders' Mixed Emotions

The harvesting and use of personal data across businesses of all kinds are now a reality, whether we like it or not. That does not mean the public should passively accept every new effort to expand their collection. Customers should know what companies are doing, and should have the final say in how it is shared. With societal boundaries on personal data still largely undefined, the potential for abuse is strong.

Fears that marketers will violate private spheres long predate the Internet. In *The Hidden Persuaders,* Vance Packard wrote, "It is about the way many of us are being influenced and manipulated—far more than we realize—in the patterns of our everyday life. Large-scale efforts are being made, often with impressive success, to channel our unthinking habits, our purchasing decisions, and our thought processes by the use of insights gleaned from psychiatry and the social sciences."[1]

Later he added, "The most serious offense many of the depth manipulators commit, it seems to me, is that they try to invade the privacy of our minds. It is this right to the privacy in our minds—privacy to be rational or irrational—that I believe we must strive to protect."[2] Packard wrote those words not about Google, Facebook, or other digital-age corporations. He was writing in 1957 about the growing sophistication of marketing and advertising.

A decade after Packard's book was published, Lester Wunderman, who is often credited with creating the term "direct marketing," described a future in which companies would gather vast amounts of personal data to further their marketing strategies. His 1967 speech makes fascinating reading today because much of his vision has long since come to pass:

> A computer can know and remember as much marketing detail about 200,000,000 consumers as did the owner of a crossroads general store about his handful of customers. I can know and select such personal details as who prefers strong coffee, imported beer, new fashions, bright colors. Who just bought a home, freezer, camera, automobile. Who has a new baby, is overweight, got married, owns a pet, likes romantic novels, serious reading, listens to Bach or The Beatles . . . Those marketers who ignore the implications of our new individualized information society will be left behind in what may well come to be known as the age of mass production and marketing ignorance.[3]

Wunderman, ninety-three years old at the start of 2014, was still working long after his vision became reality in the era of big data. I called him to discuss the current marketing landscape and heard a mixed assessment of how marketers use personal information today. "I get mail that I discard or I get some that offends me, where they are misusing the information that they have. But I think there are always outlaws and the outlaws in the marketing business are obviously those who would misuse data," he said. "Now we have all these dating sites or people-meeting-other-people sites. And those, I think, would be subject to abuse, where people who feel isolated may, in fact, enter data that could come back at them. . . . In a data-driven world, the potential for abuse may be something we have to spend more time considering than we used to where such information was not available."[4]

The potential for abuse makes many marketers cautious about what information they share about themselves. They know from experience both how useful personal data are for their work and how revealing they can be. "I don't know if I want all these websites to know I am visiting them," said Netta Kivilis, who for a time managed online marketing for Amazon's MYHABIT, a flash fashion sales site. "Most of online marketing is evil. . . . On the flip side, as a marketer, it is super useful.

"I sometimes find myself appalled to see where the line is constantly being moved," she said. "The line is getting farther and farther away."[5]

Changing Norms

As businesses try to move the line, social norms will evolve. In some cases, practices that once appeared invasive or creepy may become accepted. "User expectations change over time, and this decade they have changed more than they probably have in the last century," says Emanuel Pleitez of people search site Spokeo. "For example, five years ago location data on people and people's behavior—it would have been crazy to think that people would be updating it themselves and putting it out there and sharing it across networks. . . . Now anyone can aggregate Foursquare and all these other location-based—Instagram—and all these other data-aggregating systems," he says. "Any example you can give me today, in two years can be different in terms of user, consumer expectations."

In other instances, industry practices will provoke public outcry and government and legal action that may rein in certain practices. Spokeo paid an FTC fine in 2012 related to the marketing of its information for job employment purposes. At that time the site sold especially detailed dossiers that included a person's ethnicity, political affiliation, religion, hobbies, education level, wealth level, and credit estimate as part of a low-cost subscription. Since then Spokeo has decided to eliminate some of these details. "Spokeo deleted certain content from its services in 2012, in order to help stem potential misuse," cofounder Harrison Tang said.[6]

The line on what is fair game in personal data can move both ways, even if the overall trend is in the direction of more data gathering. Mary Culnan, a senior fellow at the Future of Privacy Forum and a professor emeritus at Bentley University, has been working on consumer privacy and marketing since the 1990s, when mailing lists and database marketing were the big concern. "Every time I think I have seen it all, something new comes along. There is a big flap about the latest new thing, and then people get used to it (or maybe never really knew about it), and life goes on," she says. "Sort of like the frog in the pot of cold water and you turn on the stove and the frog eventually boils to death as the water heats up slowly. The information collection proceeds the same way."

Highly degreed experts and ordinary Joes will continue to argue about what uses of data constitute great marketing and what creep into an intrusive zone. Opinions are going to differ. Former Las Vegas Mayor Oscar Goodman is outspoken on the topic. "This kind of 'Big Brotherism' I don't think has any place in America, in the free world," he says. "They find out what you like, what you dislike, then they appeal to you either personally or as a matter of advertising. That's the nature of that beast. I don't like it. I don't want people to know my business."

Everyone should reflect on the issue of personal data and decide for himself where the line should be. My prescribed solution—openness on the part of the data hunters and choice to the data hunted—accommodates a wide span of opinions, from those convinced that privacy is dead so get over it to those who want more control over what the commercial world knows about them.

The Price of Free

Consumers should expect that companies offering free services want to make money from personal data. Internet firms could do a better job of explaining what they are doing and how advertising underwrites the free stuff. The perception of underhandedness can badly damage a company or an entire industry. Facebook and Google continue to arouse suspicions by changing the rules on users from time to time.

Think before accepting free, and consider the consequences. For example, Scholarships.com tells high school students, "We can help you find money for school, even as colleges discover and recruit you. FREE!" The site includes a detailed series of pages where students add personal information, including sensitive categories like ethnicity, religion, and disabilities such as those related to cancer, obesity, or genetic

Former Las Vegas Mayor Oscar Goodman (right). Source: Author photo.

predisposition to Alzheimer's. Another page includes the information box for "Lesbian/Gay/Bisexual/Transgender (LGBT) or Parent LGBT." "Any and all of your responses during your search could impact your search results, so don't skip anything!" the site tells visitors.

Because the service is free, Scholarships.com makes money selling personal data via list broker American Student Marketing, which is located at the same address. About fifty thousand people visit the site every day, and 80 percent share information about themselves. "It's opt-in on the front page—nobody else has opt-in on the front page," says Larry Gerber, president of Scholarships.com, who calls his site a valuable service that matches students with the right funding sources.

However, some say high school students volunteering the information don't really understand that they have exposed themselves in the open marketplace. "Certainly this type of marketing poses real privacy risks to individuals, particularly young people that might be reliant on their family but not out to them," says Michael Cole-Schwartz, a spokesman for the gay rights group Human Rights Campaign.

Many firms offer free services or contests in exchange for data, often vaguely explaining their practices in lengthy fine print.[7] Online quizzes and surveys that offer insights on your health or wealth or other issues typically collect personal data. Publishers Clearing House encourages people to share details to enter lucrative sweepstakes or receive incentives such as gift cards. Some of its pharmacy offers ask about high blood pressure, smoking, sleep disorders, or diabetes. "I personally don't think there is anything taboo if you explicitly explain why you are collecting the data," says Mike Zane, senior director of online marketing.

A drawing to win more than $1,000 in PlayStation gaming goods asked for name, phone, date of birth, and email to enter. With this information Sony can easily use other commercially available data to learn more about you, as well as to sell your data if it chooses to do so. If you don't want such information on the marketplace, don't enter the contest.

"Consumer awareness is far and away the most important ingredient in consumer privacy. The more people know how things work, the more they'll be positioned to take the steps they want to protect their privacy," says Jim Harper, a founding member of the Department of Homeland Security's Data Privacy and Integrity Advisory Committee, now at the Cato Institute. Among the steps Harper takes is entering some false information when filling out Internet forms, thus potentially confusing aggregators. An example of such a practice happens when people give wrong ZIP codes to prevent stores from figuring out who they are. Harper also maintains several accounts at different social networks, and uses multiple logins and accounts on different platforms such as his Android phone, Twitter, and other services.

In the end, if you want the service for free, you may have to pay some price in personal data—or buy access. "I think we need to move away from advertising-supported business models because these models are inimical to privacy. There is a steady drumbeat for more and more personal information, for more finely grained targeting, with no end in sight," says Chris Hoofnagle, director of the Berkeley Center for Law and Technology's information privacy programs. "I'd like to move back to a subscription world—which is not a privacy utopia—to better align interests between consumers and firms, and to put consumers in a better posture with regard to consumer protection laws, some of which do not apply when the service offered is 'free.'"

Imagine, then, dishing out a monthly fee for your social network, another for your email account, perhaps a third for your data vault. That's the alternative vision. You may not like this concept and prefer free. Just know the price is personal data.

The Role of the Government

Many have seen a 2012 photo of Britain's Prince Harry, then third in line to the throne, naked in his hotel suite after playing strip billiards with some women he had met at a Las Vegas bar. R&R Partners, the advertising agency that came up with the slogan "What Happens Here, Stays Here," responded by running ads promoting discretion when it comes to personal information.

Under the slogan "Know the Code," the campaign warned against oversharing. "I promise to follow the code of Las Vegas by not tweeting, tagging, posting, telling, whispering, emoting, defining, drawing up, writing about or in any way revealing the all-powerful What Happens Here, Stays Here moment of me or anyone else in my party to others not on said trip," part of the promotional pledge says.

Matthew Mason, vice president of digital strategy and development at R&R Partners, said the campaign sought to shame the people who had broken the code. "When the Prince Harry thing happened we very explicitly felt that went over the line," he said. "We've got a set of rules we'd like to establish as a city and we'd like to enforce those rules and, of course, we do that in a tongue-and-cheek way. It's very much about pushing back against this pervasive sharing thing that seems to be okay everywhere else. We'd like it to maybe be not so okay when you come to Vegas."

Of course, the code is itself a clever marketing gambit to highlight all the fun Las Vegas can offer. Yet the same type of self-regulation and self-monitoring is mostly what guides data brokers and marketers today. Such a code is not always enough. Even some industry insiders say the government should do more to regulate what is and is not okay in the private-sector collection and proliferation of personal data.

"'No regulation, no transparency' risks having an environment where the most aggressive companies win," says Matthew Monahan of PeopleSmart.com. Even Acxiom, the master data collector itself, wants more rules. "You might be surprised, but we are in favor of regulation of the industry," says Acxiom CEO Scott Howe. "There is enough bad stuff going on that having tighter legislation around data collection, visibility, and choice would be good."

US law allows firms to share and sell most data, with some exceptions for financial, medical, and employment-related data.[8] The United States also limits the gathering of data and marketing to children. The US Congress and the Federal Trade Commission have stepped up their examination of data brokers, raising the possibility of future restrictions. Medical data remains a problematic area. Health providers face limitations on how they can share under the Health Insurance Portability and Accountability Act (HIPAA) of 1996. Yet commercial marketers collect and freely traffic in medical data, drawing details from shopping histories, web browsing, survey results, and other information.

Some say data brokers should draw the line at health and not seek out details of people's ailments. "Let's say cancer, for example. Is there some value to people understanding and having access to relevant research and new drugs when they are out searching for that stuff? Yeah," says M. K. Marsden, a senior vice president at data broker Epsilon. "But I think that's where it's got to be like, you as a pharmaceutical company or you as the cancer center have to be there when they touch you. You don't push at them. . . . When we've declared and we are explicit and we've asked for relevant messages of things like that, then it is appropriate to push. I think it's a delicate dance that we are learning the lines of every single day."

Government regulation could simplify that dance by setting out some of those lines more clearly. That could include some limitations on bulk access to public records, the core building block of data brokers' records. In Las Vegas, Clark County Clerk Diana Alba feels that instant access to public records has gone too far. She has worked for decades with public documents, as has her colleague Cheryl Vernon. "I don't know how you stop it. Before they opened up this whole Internet they should have given some thought to this," Vernon says.

The rich and famous avoid some of this exposure by creating their own companies so that their names do not appear in public records. Law enforcement officers, judges, and others petition courts to seal their records. But such filings are complicated and expensive. Many celebrities do not go through the trouble. When I visited the Clark County Recorder's office, former baseball pitcher Orel Hershiser, a Cy Young Award winner, had just registered a home purchase, an official told me. And officials say that even singer Michael Jackson's past purchase of a Las Vegas home was in their system for anyone to look at.

One approach might allow individuals to continue to look up public records but set limits on outside firms buying in bulk and reselling. That's how Las Vegas handles its police mug shots. Some local governments have also acted to limit what types of data they make available. For several years at the beginning of the 2000s, Clark County wedding licenses shown to anyone who asked included Social Security numbers. During this time someone obtained a copy of the marriage license for tennis superstars Andre Agassi and Steffi Graf, complete with Social Security numbers, and posted it on the Internet.[9] Since 2003 the clerk's office has redacted everyone's Social Security numbers in response to growing public concern about identity theft.

"The data has always been public, but it was in government storage that was much less accessible than a website. The problem today is that these data brokers are taking advantage of out-of-date public records laws," says Sarah Downey, a lawyer who worked for several years at Boston privacy company Abine.com.[10] "These laws were built around paper documents in regulated storage: you used to have to go to a town clerk's office to see them. It took time and effort that most people wouldn't bother with. The Internet has fundamentally changed what it means for something to be 'public,' and unless public record laws adapt, we're all in for a lot more privacy invasions."

Downey oversaw Abine's pay service, which helps users opt out from data brokers. Abine would make less money if people could easily erase their dossiers, but she advocates a one-stop removal option. "Whether it is established by Congress, the FTC, consumer rights organizations, or another group or entity, consumers need a simple method through which they can block their information from being sold by data brokers, something similar to the National Do Not Call Registry for telemarketing," she said. In some situations, such as those involving firms that use personal data to shame people, new laws and the courts may be the best remedy.

As the person being profiled, right now you can ask each data broker to remove you, but the process for multiple removals is cumbersome and there is no inherent right to stay off the data broker rolls. In 2010 an Indiana court dismissed a lawsuit from a woman who alleged a privacy invasion because Intelius kept a record on her.[11] Some countries have taken a different approach and enacted broad privacy-protection laws, including those in the European Union, as well as Taiwan, Vietnam, New Zealand, Malaysia, and South Korea.

Certainly, any US effort to limit a firm's ability to collect and share personal data would kick up a fight. "Businesses with which I transact should have every right to talk about me to others, just as I can speak about them, absent contractual limits to the contrary," says Tom Bell, a Chapman University law school professor who specializes in high-tech issues. "Regulations in this area do not strike me as cost-effective and raise serious First Amendment problems." Politicians and their campaign teams have a direct stake in the debate as they make increasingly sophisticated use of personal data to target messages to voters.

Some experts advocate a national privacy agency or ombudsman to shed light on how private-sector data practices affect people. "Just like we established a new agency, the Department of Homeland Security, there should be a new agency that helps people evaluate risks: the Department of Risk Assessment, or it could be called Privacy and Risk Assessment," says George Church, head of the Personal Genome Project. "Privacy itself is not a risk. It impacts on other risks. What are the odds that you will lose your job or never get a date again or have people spray paint your house because they don't like the way you look in public? Those are the real risks. Privacy is just like an air sock, right? It's telling you which way the wind blows."

Church, who asks his volunteers to make their medical records and DNA test results available to researchers on the Internet, thinks companies should do more than require a click for customers to show an understanding of the risks. They could require a test, as he does for his volunteers: "I personally think that there should be a similar exam or criterion for everything you sign because 90 percent of what people sign or tick-box or whatever they do is not read and not understood, sometimes intentionally on the part of the agency asking for signatures."

Shining the Light on Data Hunters

After researching the business of personal data for this book, I am struck not so much by the practices of any one company but by the intimate composite portrait that emerges from aggregating data from many different sources. One tile may not dazzle, but a mosaic of many tiles betrays a compelling and sometimes unexpectedly intimate portrait.

Often, all that a business needs is one or two tiles to piece together the rest of the picture. The cheerful store clerk asking for your ZIP code at checkout adds it along with the name from your credit card to the company's files. From those two pieces of information it can pinpoint your dossier from a data broker and know a lot more than a five-digit ZIP code might suggest.[12] Yet sometimes businesses do ask for ZIP codes for legitimate reasons. For example, automated gas pumps typically request ZIP codes with credit and debit cards to verify the user.[13]

Shopping clues such as subscribing to a premier cable TV package (lots of sitting) and fast food purchases (bad nutrition) may suggest obesity to health care companies or diet promoters. One data broker sells sightings of cars, complete with photo, for $10 a pop.[14] I looked up a relative's license plate number and found an image of her vehicle parked some months before in front of a medical clinic, potentially intimate information. Clues from Facebook as simple as "likes" can suggest someone's sexual orientation. One researcher has shown it is theoretically possible to reidentify people who have revealed their innermost sexual secrets in anonymous scientific surveys for the Kinsey Institute.[15]

In composite, all this information that we share does yield deep insights into what makes us tick. "I don't think consumers understand what they want and what they need in regard to online privacy," says Ted Claypoole, a Charlotte, North Carolina, lawyer who cowrote the book *Protecting Your Internet Identity: Are You Naked Online?* "They love to read Amazon suggesting new books and music to them, but they find it creepy when 'relevant advertising boxes' follow them around the Internet as they surf. They will widely share the most intimate personal details on social media, but then are genuinely surprised and rattled to think that business, government, enemies, or thieves might somehow use those details."

Companies and data brokers emphasize they are gathering all this data to better target their goods and services. They just want to sell you stuff or make money selling your data to other marketers. It is worth stressing that many officials at the firms gathering consumer data are smart, hardworking, and well-meaning. I certainly got that impression from the current and past executives at Caesars, at online ad agency Dstillery, and other companies.

"I don't think that the population we are talking about, for the most part, is populated by guys twirling their mustaches planning evil acts against good people," says Michael Fertik, CEO of Reputation.com. "This is not a Manichaean struggle between good and evil. But most people who are interested in this field on either side of the question, on the shades of gray along the spectrum of the question, are good and decent people who want to do good and decent things. . . . The basic goal is to make sure that the right ad reaches the right person, right? And I also do believe that there is no intent to foul someone up in life. But what happens is over time these data points . . . get accumulated and get spread to people and used in ways that even the guys collecting in the first place had no idea they could anticipate."

The possibility of unintended consequences highlights the reason why all consumers should care about personal data. Your data can and sometimes do get used in a way that is not in your best interest, and can even cause harm. Data brokers and marketers openly acknowledge that some businesses make unscrupulous use of personal data in ways that can damage people professionally or personally. "People have a right to be skeptical because for every person who is trustworthy in the industry there are probably a couple who are doing crazy weird things. That's the scary dark side," says Acxiom CEO Scott Howe.

A Simple Manifesto

We, the people about whom data is collected, should have a right to know who the data hunters are and what information they gather about us. Even among the vast majority of businesses making legitimate use of personal data for marketing purposes, many fall woefully short when it comes to providing insights into their activities. That is a mistake that will hurt these businesses in the long term. They should be clear about what they are doing, and customers should have a choice about the extent to which they participate. Some data brokers and marketers argue that curtailing their ability to track consumers will cripple the economy and the Internet. Such logic is patently nonsense. People will still want to buy things and consume even if they have a greater say in how others market to them.

Some of the companies and executives in this book, Caesars most prominently, have chosen to be open about how and why they gather personal information and how they use such details. And importantly, they offer benefits in return. The way they crunch the numbers may be complicated, but there is no reason for the basic data-gathering policy to confuse customers. It might be as simple as "If you join our loyalty program, we will collect lots of information about what you do in our properties. And we will buy outside information to better understand you, and, in exchange, reward you with free food, rooms, and other perks."

Companies should not be allowed to obfuscate with long and dull privacy policies. Many companies collecting data create confusion by hiding behind legalese along the lines of "Company X does not share personal information with any third-party except as permitted by law." Such notice is akin to a food company printing a nutritional label saying "We include only ingredients as permitted by law." That gives plenty of leeway to add lots of saturated fat, sugar, salt, or other potentially unhealthy elements into the blend. "Too often we've been victim of 'I agree.' It's like the thirty pages, online small-print thing; this is buried on page 22 in small letters and you have no idea where your data is going when you fill out the warranty card or something like that," says Howe. "This should be transparent."

The "as permitted by law" phrase does not necessarily mean companies promiscuously share your data. It may embody the unscholarly legal term of "covering your ass." In case things change in the future, they warned you. Other words with limited meaning include privacy texts that say the company only shares data with "third-party companies with which we have a business relationship." That could mean any company that buys or rents the data: that's a business relationship.

"Our laws should require commercial sites, and maybe others, to be specific about what data is collected, how it is used, and how you can see what the commercial entity is holding about you," says Ted Claypoole. "Of course, most consumers will not read the privacy policy, but if this data was offered in a consistent and recognizable box—like the nutrition box on food products—then consumers who care can understand and make informed decisions about what happens to their data, and go back to correct inaccuracies later." Until the time of easy nutrition label–style privacy policies, you can always call up a company and ask what it does with your data. Companies want your business, and alienating people runs counter to that. Often they will let customers opt out of data sharing.

We should understand how the company uses our data and whether and how it shares the information with others. "The information should be used only for the purposes that the customer believes that they are sharing it around," says Gary Loveman. "So, for example, if

I share information with a casino company, I shouldn't have it used for political campaign purposes, or to raise money for Planned Parenthood." In the world of casinos much personal data actually ends up staying in Vegas. What gamblers do on the casino floor as recorded by loyalty programs is not shared with others. The casinos know a lot, and they closely guard those insights as an important corporate asset.[16]

Overall, companies should be able to pass what Caesars executive Joshua Kanter sees as the key standard: the Sunshine Test. In other words, if managers embrace practices that would cause discomfort if featured on the front page of a major newspaper, perhaps they should think again about what they are doing. Yet in researching this book, I have found many firms reluctant to talk openly about their data-gathering practices, often adapting a defensive or evasive pose that raises questions about the propriety of what they are doing. In 2014, the Direct Marketing Association, the trade group of data brokers and marketers, went so far as to ban me from attending any future events (the lifetime ban was overturned a few weeks later). My questions and subsequent articles had apparently made some marketing firms uncomfortable. "Our industry is doing a lousy job marketing itself," says Howe, who surprised me by distancing himself from many of the DMA's views.[17] "If you do things that are great for customers and you deliver them choice, then those companies are going to win, and folks that survive by tricking consumers, they will eventually die because they become the most hated companies in the world."

"I do not agree with Mr. Howe—the industry doesn't do a bad job so much as it doesn't do enough of a job," says JoAnne Monfradi Dunn, president and CEO of data broker Alliant, who also serves as chair of the DMA's board of directors. "As we move from broadcast marketing to customer engagement, it will be even more important for marketers to be part of the national conversation, and to be partners with customers in their brand choices and relationships."[18]

Occasionally marketers admitted why they did not want to be open about their practices. One marketing executive told me his travel company was beginning to target advertising through browser fingerprinting. This technique recognizes people's browsers not via cookies, which can be removed, but through a computer's more durable attributes such as what programs are downloaded onto the browser. Then he asked that I not print his or his company's name: "At the end of the day, there isn't really a legal case against it, there isn't really a privacy case against it. It's really a PR thing. What are you going to do when the *Wall Street Journal* decides to write a nasty article about the practice?" he said.

Shifty practices will come to light. Much as the maker of an unsafe vehicle or adulterated food will one day have to face the music, unscrupulous personal data collectors will have to face those whose data they have abused. Advocacy groups, investigative journalists, congressional committees, and the legal system will all play a role in this process. Companies in the ecosystem of personal data can also help. For instance, search companies such as Google could give lower rankings to humiliation sites, and credit card firms could decline to process payment for objectionable businesses (moves they appear to have embraced recently for mug shot websites).

Since many companies supplement what they observe about you with outside dossiers, you should be able to go to the source and see what data brokers know. Companies such as Experian and Epsilon are still reluctant to crack open the vault. "Trust us, we have good policies" is not enough. Data brokers should allow consumers to peek in and amend or delete their files if they want to. In some cases marketers would gain if people corrected mistakes and refined their preferences to receive better targeted ads and offers. In other cases people would remove data or opt out entirely, so the files would become less all-inclusive.

One of this book's narratives tells how thoughtful data analytics experts at Caesars ultimately decided, after many years, to start using outside data from brokers such as Acxiom. When Acxiom partially opened its dossiers to the public in late 2013, it revealed plenty of mistakes, some trivial and others significant. The initiative showed that data brokers and companies, for all of their insights about us, have not become all-knowing oracles. Just days before he left Acxiom as the marketing chief to become a managing director at JPMorgan Chase, Tim Suther spoke openly about the limitations of personal data. "It's like searching for the fountain of youth," he said. "You know that people are searching for that one bit of information that reliably predicts or describes people, and it just doesn't exist. You know we are all complex human beings with changing needs, changing context."

When companies figure out a way for customers to reap real benefits from their own data, they will usher in a revolution in both marketing and self-empowerment. Consumers will increasingly take control of their own data. Some will routinely export medical and other personal records into their own managed vaults to keep better track of their lives and interface with the outside world.

Businesses should provide easy online access to download the personal data they hold about you. Such information might look like your credit card bill, with details of where and when you bought something, the amount, and category such as food/beverage or medical services. They should share a fair amount of detail: what exactly did you order at the restaurant, how many days was the car rental, how many miles did you drive? Perhaps you could set the fields of data you are interested in seeing. Some people would never bother to look up such details, but others would appreciate the easy access to such information.

Kanter, who in 2014 passed on the Caesars Total Rewards portfolio to a colleague as he focused on his new role as senior vice president of revenue acceleration, envisions Caesars sharing ever more data with customers. But he points out that eventually the raw data could overwhelm even the person whose actions generated the file. I saw this many years ago after reading about all the dull moments the Stasi notated about me in 1988, such as the several minutes I spent puzzling over a map trying to figure out where I was going.

Do Caesars customers really want a chart of how many days in advance they reserved their hotel rooms, how many minutes they sat in a restaurant on average, or even how many times they passed through the lobby (if future photo recognition technology could compute such comings and goings)? In some cases customers expect Caesars to record even more than they do, such as everything they ever uttered to a hotel clerk. Even with cheap and endless data storage, there can be information overload. "We have to show some judgment about what data is meaningful to the end consumer," Kanter said about the guidelines a company should embrace in releasing personal data. "Where does it enhance our relationship in creating value versus where does it create complexity that we don't have already?"

Recently, Internet giants have started allowing users to access their accumulated data. Twitter, for example, allows you to "request your archive," everything from your first tweet and all resulting interactions. Facebook's account settings allow people to download their data. And in December 2013, Google announced it would allow users to obtain a copy of Gmail and calendar data, as well as from YouTube and other Google services.[19]

Some companies will complain that sharing detailed customer information would prove onerous. But they already gather the information—they just need to design an interface that works for the average consumer. The point of empowering people with their own data is not to slow the mighty wheels of commerce. People will continue to buy. Businesses can still prosper while giving customers insight and choice. And if they are open about what they are doing, everyone can feel better about the whole process.

ACKNOWLEDGMENTS

I owe thanks first of all to Harvard University Professor Latanya Sweeney. She invited me to spend the 2012–13 academic year in residence as a fellow in Harvard's Department of Government, and then invited me back as a 2013–14 fellow at the Institute for Quantitative Social Science (IQSS). Few people understand the power of big data and personal information better than Sweeney, one of the nation's top experts on data reidentification. Sweeney provided me with great insight, encouragement, and good humor throughout. Without her support I would not have been able to write this book.

My 2012–13 fellowship was supported in part by Harvard's Data Privacy Lab and a grant from the National Science Foundation. I am thankful to the chairman of the Department of Government, Timothy Colton, IQSS chairman Gary King, and the Nieman Foundation for Journalism, which first brought me to Harvard as a fellow for the 2011–12 academic year. During that year I began to study the topics covered in this book. I am indebted to curator Ann Marie Lipinski, who encouraged me to pursue this project, and former curator Bob Giles, who took me into the program.

Many graciously gave their time and assistance to make this book possible, including hundreds of people interviewed, only some of whom are included in the narrative. In particular, I want to thank the main subjects of the book. Gary Loveman graciously opened the doors of Caesars casinos, allowing me access to top executives, patrons, and internal workings. Joshua Kanter, the head of Caesars Total Rewards program, proved a patient host over many months during my visits to Las Vegas and other company casinos. He provided a deep level of frank insights into the operation of a major company. Rich Mirman gave much help about the evolution of the company during his time there. Gary Thompson at Caesars also wholeheartedly supported the project.

The Monahan brothers spoke openly about their business and practices in a way still rare for the industry. Ann shared intimate details about her flirtation with Internet erotica and attempts to remain anonymous (I've left out her last name and Internet name at her request). Busted! founder Kyle Prall openly discussed his life and business in great detail, knowing he would face some tough questions. Janet La-Barba and Paola Roy generously shared intimate details about their arrest experiences. Claudia Perlich and her colleagues at Dstillery revealed the inner workings of online advertising to me. None of these participants made review of the material about them a precondition for their cooperation.

Shane Green and the team at Personal.com, Michael Fertik at Reputation.com, and Sarah Downey of Abine were generous with their time and knowledge. I gained insights from the Direct Marketing Association, which allowed me to join a two-day training session in New York to see what marketers are learning and to attend its annual conventions in Las Vegas and Chicago in 2012 and 2013, respectively. I thank Techonomy and its founder, David Kirkpatrick, for allowing me to attend its 2012 annual conference. I am thankful to former FBI agent Dennis Arnoldy for putting me in touch with Frank Cullotta, who lives under an assumed name in the witness protection program.

Many professors, students, fellows, and others at Harvard University shared their insights and suggestions with me, including Henry Louis Gates Jr., Laurence Tribe, David Moss, Harry Lewis, Jonathan Zittrain, Martha Minow, Mikolaj Jan Piskorski, Max Bazerman, Yochai Benkler, Phil Malone, Kit Walsh, Sean Hooley, and Charles Nesson. John Deighton of Harvard Business School gave useful comments on the advertising chapter and made valuable suggestions. Sunil Gupta, also at HBS, graciously allowed me to sit in on his online marketing class in the spring of 2012. Jim Waldo, Harvard's chief technology officer, helped guide me on the path to this book by letting me sit in on his excellent class "Privacy and Technology," which he coteaches with

Latanya Sweeney, during my Nieman fellowship year. I am grateful to others at the university whose teachings inspired me in other fields. These include my jazz gurus Daniel Henderson, Vijay Iyer, and Ingrid Monson and language gurus Richard Delacy and Giuliana Minghelli.

Writers Paige Williams, Neal Gabler, Ron Suskind, Nazila Fathi, and Gay Talese offered inspiration, as did my long-ago professor at Princeton, John McPhee. Liza Boyd gave me tremendously valuable suggestions on improving the structure of the book, and her many improvements are reflected in these pages. Dina Kraft, Sam Loewenberg, George Nikides, David Kim, and Patrick Hoge all offered insightful editing on some of the chapters. My agent, Alice Martell, sharpened the focus of the work with infectious enthusiasm. Clive Priddle at PublicAffairs Books made this book immeasurably better with his suggestions and edits and always embodied the image of the gentleman publisher. My family supported me wholeheartedly throughout the immersive and all-consuming focus a book inevitably demands, and listened to endless dinnertime stories about personal data as I discovered new insights.

Despite all this help and my best efforts, there may be matters I did not describe as precisely as I set out to, and I apologize in advance for any errors that may have slipped by. I'd enjoy hearing from readers, and can be reached at book@WhatStaysinVegas.us.

"YOUR CALL MAY BE MONITORED, YOUR INTERNET SEARCHES MAY BE RECORDED, YOUR EMAIL MAY BE SCANNED, YOUR WHEREABOUTS MAY BE TRACKED, YOUR CREDIT CARD PURCHASES MAY BE ANALYZED, AND YOUR MOST INTIMATE PERSONAL DETAILS MAY BE ACCUMULATED IN ORDER TO SERVE YOU BETTER."

APPENDIX

Take Control of Your Data

How to Control Your Data Flow

People have highly personal attitudes toward their own data. Some are alarmed by the privacy risks of the increasing amount of data collection; others scoff and ask why people make such a big fuss.

By telling the stories of how firms gather data and use them, I hope that readers will get a sense of what they are comfortable sharing. Some people are happy to receive targeted advertising online and off, and are comfortable letting firms gather data about them. Others may try to avoid such tracking. Or they may be comfortable sharing in some spheres but not others. At a Personal Genome Project conference, several volunteers told me they openly share their DNA and medical histories for science to study but refuse to maintain Facebook accounts because they do not want to transmit everything about their lives. In the end, it's up to you to control how much data you shed.

As with healthy eating, no one magic ingredient protects against the proliferation of personal data. Just adding oatmeal will not make a substantial health difference. You have to embrace a wide variety of foods and practices to change the health impact of what you eat. The same goes with gaining more control of personal data. Some cost or inconvenience comes with seeking to stem the flow of personal data.

Other analogies apply. "It's like a disease where there is no single drug that can heal it but there is a cocktail of drugs that would," says Vitaly Shmatikov, who specializes in privacy issues at the University of Texas. "It is sort of unpleasant because you would like to solve the problem once and for all."

Many Internet users may find the whole issue of seeking to protect their personal data tiresome. "I am a typical consumer of the baby boom generation and a busy person. I do shop online and I want to take advantage of the convenience and wider array of choices that the Internet offers," says Susan Grant, director of consumer protection at the Consumer Federation of America. "Other than following the basic safety rules . . . I don't take any special precautions or use any special programs. And I don't generally read privacy policies. That's why I want things like 'do not track' on by default, and nutrition-label-style privacy notices. Make it simple for me, please!"

On the other end of the spectrum, consider Eben Moglen, a professor at Columbia Law School and founding director of the Software Freedom Law Center. He maintains his own web server and an old-style cell phone (i.e., not a smart phone). When surfing the Internet, he encrypts his communications (via SSH), obscures monitoring of his web searches through a plug-in called TrackMeNot, uses additional privacy protection plug-ins including Adblock Plus and NoScript, and a text-based web browser like w3m or Surfraw. He avoids Google Voice and Skype and instead uses a system based on Asterisk. But he worked for a time as a programmer at IBM, so he has a special level of expertise to implement all these tools.

Alessandro Acquisti, an associate professor at Carnegie Mellon University, has done interesting work related to photo-recognition technology and Social Security numbers. He uses some privacy-enhancing tools, such as programs that increase online anonymity, but in moderation. "I do not use all those tools all the time," he says. "After a certain point, the marginal costs (as well as the opportunity costs) of trying to 'protect' more and more of your personal information increase rapidly, while the effectiveness of those protective strategies equally rapidly decreases."

Acquisti likes privacy-enhancing tools, but says they do not work alone. They need consumer awareness, market adoption, and a smart regulatory infrastructure to foster their use. "I stress that I think all those components are necessary at the same time—none is sufficient by itself," he says.

Much like the Internet itself, the tools to control personal data are constantly changing. "You have almost an arms race of people like us and people whose business models are predicated on invading the privacy of consumers. And because we can't get along, we fight in this arms race to give consumers control where it's being taken away," says Abine cofounder Rob Shavell. "And then the people that are taking away the control and trying to exploit data and inference on the part of consumers' activities come up with technologies, and then we have to come up with new technologies."

What follows are some strategies and tools for privacy protection I have come across in researching this book, although there are many more options to consider as well.

Internet Browsing

People who want some control over their personal data should start with how they surf the Internet. "I have not invited anyone to follow me around the Internet any more than I have invited marketers to listen to my phone calls, conversations, or email (unless it is the marketer who provides that email). So I keep different browsers on different settings depending upon what I am doing," says Al Raider, chair of the management, accounting, and finance department at the University of Maryland, University College. "The browser I use most often is set to reject third-party cookies and automatically clears cookies when closed out. For those sites requiring third-party cookies to access, I use another browser permitting that. Then I always clear those cookies when I am finished." Because a user can easily clear cookies from their system, more companies are seeking to place ads using techniques such as browser fingerprinting (looking at the distinguishing characteristics of your browser).

The next step, then, is to enhance Internet privacy: SurfEasy makes a small USB device that plugs into a computer to mask your IP address, location, and other details to obscure online tracking. The company has also developed the same technology for cell phones and tablet devices, and it is available for computers via VPN, which means you don't have to have a USB device. Anonymizer.com, a service that has been around for many years, routes your Internet surfing through VPN, which is basically an encrypted tunnel, as are FoxyProxy and Unspyable. There are other pay options and several free services to step up privacy while surfing the Internet. A service called Private WiFi plays up its usefulness in protecting privacy when using public Wi-Fi.

The free WhiteHat Aviator browser builds in privacy and security protections with little sacrifice in ease of use. Remote browsers provide even more privacy and security protection. You see the normal Internet results on your computer, but the surfing is actually taking place in the host company's computer, making it easier to block malware as well as online tracking. Authentic8's Silo provides such a service for $100 a year, and is geared for sensitive browsing such as on financial or medical websites. It disables audio, however, so it is not a full-service browser. Quarri's myPOQ provides a similar service without disabling audio and at present is free of charge. Cocoon (getcocoon.com) allows you to surf the Internet through its servers after signing on through a browser plug-in, although in my experience it often has to be reinstalled after Firefox or Internet Explorer introduces a new version of its browser.

Those concerned about Internet tracking and targeted advertising can also install browser plug-ins, including Abine's DoNotTrackMe and Disconnect.me. Adblock Plus keeps many ads off the Internet pages you visit. A number of experts recommend HTTPS Everywhere to boost security when viewing websites (www.eff.org/https-every-where/). Some privacy advocates recommend the NoScript browser plug-in for Firefox. It certainly makes it harder to navigate the web, but enhances security by allowing JavaScript, Java, Adobe Flash, and other plug-ins only for sites you approve. If you do try NoScript, you likely will be surprised to see how many programs are trying to execute on your computer every time you visit a web page.

More serious privacy advocates use a service called Tor, short for The Onion Router (www.torproject.org). This free software allows users to hide their location when surfing online. Revelations that the US government has tried to identify its users show that even Tor has limitations. Another example of how things could go wrong for users came in December 2013, when a Harvard undergraduate made a bomb threat against several buildings via Tor during final exams. He was quickly identified and arrested.

"Tor's still great, but the default configuration leaves some vulnerabilities open in order to preserve website functionality," says Kit Walsh, an expert on free speech and privacy at Harvard's Berkman Center for Internet and Society. "It's also very easy to accidentally leak info that can deanonymize you, like the Harvard bomb-threat kid who used his registered machine on Harvard's network to connect to Tor, send the threat, and then disconnect; it was very easy for Harvard to deanonymize him." Various apps including Orbot and Onion Browser use Tor to facilitate secure web browsing.

You can also limit data collection by online advertisers by going to the Digital Advertising Alliance's page or the following websites: www.aboutads.info/choices/, www.networkadvertising.org/choices/, or www.evidon.com/consumers-privacy/opt-out. You can adjust your Google ads at google.com/ads/preferences/. It's probably also worth reading Google's privacy policy at www.google.com/intl/en/policies/privacy/. That page has links to several places that allow you to set the amount of data you share in various ways.

Email

Some free email services such as Gmail serve up ads based on keywords found in your messages, so you should read the privacy policy before signing up. Some privacy activists go so far as to suggest avoiding sending mail to others who have Gmail accounts because those incoming mails will be scanned for contextual advertising even though the non-Gmail user did not agree to such policies.

Privacy advocates suggest using encrypted email providers. But three such services closed down after Edward Snowden's revelations about the NSA highlighted the limitations of such formats. Two of those companies, Silent Circle and Lavabit, have formed the Dark Mail Alliance (darkmail.info) to devise an even better encrypted email service in the future.

Other options include Hushmail, which offers a service for free provided you sign in at least once every three weeks. A paying version without this restriction costs $35 a year. When a hacker from the group Anonymous contacted me, it came from a Hushmail address. CounterMail advertises especially strong security that encrypts each email before you send it and costs $59 a year. ShazzleMail is another new service with an interesting concept: it sends email directly from your computer to its recipient without going through the usual Internet intermediaries, so it does not contain metadata, which is akin to the address on a package whose contents one cannot see. Your cell phone or computer needs to be on when the recipient downloads the message, however.

One email-related program that I like is Abine MaskMe, which creates temporary email addresses that bounce to your main email address. With this program, when you are shopping online and do not want to share your permanent email address, it generates a new one such as 61df3c71@opayq.com. If the merchant keeps sending you communications you no longer want to receive, you can deactivate the address. A browser add-on made by privowny.com also creates disposable email addresses.

Search Engines

Some search engines do not track your searches. These include DuckDuckGo and Ixquick, which compile results from a number of sources, and Startpage, which uses Google's search engine but without the tracking. However, sites that mirror Google anonymously sometimes work more slowly than Google, and all of these alternatives may not offer as rich results as Google. Thus one might use such search engines on occasion for more sensitive topics.

Social Networks

Privacychoice.org offers a free privacy dashboard to help set your preferred levels for Facebook, LinkedIn, Google, and other sites. Identity .com, set up by the Monahan brothers (featured in Chapter 6), is also aimed at helping shape your social media profiles. Some startups are trying to introduce privacy-friendly social networks such as Sgrouples, which advertises that it is "free of tracking and other data scraping nonsense."

Mobile Data

There are programs that tell you how widely your smart phone is sharing your information or that help boost your mobile privacy. I've tried a mobile VPN from SurfEasy, which has worked well so far. This can also help against wireless hacking. Turning off the GPS function prevents advertisers from knowing where you are. If you are concerned about the growing use of Wi-Fi tracking by retail stores of customers through cell phones, a pouch called Off Pocket blocks all signals sent from a phone (the downside: you can't receive any calls when using the pouch). Some experts say installing an alternative phone operating system such as Ubuntu will also aid users in preserving privacy.

ShazzleMail (as mentioned above) is a cell phone app that sends secure private emails (and also works on computers). WhisperSystems encrypts mobile communications for added security on voice calls and texting, and TextSecure encrypts text messages.

In 2014, several companies have introduced new cell phones preconfigured to maximize privacy, including Blackphone.

Traditional Mail and Phone Marketing

Several sites make it easy to limit or opt out of various categories of direct mail. Direct marketing offers such catalogs, subscription offers, donation requests, and various promotions (www.dmachoice.org). Do Not Call Registry allows Americans to opt out of receiving most telephone solicitations (www.donotcall.gov).

Banks and Credit Cards

Credit card transactions are a major source of transaction data about you. You can opt out of certain targeting by credit card companies. MasterCard allows you to opt out of web analytics, marketing email, and data analytics at www.mastercard.us/privacy. Visa allows you to opt out of its anonymous marketing analytics for five years (usa.visa .com/sitewide/privacy_policy_optout.html). American Express lists its opt-out policies at http://tinyurl.com/czdzubp. Also, check with your bank to learn what data it shares about you and how you can opt out of that sharing.

Those "prescreened" credit card offers that pile up in the mail come from data collected by credit reporting agencies Experian, Equifax, and TransUnion. You can opt out by phone at (888) 567-8688, which removes you for five years. You can also opt out for five years of credit card and insurance offers at www.optoutprescreen.com.

Abine will process credit card transactions on your behalf so that none of your personal information is recorded. In the future, some firms may realize a market advantage by offering credit cards that do not collect personal data on their users. Personal.com says it is considering introducing such a card.

Privacy Rights Clearinghouse offers sample opt-out letters you can send to your financial institutions asking that they refrain from sharing your financial data. They are available at www.privacyrights.org/fs /fs24a-letter.htm.

Data Brokers

Companies like Reputation.com and Abine offer services to remove you from people-search databases. In the end I had the impression that these services hack away at the weeds but do not remove the roots of your personal information. And because personal data are collected and spread in so many places, they will continue to sprout into new dossiers about you. "The root problem is the public records laws that enable data brokers to exist: they came about in an era of paper records, limited access, and limited visibility," says Sarah Downey, a lawyer who worked as Abine's chief privacy strategist. "Until they're modernized to align with the web's capabilities and people's reasonable expectations about the privacy of their personal information, they're going to cause a lot of problems for a lot of people. Technological solutions can only go so far when there's an underlying legal hole as big as this one."

You can also opt out by contacting data brokers one by one, but that's a huge task. Abine maintains a list of leading brokers (abine .com/optouts.php), as does Privacy Rights Clearinghouse (www.privacy rights.org/online-information-brokers-list).

You may find it interesting to see how much information a major data broker like LexisNexis has about you. Details of how to do that are at www .lexisnexis.com/privacy/for-consumers/request-personal-information .aspx. Unfortunately, its Accurint dossier service only allows very few people to remove themselves from the database, such as victims of identity theft or those at risk of physical harm. You can opt out of marketing products from one of the biggest databases, Acxiom, at isapps.acxiom .com/optout/optout.aspx, and see your file at Aboutthedata.com.

Traditional Shopping

If you are making a sensitive purchase that you do not want recorded for posterity and potentially shared with other merchants, go in person and pay in cash.

Data Vaults and Form Filling

Personal.com allows you to encrypt and store important personal documents and details on Dropbox. Gordon Bell, the author of *Total Recall: How the E-Memory Revolution Will Change Everything*, suggests, for example, that people embrace health logging, keeping track of all their medication information. Personal.com's browser plug-in Fill It allows you to use some of this data to fill out online forms. Abine also has a good password and form-filling plug-in, and allows you to create multiple identities so that not every site needs to know your real name.

More Information

Privacy Rights Clearinghouse (www.privacyrights.org) offers many useful detailed background papers on issues such as online privacy and technology, Social Security numbers, and privacy for in-store shoppers. It also has a series of sample opt-out letters for companies, financial institutions, charities, and others asking them not to share your information.

The Electronic Privacy Information Center lists various privacy tools at epic.org/privacy/tools.html. Another list of suggestions is at www.cotse.net/privacytools.html. DataBanker.com also has helpful links on privacy.

NOTES

Introduction

1. California data broker Infocore tracks a huge volume of international dossiers for its US clients. At present the company tracks more than 7.6 billion records from more than 1,100 separate datasets owned by more than 720 data companies around the world, according to CEO Kitty Kolding. Email to author, January 1, 2014. For more information on her company, see Adam Tanner, "U.S.-Style Personal Data Gathering Is Spreading Worldwide," Forbes.com, October 16, 2013.

2. James Glanz, Jeff Larson, and Andrew Lehren, "Spy Agencies Tap Data Streaming from Phone Apps," *New York Times,* January 27, 2014.

3. "Rovio Does Not Provide End User Data to Government Surveillance Agencies," Rovio press release, January 30, 2014.

Chapter 1: What Happens Here, Stays Here?

1. For example, James McElroy, who started working as a Las Vegas dealer in 1973, says he would address important clients only by the first initial of their last name, such as "Mr. C." or "Mrs. S." "Maybe the person did not want to be known," says McElroy, who rose through the ranks to become the assistant casino manager at Caesars Palace. "I very seldom call a person by their actual name, unless I know them very well."

Chapter 2: A Harvard Professor Comes to Vegas

1. The cost of attending HBS has risen steadily since Loveman's years there. The class of 2016 faces total costs of more than $95,000 a year, although many receive some form of financial aid. See www.hbs.edu/mba/financial-aid/Pages/cost-summary.aspx. Students often interrupt careers in which they earn more than $100,000 a year, some with base salaries of

more than $135,000, not including bonuses, according to statistics from the school. See www.hbs.edu/about/facts-and-figures/Pages/mba-statistics .aspx. Naturally, students have high expectations for their professors.

2. *Harvard Business Review* still sells his cases today at hbr.org/search /gary+loveman/4294958507/?Nao=30. He also coauthored a book about economic changes in post-Communist Eastern Europe.

3. "An Assessment of the Productivity Impact of Information Technologies," Graduate School of Business Administration, Harvard University, June 1990. Asked about the paper today, Loveman says, "It didn't necessarily say computers weren't important, it just said it didn't seem to lead to productivity. . . . Since then everyone agrees that technology has been applied in ways that are dramatically improving productivity rates."

4. In 1992 Bob Metcalfe, publisher of *InfoWorld,* described Loveman as "the probable father of the Paradox—the devil himself." "Productivity Paradox 'Devil' Slides Data Past the Debunkers," *InfoWorld,* August 24, 1992, 43. In 1994, *CIO Magazine* referred to Loveman's "now-infamous macroeconomic study" and concluded, "Reports on the dearth of IT impact may have been greatly exaggerated." "Bye-Bye Productivity Paradox," *CIO Magazine,* October 15, 1994, 42.

5. "Putting the Service-Profit Chain to Work," *Harvard Business Review,* March 1994.

6. Author interview, January 17, 2013.

7. Author interview, January 2, 2013.

8. "Harrah's to Merge with Rio," press release, August 10, 1998.

9. Author interview with former Harrah's executive Rich Mirman, January 3, 2012, and confirmed by Loveman.

10. Because slot machines are so profitable, they dominate most casinos. There are about one million slot machines in the United States, according to Patti Hart, CEO of slot machine maker IGT (author interview, November 12, 2012). Nevada Gaming Commission statistics show there were about 155,000 slot machines in Nevada alone as of the end of January 2014. See "Gaming Revenue Report," Nevada Gaming Commission, January 31, 2014, at http://gaming.nv.gov/modules/showdocument .aspx?documentid=8701.

11. In 2004 Harrah's Entertainment agreed to buy Caesars Entertainment for $9.4 billion. After concluding the deal the following year, it became the world's largest casino company. In 2010 Harrah's Entertainment

changed its name to Caesars Entertainment Corporation, giving center stage to the name of the best-known property in the chain, Caesars Palace in Las Vegas. I refer to the company as Caesars today and Harrah's in references before 2010. There are some references to Caesars Entertainment before 2004 in this book about the company centered on Caesars Palace at the time. The corporate picture became even more complicated in late 2013 as part of restructuring efforts amid its massive debt load. The main company became Caesars Entertainment Operating Company, and it created Caesars Entertainment Resort Properties and Caesars Growth Partners. "Confused? Card counters likely have an easier time keeping track," Spencer Jakab wrote in *The Wall Street Journal* about the related companies and their finances on March 11, 2014.

12. Nevada State Gaming Control Board statistics for the twelve months ending January 31, 2014, show an average hold percentage at Las Vegas Strip casinos for the prior year at about 7.5 percent. Penny slots returned the least amount, only 88 cents per dollar, whereas $100 slot machines offered the best odds on average, returning 95 cents for every dollar wagered. See http://gaming.nv.gov/modules/showdocument .aspx?documentid=8701.

13. The big-picture estimate comes from Gary Loveman: "That has allowed us to re-price slot machines over the years very dramatically and has made us hundreds [of millions] if not billions of dollars over that period. And the whole industry has followed us and done the same thing." Author interview, December 12, 2012.

14. The mean is the average payout across the cycle of spins. Yet there will be a variance of results. So some people will win more money and others will lose more money than average during their time at the slot machine. Greater variance makes it harder to accurately assess the distribution from repeated observations.

Chapter 3: Loyalty

1. Binion quotes recalled by John Acres. Author interview, May 23, 2013.

2. In 2013, slots and related devices brought in 65 percent of total Nevada gaming revenue for casinos making at least $1 million, according to the 2013 Nevada Gaming Abstract put out by the State Gaming Control

Board. On average, each casino resort earned $156 in daily slot revenue per hotel room, compared to $76 per room daily for pit games. See http://gaming.nv.gov/modules/showdocument.aspx?documentid=8566.

3. James Nagle, "Trading Stamps: A Long History; Premiums Said to Date Back in U.S. to 1793," *New York Times,* December 26, 1971.

4. The company had introduced a more rudimentary version of the loyalty program some years before that. Caesars, then a separate company from Harrah's, introduced the slot players loyalty program, called Emperors Club, in 1992.

5. Jamie McKee, "Believing in the Brand," *Casino Journal,* March 1997.

6. Many years later Booz Allen Hamilton made international headlines when Edward Snowden, one of the firm's employees who was working as a contractor for the National Security Agency, leaked information about the government's covert surveillance program that monitored private communications and traffic on leading websites such as Google and Facebook as well as phone logs. Mirman said he worked on the commercial side of the consulting business, not the government side.

7. Author interview with Mirman, January 3, 2013. Nowadays, Caesars set up special lines for top-tier members in some of their restaurants, much as airlines check in first- and business-class passengers before others.

8. "Harrah's Entertainment Unveils New Customer-Loyalty Program," press release, April 4, 2000.

9. Author interview, December 4, 2012.

Chapter 4: Casino Data Gathering in Action

1. The buffet price sometimes changes during holiday periods, when demand spikes. There are also some restaurants in big properties not owned by Caesars that do not offer preferential prices for Total Rewards members.

2. "Of course we have surveillance if we need to go back and check our judgment; we can do that with surveillance. And we rate you," Loveman says.

3. In the episode Franklin falls to his death from his hotel window. In an eerie twist, Everett Sloane, the actor who played Franklin and who had

appeared in the movie *Citizen Kane*, took his own life in desperation five years later, in 1965.

4. Casinos also distribute informational brochures on addictive gambling and invite gambling addicts to put themselves on an excluded list so that they will not be allowed to wager in the future.

5. The *Hangover* series is popular enough to lure a steady stream of guests who rent the duplex apartment that inspired the suite shown in the film. Sometimes they damage the room. Unlike in Hollywood, there are real consequences. For most fans of the movie, however, it is enough to jokingly ask the receptionist, "Did Caesar live here?" as the Zach Galifianakis character does in the film, or just buy a *Hangover* T-shirt in a lobby gift shop.

Chapter 5: A Celebrity, a Private Eye, and a Hit Man

1. In this case I used Accurint, which is part of LexisNexis.

2. Details provided from Criss Cross advertisement, at http://digital collections.mypubliclibrary.com/digital/13/16708/1/120.pdf.

3. Author interview, June 7, 2013.

4. Author interview, July 9, 2013.

5. Cullotta's debriefer, Dennis Arnoldy, was an FBI agent from 1971 to 1997. He moved to Las Vegas in 1980 during the end of the mob's era of widespread influence. He investigated Tony Spilotro and ended up overseeing Cullotta when he decided to work as a cooperating witness. Arnoldy envies the amount of personal information law enforcement officials can acquire today. "There was a lot of the stuff we would have to get, like to subpoena telephone records from the telephone companies and all that," he said. "Nothing, but nothing, like they have now. I mean, I think it would be so nice to be an FBI agent now." For private investigators, the huge increase in personal information facilitated by the Internet turned out to be a double-edged sword. "Times changed, and along comes the computer. They are the best thing and the worst thing that ever happened," LaRue says. "You could look up everything. The problem is that everyone who owns a computer thinks they are a detective. Business has dropped off somewhat."

6. Nina Bernstein, "On Line, High-Tech Sleuths Find Private Facts," *New York Times*, September 15, 1997.

7. Another example: more than four times more couples marry in Vegas than in Seattle and its surrounding county, an area with an almost

identical population. Comparative statistics from 2013 at www
.clarkcountynv.gov/depts/clerk/Pages/Statistics.aspx.

8. The search page for marriages in Clark County is at https://aivitals
.co.clark.nv.us.

9. Wynn sought the same records from two different offices about
the same weddings because about 3 percent of those who get a marriage
license do not go through with the marriage. The recorder's office regis-
ters those who do actually wed, but the license application contains more
personal information.

10. I contacted Terry Murphy, the outside consultant to Wynn who
had worked on the campaign. "It's a matter of guest privacy," she told me
when she declined to talk about the marketing campaign.

11. The company has since changed its slogan to "Search People.
Reunite."

12. A Spokeo official agreed some weeks later to speak by telephone.

13. He did finally respond by email more than a year later during the
final fact checking for this book.

14. Adler left the position in 2013 to become vice president of products at Metanautix, a big data startup.

15. See www.peoplefinders.com/about/leadership.

Chapter 6: Dossiers on (Virtually) Everyone

1. Buffett's and Munger's answers are quoted in Whitney Tilson's 2007
Berkshire Hathaway Annual Meeting Notes, May 5, 2007, at www
.tilsonfunds.com/Berkshire_Hathaway_07_annual%20meeting_notes
.pdf. These notes correspond with Monahan's recollection as well.

2. As the company has grown and industry prices have fallen, they
now pay far less for the data, in the neighborhood of 12 to 20 cents per
cell phone lookup, Matthew says.

3. Intelius S-1 filing to Securities and Exchange Commission, October 19, 2009. In the end, Intelius canceled the initial public offering, so it
did not announce financial results in subsequent years.

4. See http://corp.intelius.com/intelius-facts.

5. In its IPO filing, Intelius wrote that "total advertising expenses were
approximately $30.3 million, $39.9 million and $58.2 million for the
years ended December 31, 2006, 2007 and 2008, respectively." Their total

expenses in those years were $47.7 million, $71.6 million, and $102.5 million.

6. "One wrong turn and you're enrolled in a membership program that costs you $20 or more each month. And you'll never know until you scrutinize your credit card bill," then Washington State Attorney General Rob McKenna said of Intelius. See www.atg.wa.gov/uploadedFiles/Home /News/Press_Releases/2010/InteliusConsentDecree2010-08-10.pdf. Consent decree at http://is.gd/RTRXvx.

7. "State General Fund Benefits from Intelius' Bad Business Practice," Washington State Office of the Attorney General, press release, February 2, 2011, at www.atg.wa.gov/pressrelease.aspx?&id=27274.

8. Author interview, March 13, 2014.

9. Of the 2.1 million firms about which the Council of Better Business Bureaus has current ratings and information as of mid-March 2014, 62 percent have an A+, according to statistics provided by Katherine Hutt, director of communications for the Council of Better Business Bureaus, on March 17, 2014.

10. *Thomas Dreiling v. Naveen Jain and Anuradha Jain and Info-Space*, US District Court, Western District of Washington at Seattle, August 22, 2003, ruling at www.symslaw.com/infospace/order_on _summary_judgment_082203.pdf.

11. *Thomas Dreiling v. America Online; InfoSpace*, US Court of Appeals for the Ninth Circuit, August 19, 2009, ruling at http://cdn.ca9 .uscourts.gov/datastore/opinions/2009/08/19/08-35095.pdf.

12. Jain stresses that this cofounder was dismissed immediately after the company learned of the case. Email to author, March 13, 2014.

13. Author interview with Spokeo chief strategist Emanuel Pleitez, November 29, 2012.

14. See www.ftc.gov/opa/2012/06/spokeo.shtm. In 2014, Spokeo suffered another setback when the US Court of Appeals for the Ninth Circuit ruled that a man who had trouble finding a job can sue the company for publishing inaccurate information about him even if he cannot prove actual harm. *Thomas Robins v. Spokeo Inc.*, US Court of Appeals for the Ninth Circuit, February 4, 2014.

15. See http://www.courthousenews.com/2011/08/17/MyLife%20 complaint.pdf. See also Section 4, www.mylife.com/privacy-policy.

16. "It was settled, aided by the facts we shared with plaintiffs," Tinsley said. "MyLife.com (formerly Reunion.com), has been in business for more than 12 years. We pride ourselves on providing valuable services to our customers, and work hard to maintain an A+ rating with the Better Business Bureau." Email to author, March 12, 2014. The company declined to disclose the settlement details.

17. Details at www.sec.gov/litigation/litreleases/2012/lr22536.htm.

18. See SEC announcement, at www.sec.gov/litigation/litreleases /2013/lr22629.htm.

19. See www.peoplesmart.com/about.

20. Figure provided by Courtney Hill, a computer systems administrator in the Clark County Recorder's office.

21. See www.corelogic.com/about-us/news/corelogic-reports-fourth -quarter-and-full-year-2013-financial-results.aspx.

22. See www.lssidata.com/data-sets/wireless-data.html.

23. See www.lssidata.com/data-sets/landline-plus.html.

24. See www.lssidata.com/why-lssidata.html. A CLEC is a competitive local exchange carrier.

25. See peoplesmart.pissedconsumer.com/our-private-information -their-so-called-public-information-20110207220356.html.

26. Inflection sets out its easy-to-understand privacy policies at http:// inflection.com/privacy.

27. Pop-up screen as accessed on the site March 25, 2014.

28. See www.instantcheckmate.com/features/, accessed March 25, 2014.

29. The founder of Intelius, Naveen Jain, said his company, which operates a series of people search sites, remains the industry's biggest player overall, with twenty-eight million unique visitors in January 2014. Email to author, March 13, 2014.

30. Number of searches as given on March 25, 2014.

31. "InstantCheckmate.com Offers a Tool That Could Help Protect Your Child's Safety," Marketwire news release, April 5, 2011, at http://finance.yahoo.com/news/InstantCheckmatecom-Offers-a -iw-2840624434.html.

32. Company blog post, December 13, 2012, at http://blog.instant checkmate.com/5-people-to-run-a-criminal-background-check-on/.

33. Email from Kibak to the author, October 16, 2013.

34. See http://www.fbi.gov/scams-safety/registry.

35. Email from Kibak to the author, March 24, 2014.

36. See www.instantcheckmate.com/about/.

37. "BreederRetriever.com Goes Live: Disgruntled Investment Banker and Internet Guru Team Up to Launch Ambitious New Website," October 24, 2006, at www.prweb.com/releases/entrepreneur/breederretriever /prweb454675.htm.

38. See http://blog.instantcheckmate.com/need-to-give-away-your-pet -make-sure-it-goes-to-a-good-home-with-instant-checkmate/.

39. See http://blog.instantcheckmate.com/instant-checkmate-why -you-should-run-a-background-check-on-yourself/.

40. See http://blog.instantcheckmate.com/this-what-work-fridge -supposed-look-like/.

41. According to a tweet from Kibak, thecontrolgroup.com went online in May 2013.

42. Email from Kibak to the author, October 16, 2013.

43. See http://is.gd/yu422S and http://is.gd/diO7YA, whose conditions include in all caps: "PLEASE NOTE: ALL AD-COPIES/ CREATIVES AND LANDING PAGES MUST BE APPROVED. . . . ONLY AFTER YOUR AD COPIES/CREATIVES ARE APPROVED WILL YOU BE ALLOWED TO RUN THIS OFFER."

44. See www.peerflyoffers.com/offer.php?id=6598. That campaign said Instant Checkmate would absolutely not allow "unapproved/false/ deceptive subject lines" in the promotional emails.

45. See www.neverblueescape.com/.

46. "All-expenses Paid Trip to Croatia for Publishers in Performance Marketing," PRWEB release, February 5, 2014, at www.prweb.com /releases/2014/02/prweb11549124.htm.

47. Email from Kibak to the author, March 24, 2014.

48. Ibid., October 16, 2013.

49. AdWords are Google ads that appear on Google's search pages. AdSense delivers ads for searches on other firms' websites such as About .com. For simplicity here I am describing both as Google ads.

50. In 2013 the company was expanding its vision, with Kibak and a partner leading the Control Group, "the company who developed the

popular website, Instant Checkmate." It called itself "a San Diego–based startup that specializes in large-scale data aggregation, marketing, and design." See "The Control Group, Developer for Instant Checkmate, Expands Professional Development Program," press release, July 23, 2013.

51. See www.thecontrolgroup.com/drafternoon-recap-revealing -the-new-office/.

52. Lowrey email to the author, October 9, 2012.

53. Email from Kibak to the author, October 16, 2013.

54. *Meagan Simmons v. Instant Checkmate,* filed February 25, 2014, in Hillsborough County, Florida.

55. Email from Kibak to the author, March 24, 2014.

56. See press releases at http://is.gd/wCBtNV.

57. Complaint at http://is.gd/j51e6J.

58. Company statement emailed to author April 9, 2014.

Chapter 7: Direct Marketing

1. For an example of these categories, see www.aslmarketing.com /list_high_school_students.php.

2. See www.aslmarketing.com/list_high_school_students.php.

3. Figures provided by Joshua Kanter as of March 2014.

4. MGM Resorts statistic from Adam Bravo, MGM's director of campaign operations, March 17, 2014, email to author.

5. Bravo made the comment at the 2012 annual Direct Marketing Association conference.

6. I sent this quote to American Express for reaction. Marina Hoffmann Norville, the company's vice president for corporate, financial and risk public relations, declined to comment in an email dated January 18, 2013.

7. Boris Emmet and John E. Jeuck, *Catalogues and Counters* (Chicago: University of Chicago Press, 1950), 2–3.

8. Details drawn from an article in *Printers' Ink: A Journal for Advertisers*, November 25, 1903, 3. "To get all the telephone directories in a given state and copy the names seems like a simple proceeding," said company president J. N. P. Cramer. "You would naturally suppose that the advertiser who wanted to reach these people could do that himself." However, he went on to say that gathering all the phone books from smaller communities in places such as Ohio and New York was difficult, so his

company provided a valuable service to marketers. Phone directories have remained an important source of personal data ever since.

9. The company reported worldwide revenue of $1.38 billion in 2013, up 39 percent from $996 million in 2012.

10. Epsilon letter to Congressional Bipartisan Privacy Caucus, then headed by Ed Markey and Joe Barton, August 14, 2012.

11. See www.epsilon.com/about-us.

12. Details about Acxiom's reach come from a company letter to Congressman Edward Markey, August 15, 2012.

13. Presentation to Direct Marketing Association panel in Las Vegas, October 14, 2012. In 2013 Suther left Acxiom after eight years to become a managing director at JPMorgan Chase.

14. Author interview, November 8, 2012.

15. Ibid.

16. See the 2013 UNAIDS report on the global AIDS epidemic at www.unaids.org/en/media/unaids/contentassets/documents /epidemiology/2013/gr2013/UNAIDS_Global_Report_2013_en.pdf.

17. Mike McIntire, "Clinton Backer's Ties to Powerful Cut Both Ways," *New York Times,* July 14, 2007.

18. See everestcpi.com/entrepreneurs.html.

19. Details from the SEC complaint at www.sec.gov/litigation/ complaints/2010/comp21451-gupta.pdf.

20. Ibid.

21. "SEC Charges Former Executives in Illegal Scheme to Enrich CEO With Perks," SEC press release, March 15, 2010.

22. "Gupta agreed to pay disgorgement of $4,045,000, prejudgment interest of $1,145,400, and a penalty of $2,240,700," according to an SEC statement on March 15, 2010, at www.sec.gov/news/press/2010 /2010-39.htm. Gupta did not want to discuss this episode in his life when we met or when we later spoke on the phone and exchanged emails.

23. "102 Million Cell Phone Numbers to be Available from Database USA.com," press release, October 25, 2012.

24. Woolley was acting CEO at the time; in 2013 she formally became CEO.

25. DMA cited these statistics many times in 2012. See, for example, www.the-dma.org/cgi/disppressrelease?article=1565.

26. The clients of all this personal data are not just companies trying to sell products. Politicians, from President Barack Obama on down, are making increasingly sophisticated use of data from Acxiom and many other firms to target their messages to receptive voters. Health care organizations can even buy data predicting how likely you are to keep taking your medications over the next year. For example, Fair Isaac sells such data in its FICO Medication Adherence Score.

27. Acxiom letter to Congressman Edward Markey, August 15, 2012.

28. Asked about the impact of Acxiom on the company's marketing, Wynn spokesman Michael Weaver said, "Regarding the number of room nights generated by partnerships with Acxiom, our records dating to back to our opening do not substantiate those numbers."

29. Author interview with Tim Suther when he was still at Acxiom.

Chapter 8: Recession

1. In the two decades before the 2008 financial crisis hit, casino assets in Nevada increased more than tenfold. David G. Schwartz and Riva Churchill, *Nevada Gaming: Assets, Liabilities, and Expenses, 1984–2011* (Las Vegas: Center for Gaming Research, University Libraries, University of Nevada Las Vegas, 2013).

2. Ibid.

3. Norton later became the chief analytics officer at clothing retailer Urban Outfitters.

4. As reported in the company's annual 10-K statements.

Chapter 9: The Puzzle of Your Identity

1. Stanley Milgram, "The Small World Problem," *Psychology Today*, May 1967, 61–67.

2. This narrative is based on interviews with Harry Lewis, who also shared with me his email correspondence with Mark Zuckerberg from that time. Those Zuckerberg emails have not previously been made public, Lewis said.

3. For more details about the project, see mypersonality.org/wiki/doku.php?id=about_mypersonality.

4. Michal Kosinski, David Stillwell, and Thore Graepel, "Private Traits and Attributes Are Predictable from Digital Records of Human Behavior," *Proceedings of the National Academy of Sciences*, March 6, 2013, at www .pnas.org/content/early/2013/03/06/1218772110.full.pdf.

5. Author interview, March 21, 2013.

6. Facebook communications manager Jay Nancarrow said the company had no comment to make on the study. Email to author, March 14, 2014.

7. Intelius-operated sites include USSearch, ZabaSearch, Public Records, PeopleLookup, PhonesBook, and LookupAnyone.

8. Author interview, December 18, 2012.

9. Because rules governing the industry are limited, data brokers have a lot of leeway as to where to draw the line on what they sell. Some feel comfortable listing religion or sexual orientation. Others impose far greater self-restrictions. US Farm Data, a Nebraska-based data broker that rents lists of 2.5 million farmers, does not list cell phone numbers because it does not want to burden farmers with the cost of incoming calls. As a result, its listings are becoming less complete as some farms abandon landlines for cellular service.

10. Carter Jernigan and Behram Mistree, "Gaydar: Facebook Friendships Expose Sexual Orientation," *First Monday* 14, no. 10-5 (October 2009).

11. The study did not find the same patterns for lesbians, either because they represented a small sample in the survey or because of different interactions in lesbian communities.

12. Author interview with Mistree, February 27, 2013.

13. Ibid.

14. Weld declined to respond for comment when contacted.

15. Ninety tries to pass the twenty questions may seem high at first, but it's not that bad, all things considered. For twenty questions with five choices each, it would take, on average, 119 trillion tries to get a perfect score by guessing randomly.

16. The study assumed that people could read 250 words a minute. Aleecia M. McDonald and Lorrie Faith Cranor, "The Cost of Reading Privacy Policies," *I/S: A Journal of Law and Policy for the Information Society,* 2008 (Privacy Year in Review issue).

17. Sweeney describes her findings at dataprivacylab.org/projects /pgp/.

18. Despite the warnings the Personal Genome Project gives volunteers, Church does not see a great danger from sharing one's DNA with the world. He cites the 2008 Genetic Information Nondiscrimination Act's protections against health insurance and job discrimination, and he says there is no evidence of adverse impact on insurance. "Rumor has it is working in the opposite direction, which is there are people who are getting the DNA sequence and then deciding on their life insurance and long-term care based on the stuff they know and the insurance company does not know, and there is no law that restricts that," he says. What about the impact from financial institutions? For example, might a bank want to decline a loan to someone unlikely to live very long? "These companies are not yet highly motivated to do that and . . . they would be ill advised to do that from a public relations standpoint," he says. For his part, Church embraces a philosophy of posting intimate data about himself on his personal website (arep.med.harvard.edu/gmc/pers.html). He tells the world he has suffered from a heart attack, carcinoma, narcolepsy, dyslexia, pneumonia, and motion sickness. He gives the exact coordinates of his home as well as his birth and marriage details, in addition to the names of his genetic and adoptive parents. He also posts a document that many others might have wanted to hide or even burn: a 1976 letter from Duke University expelling him for getting an F in his graduate major subject.

19. See stevenpinker.com/biocv.

20. Personal Genome Project volunteer Gamble consented to having his name published in his book.

21. *IMS Health Incorporated v. CVS Pharmacy Inc., Caremark, L.L.C., Caremark Pcs Health, L.L.C., and Caremark PHC, L.L.C.,* No. 6174-VCL, Chancery Court of Delaware, filed April 27, 2011.

22. See www.netflixprize.com//rules.

23. Comments from unnamed reviewer No. 1 in email to Vitaly Shmatikov from Birgit Pfitzmann and Patrick McDaniel, January 26, 2007.

24. The Netflix contest sought to improve the "measurement of how closely predicted ratings of movies match subsequent actual ratings," thus better predicting movies a customer would like. See www.netflixprize .com//rules.

25. *Jane Doe, Nelly Valdez-Marquez, Anthony Sinopoli, Paul Navarro v. Netflix and Does 1 Through 50,* filed in US District Court for Northern California, San Jose Division, December 17, 2009.

26. Netflix officials declined to discuss the lessons of the contest for this book.

27. Michael Barbara and Tom Zeller Jr., "A Face Is Exposed for AOL Searcher No. 4417749," *New York Times,* August 9, 2006.

28. Author interview, November 12, 2012.

Chapter 10: The Hunt for a Mystery Woman

1. The page was still up at the start of 2014.

2. I did find a Kristen Bright working as a publicist in North Carolina, but she said she had never heard of Instant Checkmate nor done any work for the company.

3. Author interviews, December 21 and December 23, 2012, and January 4, 2013. I have withheld her real last name and Internet stage name at her request.

4. Instant Checkmate founder Kibak says, "Our member care representatives use their real first names, but do not provide their last names." Email to the author, October 16, 2013.

5. Why would a company create a fictitious name and face for the company? An executive at a well-known Silicon Valley Internet company says some startups create fictional spokespeople for two reasons. One is that an invented name can show continuity in company statements, even though frequent churn at startups means real people are coming and going all the time. The other reason is that company officials sometimes want to distance themselves from a business they may eventually sell. In 2013, Instant Checkmate started working with an actual spokesperson.

6. Email from Kibak to the author, October 16, 2013.

Chapter 11: Thousands of Eyes

1. James Moore, vice president of iView Systems, says his company's license plate recognition technology works accurately 94 percent of the time. Of course, even if it identifies the license plate, it will not know the owner if the car is rented, which is often the case among Las Vegas casino visitors.

2. Head of security Tom Flynn says Caesars Palace has three thousand cameras and that larger new casinos have as many as four thousand or five thousand cameras. MGM Resorts has about three thousand at each of its big casinos, such as Bellagio, ARIA, and Luxor, according to Yvette Monet in MGM Resorts public affairs. Mike Pfahler, director of corporate security at Fifth Street Gaming, said the Stratosphere, where he used to work, had more than 1,500 cameras in nongaming areas—key to watching the staff—and another thousand in the casino. He said the number has likely increased since he worked there. Officials typically agree that three thousand is about average for a large casino.

3. No one knows for sure how many surveillance cameras exist in the United States, but experts say casinos are likely at the top of the list because they have the money to afford them and the need with all that cash around. "I don't know how heavily cameras are used in prisons, or banks, or nuclear facilities. I think you would be safe to say that the Las Vegas casinos are probably the most densely 'camera-ed' civilian environments that we know of (and for good reason)," said Jim Waldo, the chief technology officer at Harvard University.

4. Video cameras once stuck out as unusual objects. I remember walking around East Berlin during the final years of Communism, jarred by the many cameras perched above the capital's wide avenues.

5. See http://gaming.nv.gov/index.aspx?page=72.

6. See www.richardmarcusbooks.com/.

7. The Imperial Palace has since been renamed the Quad Resort and Casino.

8. MGM Resorts has ten hotels on the Las Vegas Strip. Caesars has eight, not including the Rio, which is a few blocks away on the other side of the highway.

9. In a December 12, 2012, speech to investors in Boston, Loveman said Caesars charter three thousand flights a year for their best customers.

10. One of the murders was recorded by surveillance cameras in 2006 and eventually posted on the Internet. See www.youtube.com /watch?v=y0QlZm_zVSw.

11. Other than the Silver Nugget, these casino are the Opera House, Lucky Club, and Siegel Slots.

12. Details of the Tony Ahn case come from the author's interview with Ted Whiting on May 31, 2013, and news releases related to the case.

13. United States Attorney's Office, District of Nevada, "Former Casino Employee Sentenced to 57 Months in Prison for Stealing Player's Card Information," press release, August 6, 2012.

14. Whiting says he does not have a personal Facebook page, but he does have a LinkedIn profile.

Chapter 12: Mugged

1. Kyle Prall email to Don Field, November 11, 2008.

2. "Busted! In Austin" is also the title of a Texas blues song by veteran rocker Johnny Winter. "Busted in Austin, walking around in a daze," he sang. Prall says he had never heard of the tune.

3. "We are working to make bustedmugshots.com the premier website for local crime and arrest information. Our goal is to provide greater transparency to the activities of local law enforcement and provide never-before available criminal justice information to the public," the site told readers in 2012. "In the near future, you will be able to view not only arrest information, but also the outcome of the arrests, incident reports, sex offender information and other local court records customized to your locality. This will be nothing less than a criminal justice information revolution. Never before has the public had access to the inner workings of law enforcement. Public information that has been stored in police stations and courthouses is, for the first time in history, being made available by Busted free of charge to the general public."

4. As the company's mission statement explained in 2012, "At Busted we have a simple process to initiate a review of your case for removal from our database for a one-time nominal fee. We gladly waive this fee for those who demonstrate that they have been exonerated or found not guilty of the charges. On the other hand, we do not allow the removal of serious violent or sex crime arrests that have not been exonerated or found not guilty." See web.archive.org/web/20121023164307/http://www.bustedmugshots.com/mission-statement.

5. When I went with LaBarba on a short drive in Dallas she partially drove over an elevated medium in the middle of the road, then did not notice pedestrians in a white-lined designated crosswalk until just seconds before they stepped in front of the car. I felt slightly carsick. "I know I'm not a great driver," she said sheepishly.

6. Author interview with friend-turned-informant, November 1, 2012.

7. University of Illinois at Urbana-Champaign transcript, October 1, 2008, as submitted in Prall's 2010 clemency petition.

8. When I initially asked to visit, I was told I would have to sign a non-disclosure agreement barring me from ever revealing the company's address. In the end Prall did allow the visit to take place without me signing the release, with a promise that I not disclose the office's exact location.

9. According to FBI statistics for the last several years. See www.fbi .gov/about-us/cjis/ucr/ucr.

10. See www.fbi.gov/about-us/cjis/fingerprints_biometrics/iafis/iafis _facts, accessed March 7, 2014.

11. Each state maintains its own public records laws. For a state-by -state rundown of what is made public, see http://www.lc.org /hotissues/2001/aba_1-18/public_records_laws_by_state.htm.

12. See www.newyorkpersonalinjuryattorneyblog.com/2012/09 /is-kyle-prall-an-extortionist.html.

13. By 2014 Prall was charging subscribers $12.95 a month with a six-month commitment though his site bustedgrid.com.

14. "Nevada has a rather archaic public records law which is very vague, so we have not had much success working with agencies in this state," Prall says.

15. "Busted! Grid Establishes Strong Relationships at Crime Stoppers International Conference," press release, November 9, 2012, at www .prweb.com/releases/2012/11/prweb10112237.htm.

16. See, for example, bustedgrid.com/uncategorized/bustedgrid -com-announces-milestone-of-over-9-million-arrest-records-in-the -busted-mugshots-database.

17. Details of one class-action case are at www.counselor.pro/practice -areas/class-action-lawsuit-against-mugshot-websites/. Another site, classactionagainstmugshotwebsites.com/wp/, gives more details on the latest developments related to mug shot businesses.

18. *Inside Edition* (CBS), November 19, 2013.

Chapter 13: Internet Advertising

1. Pamela E. Swett, S. Jonathan Wiesen, and Jonathan R. Zatlin (eds.), *Selling Modernity: Advertising in Twentieth-Century Germany* (Durham, NC: Duke University Press, 2007), 16–17.

2. As listed in early 2013 at m6d.com/who-we-are/press/.

3. The company also allows people to opt out of advertising delivered by Dstillery. See http://dstillery.com/privacy.php.

4. Dstillery is just one of many companies seeking to profit off insights gained from tracking users' online activities. If you want to track the companies tracking you, you can install a browser plug-in such as disconnect.me or Ghostery. For example, when I visited the celebrity gossip site TMZ.com, Ghostery indicated a swarm of tracking under way: eighteen ad networks, behavioral data providers, and web publishers, some well-known, such as disconnect.me or Google and Facebook, others obscure. These included Audience Science, Criteo, DoubleClick, Facebook Connect, Google+1, gumgum, Kaltura, MediaMind, Meebo Bar, NetRatings, CiteCensus, Omniture, Quantcast, Quigo AdSonar, Realtime, ScoreCard Research Beacon, StumbleUpon Widgets, and Tynt Insight.

5. Author interview with Andrew Pancer, February 13, 2013.

6. This site appears to have come into existence in 2012 and gone offline in mid-2013, according to the Internet Archive Wayback Machine. The site at the time had a tag on the bottom reading, "Copyright © 2012 Alphabird, LLC." See web.archive.org/web/20130515000000*/http://www.iamcatwalk.com.

7. This site lists Brad Feniger as "Founder/Photographer/Editor." He said the site is part of Bluefin Media, which operates sites including GossipCenter.com, DIYFashion.com, RecipeCorner.com, Celebrity-Gossip.net, HighFashionMagazine.com, and CelebSpin.com. He said the company's sites together attract fifty to sixty million visitors a month, often through banner ads on its different sites. When I asked about click fraud, he referred me to the CEO of Bluefin Media, Brad Mandell, and then hung up. Mandell later said his site had acquired therisinghollywood.com in late 2013 from Feniger, so he would not know about the period during which the site came to the attention of data scientist Perlich. "There is no way that I can speak on behalf of TRH for any activity on the site prior to Bluefin Media recently taking over," he said. "When it comes to sites operated by Bluefin Media, we work with multiple third-party companies who provide real-time solutions to prevent non-human traffic from ever reaching our sites." Email to author, March 15, 2014. Feniger did not return subsequent calls for further comment.

8. This site appears to have gone offline in 2013.

9. This site also went offline sometime after Perlich and Stitelman learned of it in their models.

10. Finding a human running the site is not easy. Efforts to contact someone at ChinaFlix.com failed as email addresses given on its privacy policy and other sections of the site bounced back.

11. See www.linkedin.com/company/AlphaBird and news releases from 2012 and 2013, including http://is.gd/uQjyui and http://is.gd/bB7ZAO.

12. Author interview, February 7, 2013.

13. See www.youtube.com/watch?v=dMOKOZEktxg&feature=youtu.be.

14. See www.upgradevisits.com/how-it-works/.

15. Conference call with author, March 18, 2013.

16. See www.fulltraffic.net/global, accessed December 29, 2013.

17. "Alphabird changed its name to Emerge Digital Group last year based on an acquisition we did in the APAC region and to better reflect our status (as a holding company for a portfolio of international digital marketing assets that we've acquired over the past few years)," Norlin said. Email to author, March 17, 2014.

18. Email to author, March 14, 2014.

19. See Whiteops.com, accessed on January 4, 2014.

14: Seeking the Goldilocks Balance

1. Adam Tanner, "Data Monitoring Saves Some People Money on Car Insurance, but Some Will Pay More," *Forbes,* September 2, 2013.

2. Author interview with Gary Loveman, December 12, 2012.

3. Marketing to magazine subscriber lists remains a popular if basic technique largely unknown to those whose names are for sale. After the American Civil Liberties Union sent me a solicitation letter, I contacted the group's executive director to see where he had gotten my details. It turned out the organization bought the subscriber list from *Columbia Journalism Review*. Getting my name cost 10.5 cents. Adam Tanner, "I Caught the Guys Selling My Personal Information to the ACLU," *Forbes* online, August 9, 2013.

4. In 2013 Eskin became director of direct marketing at Time Warner Cable.

5. Direct Marketing Association, customer relationship management and database marketing seminar, New York City, September 10–11, 2012.

6. Eskin expressed her concerns in 2012. Today, those signing up for Godiva's Rewards Club must provide more details: a mailing address and birth date as well as name and email. This information makes it easy to cross-reference the dossier with that of other data brokers, or to sell the information to a data broker who might note that someone is a chocolate lover.

7. Tim Suther, "Not all Data is Created Equal (ii)," Acxiom PowerPoint presentation, February 21, 2013.

8. Author interview, March 7, 2014.

9. Number of Total Rewards members from Joshua Kanter. Author interview, December 26, 2013.

10. Caesars do not know exactly what percentage of total gamblers do not sign up, as they do not have a unique identifying number for such customers. Author interview with Joshua Kanter, December 26, 2013.

11. That number is about average for casinos across Clark County, which allocated 20.8 percent of their expenses on comps, according to the 2013 State Gaming Abstract of the Nevada Gaming Control Board. A fifth of all rooms and food are given away, and 39 percent of all drinks are comped in Las Vegas and its surrounding county.

12. Figure on active Total Rewards members from Jacqueline Beato, Caesars vice president of finance, from December 5, 2013, presentation to Bank of America Merrill Lynch, 2013 Leveraged Finance Conference. See http://is.gd/5OEhef.

13. John Koster email to Joshua Kanter, November 14, 2012. As he learned more about the changes over the following days, Koster's fears lessened.

15: New Frontiers in Customer Data

1. Scott Dowty, email to author, March 18, 2014. Dowty estimates his company's market share at 65–70 percent.

2. The company only gains personal information on ATM withdrawals when the person has also gotten credit or debit card or cash-checking services from GCA, something that happens infrequently, according to Dowty.

3. CGA promotional video, at www.youtube.com/watch?v=cRA84 bbJc7k. The company sets certain conditions on what data it will share: "Individual patron names and addresses cannot be queried unless they already exist in the customer's database or have made a GCA identified withdrawal at the client's property." See "Proprietary Data Analysis Tool Gives Casino Operators True Understanding of Gaming Patrons," press release, May 3, 2010.

4. See www.gcainc.com/business-intelligence-and-marketing/casino -share-intelligence/.

5. How does Dowty respond to Kanter's remarks? "I'm not really interested in what they think about our service because they have already made it clear they don't want to use it. We opted them out a while ago," he says.

6. Adam Tanner, "The Revolutionary Way Marketers Read Your Financial Footprints," *Forbes,* December 16, 2013.

7. Brubaker, *The Eye in the Sky* (J. M. Brubaker).

8. Author interview, March 7, 2014.

9. As of now the company sets limits on its card of $2,000 per day, $4,500 per week, $10,000 per month.

10. See www.mgmresorts.com/mobile/mirage.aspx.

11. Jumptap was renamed Millennial Media after that company acquired it in 2013.

12. "Catalina Launches Personalized Mobile Advertising for CPG Brands," press release, March 11, 2013.

13. Statistic from Catalina spokeswoman Ally Peebles.

14. Ibid.

15. About the demographics of gamblers Kanter says, "It's a great exaggeration that customers are dying out."

16. Adam Tanner, "House of Cards," *Worth Magazine,* February/ March 2014.

Chapter 16: Casino Adventures in Three Cities

1. Overall 2013 turned out to be an exceptionally lucky year for Kostel. He estimates he won $8,000 to $9,000 between Caesars and other casinos, with that June night at Caesars Palace a major contributor to his total winnings. Author interview, March 16, 2014.

2. Caesars sold about $200 million in new shares in late 2013.

3. Debt figure given on Caesars Entertainment Corporation Q4 2013 earnings call, March 11, 2014, at http://is.gd/SuMaTv.

4. Sign-up statistics from Joshua Kanter, March 13, 2013.

5. Statistic from Gary Loveman, March 11, 2014, conference call on fourth-quarter and full-year 2013 results.

Chapter 17: Embracing Outside Data

1. David G. Schwartz, *Major Gaming Jurisdiction: Ten-Year Comparison* (Las Vegas: Center for Gaming Research, University Libraries, University of Nevada Las Vegas, 2011).

2. Loveman recalled the conversation in an interview with the author, December 12, 2012. Through a spokesman, Wynn said he did not remember the specific dialogue.

3. Schwartz, *Major Gaming Jurisdiction*.

4. Statistics from Macau Gaming Inspection and Coordination Bureau, at www.dicj.gov.mo/web/en/information/DadosEstat/2013/content .html#n1. In another contrast with Las Vegas, slot machines make up only a small fraction of total casino revenue in Macau (4 percent in 2013). More than 90 percent of Macau's casino revenue came from the card game baccarat.

5. "The average daily number of visitors is up 33 percent, the average daily food and beverage revenue rose 35 percent and the average daily gaming volume increased 23 percent. For the weeks Celine is performing, assuming normalized slot and table hold, these results translate into incremental daily revenue of approximately $200,000, compared to the three months before opening," the company stated in a press release. "Park Place Reports Financial Results for First Quarter 2003," press release, May 1, 2003.

6. Email to David Schwartz from Caesars Entertainment Las Vegas, May 24, 2013.

7. Leading the personal data revolution in gaming proved lucrative for the former professor, who still commutes back to his family in the Boston area. The company's annual reports highlighting its continued growth also list his total compensation: more than $15 million in 2007, rising to almost $40 million in 2008, according to Harrah's annual

10-K report for 2008. The amount fell to almost $6 million in 2009 and jumped back to more than $20 million two years later, according to Caesars' Form 10-K annual report, filed March 15, 2012. The company paid more than $500,000 a year for him to commute from Boston to Las Vegas on company jets, and spent another couple hundred thousand dollars a year on a bodyguard. "For security reasons, Mr. Loveman is required to use our aircraft for personal and business travel," the company wrote. "The decision to provide Mr. Loveman with the personal security benefit was prompted by the results of an analysis provided by an independent professional consulting firm specializing in executive safety and security."

8. Statistics from Joshua Kanter, January 8, 2013. But he later cautioned that such numbers are "notoriously difficult to quantify with accuracy" because Caesars do not know with certainty how much their customers spend elsewhere and because "people don't generally have a good sense of how much they 'spend' when they visit us." Kanter email to author, December 26, 2013.

9. The number of properties changes frequently. In Las Vegas the company's properties include Bally's Las Vegas, Caesars Palace, the Cromwell (formerly known as Bill's Gamblin' Hall and Saloon), Flamingo Las Vegas, Harrah's Las Vegas, Paris Las Vegas, Planet Hollywood Resort and Casino, the Quad Resort and Casino ("The Quad"), and Rio All-Suites Hotel and Casino. Among the brands in the company stable are Harrah's, Grand Biloxi, Bally's, Flamingo, Paris, Caesars Palace, Rio, Showboat, and Harveys. In early 2014, as part of the company's complicated restructuring that created Caesars Entertainment Operating Company, Caesars Entertainment Resort Properties, and Caesars Growth Partners, several of these properties changed hands.

10. In casinos in the United States, Canada, Britain, Egypt, and South Africa, as well as online in France and Italy.

11. Jacqueline Beato (Caesars vice president of finance), presentation to Bank of America Merrill Lynch 2013 Leveraged Finance Conference, December 5, 2013, at http://is.gd/5OEhef.

12. Comparative statistics from Acxiom CEO Scott Howe, email to author, March 10, 2014. Google spokesman Jason Freidenfelds said the company conducts more than a hundred billion searches a month but declined to give exact numbers. Email to author, March 10, 2014.

13. Author interview with Scott Howe, November 1, 2013.

14. Other data brokers have reacted similarly, with rivals such as Experian not showing any interest in following Acxiom's lead.

Chapter 18: The Not-So-Enriching Business of Privacy

1. These quotes are as recalled by Shane Green. In a separate interview, Dyson said she does not recall the exact conversation but said his recollection accurately reflected her sentiments. She cited Mint.com as an exception to those companies that encourage people to give them personal information but have not gone to the dark side. After initially declining to invest, Dyson agreed to join Personal.com's board of directors and invested in the company in 2013.

2. Another example of a successful company in a related field is LifeLock, which offers identity theft protection services. They reported a profit in 2012, a year in which they also went public, as well as in 2013.

3. One Reputation.com ad reads, "Do you know what potential customers see when they Google you or your business? You should. Because negative results or reviews—true or not—could be driving them to your competitors, costing you real money."

4. The company declined my request to send a mailing to some of its clients asking them if they realized they were on such a mailing list and to seek out their opinions on direct marketing. For a description of their mailing lists for sale, see http://is.gd/EO19vb.

5. "While we won't share your email address with other companies, we may rent, sell or exchange your postal mailing address and information about your transactions with businesses that we believe to be reputable and that can provide you with offers and information that we think will be of interest to you." See www.adameve.com/t-faq.aspx.

6. Comments posted at www.reddit.com/r/sex/comments/1diciq/.

7. In 2013 Saracevic moved on, leaving his full-time job at Personal .com to focus on making Sarajevo an IT development hub (he remains a shareholder in Personal.com).

8. Email from CEO Shane Green to author, March 16, 2014.

9. Adam Tanner, "Others Take Your Data for Free, This Site Pays Cash," *Forbes,* March 3, 2014.

10. Author interview with Scott Howe, March 3, 2014.

Chapter 19: Empowerment

1. Vance Packard, *The Hidden Persuaders* (New York: D. McKay Company, 1957), 3.

2. Ibid., 266.

3. Lester Wunderman, *Being Direct* (New York: Random House, 1996), 164.

4. Author interview with Lester Wunderman, January 22, 2013.

5. Customer Loyalty panel, "One To One Marketing Conference," Harvard Business School, December 4, 2011.

6. Email to author, March 18, 2014. "Spokeo deleted the 'Wealth' section from personal profiles. This section previously contained certain data relating to credit estimates and estimated wealth levels. All financial related estimates now relate solely to the neighborhood in which the individual resides," Tang said. "Spokeo also deleted the 'Lifestyle and Interests' section from personal profiles. This section previously contained certain attributes based upon an individual's interests and purchasing behaviors."

7. For example, Zinch.com helps link up students with universities and scholarships. Its privacy policy is 6,269 words long, longer than many chapters in this book. The kernel of the policy is not unexpected. The company supplements information users provide with outside data to target offers and advertising from them and third-party providers.

8. One additional area where your data are protected is video rental records, thanks to a law passed in 1988 after a newspaper obtained and published details of Supreme Court nominee Robert Bork's video rentals.

9. Author interview with Diana Alba, May 22, 2013.

10. Downey changed jobs in 2014 to become director of marketing at Ovuline.

11. *Fowler v. Intelius,* No. 3:10-CV-15-TS (US District Court, N.D. Indiana), January 13, 2010.

12. When I explained how this process worked in a 2013 article for *Forbes,* the story quickly went viral online, with many readers expressing their indignation and surprise. Adam Tanner, "Never Give Stores Your ZIP Code. Here's Why," *Forbes,* June 19, 2013, at http://is.gd/RP8knj.

13. Adam Tanner, "Yes, Gas Pumps Really Do Need Your ZIP Code (Even If Stores Usually Do Not)," *Forbes,* July 12, 2013.

14. Adam Tanner, "Data Brokers Are Now Selling Your Car's Location for $10 Online," Forbes.com, July 10, 2013.

15. Adam Tanner, "Anonymous Sex Survey Takers Get Identified in Data Dive," Forbes.com, October 11, 2013. The researcher showed it was theoretically possible but did not actually reidentify people.

16. By contrast, the antics of celebrities in Vegas often become public knowledge. Golfer Tiger Woods's affairs in the city eventually became widely known. O. J. Simpson was sentenced to a lengthy time in prison for breaking into a sports memorabilia dealer's hotel in 2007, convicted of robbery and kidnapping, among other charges.

17. Presentation to Harvard's Data Privacy Lab, March 3, 2014.

18. Email to author, March 15, 2014.

19. See www.google.com/settings/takeout/custom/gmail,calendar.

BIBLIOGRAPHY

This book is based on original reporting and interviews with hundreds of people. At the same time it is informed by previous scholarship and journalistic reporting on related subjects.

Books

Andrews, Lori B. *I Know Who You Are and I Saw What You Did: Social Networks and the Death of Privacy.* 1st Free Press hardcover ed. New York: Free Press, 2012.

Ayres, Ian. *Super Crunchers: Why Thinking-by-Numbers Is the New Way to Be Smart.* New York: Bantam Books, 2007.

Bell, C. Gordon, and Jim Gemmell. *Total Recall: How the E-Memory Revolution Will Change Everything.* New York: Dutton, 2009.

Bennett, Colin J. *The Privacy Advocates: Resisting the Spread of Surveillance.* Cambridge, MA: MIT Press, 2008.

Binkley, Christina. *Winner Takes All: Steve Wynn, Kirk Kerkorian, Gary Loveman, and the Race to Own Las Vegas.* New York: Hyperion, 2008.

Brubaker, John M. *The Eye in the Sky: A Casino Surveillance Guide for Management, Directors, and Other Casino Executives and Personnel.* J. M. Brubaker, 1993.

Claypoole, Ted, and Theresa Payton. *Protecting Your Internet Identity: Are You Naked Online?* Lanham, MD: Rowman & Littlefield, 2012.

Davenport, Thomas H., and Jeanne G. Harris. *Competing on Analytics: The New Science of Winning.* Boston: Harvard Business School Press, 2007.

Duhigg, Charles. *The Power of Habit: Why We Do What We Do in Life and Business.* 1st ed. New York: Random House, 2012.

Durham, Steve, and Kathryn Hashimoto. *Casino Financial Controls: Tracking the Flow of Money.* 1st ed. Casino Management Essentials Series. Upper Saddle River, NJ: Prentice Hall, 2010.

Earley, Pete. *Super Casino: Inside the "New" Las Vegas*. New York: Bantam Books, 2000.

Edwards, Douglas. *I'm Feeling Lucky: The Confessions of Google Employee Number 59*. Boston: Houghton Mifflin Harcourt, 2011.

Emmet, Boris, John E. Jeuck, Edith Goodkind Rosenwald, and Lessing J. Rosenwald Collection (Library of Congress). *Catalogues and Counters: A History of Sears, Roebuck and Company*. Chicago: University of Chicago Press, 1950.

Fertik, Michael, and David Thompson. *Wild West 2.0: How to Protect and Restore Your Online Reputation on the Untamed Social Frontier*. New York: American Management Association, 2010.

Franks, Bill. *Taming the Big Data Tidal Wave: Finding Opportunities in Huge Data Streams with Advanced Analytics*. Hoboken, NJ: John Wiley. 2012.

Garfinkel, Simson. *Database Nation: The Death of Privacy in the 21st Century*. 1st ed. Beijing: O'Reilly, 2000.

Gellman, Robert, and Pam Dixon. *Online Privacy: A Reference Handbook*. Contemporary World Issues. Santa Barbara, CA: ABC-CLIO, 2011.

Harvard Business Review on Increasing Customer Loyalty. Harvard Business Review Paperback Series. Boston: Harvard Business Review Press, 2011.

Henderson, Harry. *Privacy in the Information Age*. Rev. ed. Library in a Book. New York: Facts on File, 2006.

Hughes, Arthur Middleton. *Strategic Database Marketing: The Masterplan for Starting and Managing a Profitable, Customer-Based Marketing Program*. Chicago: Probus Pub. Co., 1994.

Johnson, Simon, and Gary Loveman. *Starting over in Eastern Europe: Entrepreneurship and Economic Renewal*. Boston: Harvard Business School Press, 1995.

Kremers, Edward, and George Urdang. *History of Pharmacy: A Guide and a Survey*. Philadelphia: J. B. Lippincott, 1940.

LaWall, Charles H. *Four Thousand Years of Pharmacy: An Outline History of Pharmacy and the Allied Sciences*. Philadelphia: J. B. Lippincott, 1927.

Macrakis, Kristie. *Seduced by Secrets: Inside the Stasi's Spy-Tech World*. Cambridge, MA: Cambridge University Press, 2008.

Maex, Dimitri, and Paul B. Brown. *Sexy Little Numbers: How to Grow Your Business Using the Data You Already Have*. 1st ed. New York: Crown Business, 2012.

Mayer-Schonberger, Viktor. *Delete: The Virtue of Forgetting in the Digital Age.* Princeton, NJ: Princeton University Press, 2009.

O'Harrow, Robert. *No Place to Hide.* New York: Free Press, 2005.

Ogilvy, David. *An Autobiography.* New York: Wiley, 1997.

———. *Ogilvy on Advertising.* 1st Vintage Books ed. New York: Vintage, 1985.

———. *Confessions of an Advertising Man.* Rev. ed. Harpenden, Herts, UK: Southbank, 2011.

Packard, Vance. *The Hidden Persuaders.* New York: D. McKay Company, 1957.

Pearson, Bryan. *The Loyalty Leap: Turning Customer Information into Customer Intimacy.* New York: Portfolio/Penguin, 2012.

Powell, Gary L., Louis A. Tyska, Lawrence J. Fennelly, and ASIS International. *Casino Surveillance and Security: 150 Things You Should Know.* Alexandria, VA: ASIS International, 2003.

Ratneshwar, S., and David Glen Mick. *Inside Consumption: Consumer Motives, Goals, and Desires.* London: Routledge, 2005.

Schull, Natasha Dow. *Addiction by Design: Machine Gambling in Las Vegas.* Princeton, NJ: Princeton University Press, 2012.

Searls, Doc. *The Intention Economy: When Customers Take Charge.* Boston: Harvard Business Review Press, 2012.

Shook, Robert L. *Jackpot: Harrah's Winning Secrets for Customer Loyalty.* Hoboken, NJ: John Wiley & Sons, 2003.

———. *The Future of Reputation: Gossip, Rumor, and Privacy on the Internet.* New Haven, CT: Yale University Press, 2007.

Swett, Pamela E., S. Jonathan Wiesen, and Jonathan R. Zatlin, eds. *Selling Modernity: Advertising in Twentieth-Century Germany.* Durham, NC: Duke University Press, 2007.

Turow, Joseph. *The Daily You: How the New Advertising Industry Is Defining Your Identity and Your World.* New Haven, CT: Yale University Press, 2011.

Vogel, Harold L. *Entertainment Industry Economics: A Guide for Financial Analysis.* 7th ed. Cambridge: Cambridge University Press, 2007.

Weber, Larry. *Sticks & Stones: How Digital Reputations Are Created over Time and Lost in a Click.* Hoboken, NJ: Wiley, 2009.

Wunderman, Lester. *Being Direct: Making Advertising Pay.* 1st ed. New York: Random House, 1996.

Zittrain, Jonathan. *The Future of the Internet and How to Stop It*. New Haven, CT: Yale University Press, 2008.

Magazines, Newspapers, and Studies

Annual Nevada Gaming Abstract Reports, Nevada State Gaming Control Board Gaming Commission, 1990–2013.

Barth-Jones, Daniel. *The "Re-Identification" of Governor William Weld's Medical Information: A Critical Re-Examination of Health Data Identification Risks and Privacy Protections, Then and Now*. June 4, 2012, at papers.ssrn.com/sol3/papers.cfm?abstract_id=2076397.

Chang, Victoria and Jeffrey Pfeffer. *Gary Loveman and Harrah's Entertainment*. Stanford Graduate School of Business case study, OB-45, November 4, 2002.

Commission to the European Parliament, the Council, the Economic and Social Committee and the Committee of the Regions. *A Comprehensive Approach on Personal Data Protection in the European Union*. November 4, 2010, at ec.europa.eu/justice/news/consulting_public/0006/com_2010_609_en.pdf.

Deighton, John. "Market Solutions to Privacy Problems?" In Christopher J. Nicoll, E. J. Prins, and Miriam J. M. van Dellen, eds. *Digital Anonymity and the Law: Tensions and Dimensions*. Cambridge: Cambridge University Press, 2003.

Delong, Thomas and Vineeta Vijayaraghavan. "Harrah's Entertainment, Inc.: Rewarding Our People." Harvard Business School case study 9-403-008, January 7, 2003.

Etzioni, Amitai. "The Privacy Merchants: What Is to Be Done?" In *University of Pennsylvania Journal of Constitutional Law* 14, no. 4 (March 2012), 929–953.

Foxman, Ellen R., and Paula Kilcoyne. "Information Technology, Marketing Practice, and Consumer Privacy: Ethical Issues." In *Journal of Public Policy & Marketing* 12, no. 1 (Spring 1993), 106–119.

Frankland, Dave. *The Forrester Wave: US Database Marketing Service Providers*. Forrester Research, January 12, 2011.

Froomkin, A. Michael. "The Death of Privacy?" In "Symposium: Cyberspace and Privacy: A New Legal Paradigm?" *Stanford Law Review* 52, no. 5 (May 2000), 1461–1543.

Gellman, Robert, and Pam Dixon. *Many Failures: A Brief History of Privacy Self-Regulation in the United States.* World Privacy Forum, October 14, 2011, at www.worldprivacyforum.org/pdf/WPFselfregulationhistory.pdf.

Heskett, James L., Thomas O. Jones, Gary W. Loveman, W. Earl Sasser Jr., and Leonard A. Schlesinger. "Putting the Service-Profit Chain to Work." In *Harvard Business Review,* July 2008.

Lal, Rajiv. *Harrah's Entertainment, Inc.* Harvard Business School case study, 9-502-011, revised June 14, 2004.

Laudon, Kenneth. *Markets and Privacy.* Association for Computing Machinery. Communications of the ACM, September 1996.

Lovat, Oliver. *Pyramids to Players Clubs: The Battle for Competitive Advantage in Las Vegas.* Occasional Paper Series 19. Las Vegas: Center for Gaming Research, University Libraries, University of Nevada Las Vegas, 2012.

Loveman, Gary. "Diamonds in the Data Mine." In *Harvard Business Review,* May 2003.

MacDonald, Andrew, and William Eadington. *Macau—A Lesson in Scarcity, Value and Politics,* posted by the University of Macau at www.umac.mo /iscg/publication/Publications/ExternalResources/Macau%20scarcity .pdf.

Macomber, Dean. *The Fiscal Forensics of the Las Vegas Strip: Lessons from the Financial Crisis.* Occasional Paper Series 17. Las Vegas: Center for Gaming Research, University Libraries, University of Nevada Las Vegas, 2012.

Milne, George R. "Privacy and Ethical Issues in Database/Interactive Marketing and Public Policy: A Research Framework and Overview of the Special Issue." In *Journal of Public Policy & Marketing* 19, no. 1 (Spring 2000), 1–6.

Nagle, James. "Trading Stamps: A Long History," *New York Times,* December 26, 1971.

Nobel, Carmen. *Why We Blab Our Intimate Secrets on Facebook.* Harvard Business School Working Knowledge, December 10, 2012.

Ohm, Paul. "Broken Promises of Privacy: Responding to the Surprising Failure of Anonymization." In *UCLA Law Review* 57 (2010), 1701.

PricewaterhouseCoopers LLP. *Transforming Healthcare Through Secondary Use of Health Data,* 2009.

Reidenberg, Joel R. "Resolving Conflicting International Data Privacy Rules in Cyberspace." In "Symposium: Cyberspace and Privacy: A New Legal Paradigm?" *Stanford Law Review* 52, no. 5 (May 2000), 1315–1371.

Schwartz, David. *Seeking Value or Entertainment? The Evolution of Nevada Slot Hold, 1992–2009, and the Slot Players' Experience*. Occasional Paper Series 1. Las Vegas: Center for Gaming Research, University Libraries, University of Nevada Las Vegas, 2010.

Schwartz, Paul M. "Property, Privacy, and Personal Data." In *Harvard Law Review* 117, no. 7 (May 2004), 2056–2128.

Shaw, Jonathan. "Exposed: The Erosion of Privacy in the Internet Era." In *Harvard Magazine,* October 2009.

Solove, Daniel J., "Access and Aggregation: Public Records, Privacy and the Constitution." In *Minnesota Law Review* 86, no. 6 (2002).

Solove, Daniel J., and Chris Jay Hoofnagle. "A Model Regime of Privacy Protection." GWU Law School Public Law Research Paper No. 132; GWU Legal Studies Research Paper No. 132, April 5, 2005.

Stein, Joel. "Data Mining: How Companies Now Know Everything About You." In *Time Magazine,* March 10, 2011.

Sweeney, Latanya. *Patient Identifiability in Pharmaceutical Marketing Data*, Data Privacy Lab Working Paper 1015. Cambridge, 2011.

———. *Discrimination in Online Ad Delivery,* at http://dataprivacylab.org/projects/onlineads/1071-1.pdf, January 28, 2013.

Turdean, Cristina. *Computerizing Chance: The Digitization of the Slot Machine (1960–1984)*. Occasional Paper Series 15. Las Vegas: Center for Gaming Research, University Libraries, University of Nevada Las Vegas, 2012.

Wall Street Journal. "What They Know" series and other reporting.

INDEX

Adam Tanner writes about the business of personal data. He is a fellow at the Institute for Quantitative Social Science at Harvard University and was previously a Nieman fellow there. Tanner has worked for Reuters News Agency as Balkans bureau chief (based in Belgrade, Serbia), as well as San Francisco bureau chief, and has had previous postings in Berlin, Moscow, and Washington, DC. He also contributes to *Forbes* and other magazines.

PublicAffairs is a publishing house founded in 1997. It is a tribute to the standards, values, and flair of three persons who have served as mentors to countless reporters, writers, editors, and book people of all kinds, including me.

I. F. STONE, proprietor of *I. F. Stone's Weekly*, combined a commitment to the First Amendment with entrepreneurial zeal and reporting skill and became one of the great independent journalists in American history. At the age of eighty, Izzy published *The Trial of Socrates*, which was a national bestseller. He wrote the book after he taught himself ancient Greek.

BENJAMIN C. BRADLEE was for nearly thirty years the charismatic editorial leader of *The Washington Post*. It was Ben who gave the *Post* the range and courage to pursue such historic issues as Watergate. He supported his reporters with a tenacity that made them fearless and it is no accident that so many became authors of influential, best-selling books.

ROBERT L. BERNSTEIN, the chief executive of Random House for more than a quarter century, guided one of the nation's premier publishing houses. Bob was personally responsible for many books of political dissent and argument that challenged tyranny around the globe. He is also the founder and longtime chair of Human Rights Watch, one of the most respected human rights organizations in the world.

·   ·   ·

For fifty years, the banner of Public Affairs Press was carried by its owner Morris B. Schnapper, who published Gandhi, Nasser, Toynbee, Truman, and about 1,500 other authors. In 1983, Schnapper was described by *The Washington Post* as "a redoubtable gadfly." His legacy will endure in the books to come.

Peter Osnos, *Founder and Editor-at-Large*